高等院校互联网+新形态教材·经管系列(二维码版)

国际贸易实务(双语)
(微课版)

韦苏健　朱振东　主　编

王　敏　李　为　　副主编

包晓宁　杨倩雯

U0368619

清华大学出版社

北京

内 容 简 介

本书结合我国的进出口贸易实践，以培养国际经济与贸易高级管理人才为目标，以货物进出口贸易中的习惯做法、贸易惯例和法律为依据，详细介绍了国际货物买卖合同的订立、合同中的主要交易条款和条件、货物的交付、货运保险、货款结算，以及合同履行过程中的制单和争议的解决等内容。

为了与进出口贸易的实际尽可能地接近并满足现实的需求，本书采用双语(中英文)编写，引导读者从整体上把握进出口业务流程、相关的法律法规和惯例，针对重点和难点内容设计了译文，选用了相关问题和案例，并配有在线课程学习资源，以方便读者学习使用。

本书可作为高等院校经济类专业师生学习国际贸易实务课程的教材，也可作为国际贸易从业人员的自学或参考书。

图书在版编目(CIP)数据

国际贸易实务：微课版：汉文、英文/韦苏健，朱振东主编. —北京：清华大学出版社，2022.5
高等院校互联网+新形态教材. 经管系列：二维码版
ISBN 978-7-302-60535-5

Ⅰ. ①国… Ⅱ. ①韦… ②朱… Ⅲ. ①国际贸易—贸易实务—高等学校—教材—汉、英 Ⅳ. ①F740.4

中国版本图书馆 CIP 数据核字(2022)第 062057 号

责任编辑：梁媛媛
装帧设计：李　坤
责任校对：李玉茹
责任印制：宋　林

出版发行：清华大学出版社
　　　　网　　　址：http://www.tup.com.cn, http://www.wqbook.com
　　　　地　　　址：北京清华大学学研大厦 A 座　　　邮　　编：100084
　　　　社 总 机：010-83470000　　　　邮　　购：010-62786544
　　　　投稿与读者服务：010-62776969, c-service@tup.tsinghua.edu.cn
　　　　质量反馈：010-62772015, zhiliang@tup.tsinghua.edu.cn
　　　　课件下载：http://www.tup.com.cn, 010-62791865

印 装 者：三河市东方印刷有限公司
经　　销：全国新华书店
开　　本：185mm×260mm　　　印　张：13.25　　字　数：322 千字
版　　次：2022 年 6 月第 1 版　　印　次：2022 年 6 月第 1 次印刷
定　　价：39.80 元

产品编号：092413-01

前　　言

　　随着经济的全球化发展，全球市场竞争越来越激烈，国际贸易在世界经济中的作用不断加强，国际贸易量不断增加，进出口贸易的风险也随之增加。历史、习俗、法律规定和经济发展程度的不同，使得参与国际贸易的各个国家之间在贸易实践上存在巨大的差异。尽管许多国际组织一直致力于推进国际贸易法律和惯例的统一，但仍然任重而道远。相对国内贸易而言，国际贸易的潜在风险更多。这就要求国际贸易从业人员具备足够的专业知识，熟悉与国际贸易相关的法律、惯例、规定和习惯，快速、准确地识别潜在的利益和风险。本书旨在激发学习者对国际货物贸易实践的学习兴趣，引导学习者从总体上把握进出口业务流程，熟悉相关的法律法规和惯例。

　　跨文化沟通能力也是国际贸易从业人员需要具备的能力。英语是国际货物买卖中使用最为广泛的语言，因此，国际贸易实务课程有必要采用双语或英语教学。英文教材的缺失和不足一直是课程建设和发展的瓶颈。国家之间贸易政策和实践的差异使得引进的英文版教材并不完全适用于国内高校的教学，而国内现有英文教材的内容有待深化。因此，我们编写本书以供国内高校学生学习和国际贸易领域的从业人员使用。

　　本书主要从国际货物贸易出发，分析了国际贸易的一般特征和风险，介绍了货物进出口的一般流程。具体来说是以习惯做法、贸易惯例和法律为指导，详细介绍了国际货物买卖合同的订立、合同的主要交易条款和条件、合同履行过程中的制单和争议解决等内容。全书主要包括九个部分。

　　第一章　国际贸易概述：主要介绍国际贸易的起源、作用、形式以及国际贸易中的主要问题。

　　第二章　价格条款：结合国际商会制定的 *Incoterms 2020*(《国际贸易术语解释通则 2020》)阐明不同价格术语条件下买卖双方的风险和责任分担问题。

　　第三章　商品的品名、品质、数量和包装：围绕商品介绍合同的主要条款(品名、品质、数量和包装等)，同时介绍相关的应用知识。

　　第四章　国际货物的运输：介绍国际货物运输的不同方式。

　　第五章　国际货运保险：介绍我国海洋货物运输保险条款的内容和英国伦敦保险业协会海运货物条款，以及如何投保和进行保险索赔。

　　第六章　国际货款支付：对国际贸易中的常用票据进行讲解。此外，对汇付、托收和跟单信用证三种主要结算方式也进行了详细介绍。

　　第七章　商品的检验和报关：介绍商品检验的内容和作用，商品检验的主要条款，订立检验条款应注意的问题，报关的概念、范围和分类，以及进出口货物的报关程序。

第八章　争议、索赔和仲裁：介绍争议索赔和仲裁的相关知识。

第九章　国际贸易单证：介绍国际贸易单证种类，并详细介绍主要单证。

为提高学习者的学习效率，本书针对重点和难点内容设计了案例和问题，启发学习者通过思考和分析习得相关知识。

此外，本书还提供配套的在线课程学习资源，包括课件、微课等，方便学习者自觉使用，或作为翻转课堂教学实践的一个环节。

本书由韦苏健、朱振东担任主编，王敏、李为、包晓宁、杨倩雯担任副主编。其中，第三章和第四章的内容由朱振东编写，第五章的内容由王敏编写，第六章的内容由李为编写，第七、第八、第九章三个部分的内容由包晓宁和杨倩雯编写，其余部分的内容和全书的统稿工作由韦苏健完成。感谢在本书编写过程中进行校对的广西大学硕士生陈彬彬以及提出宝贵修改意见的学生和老师，同时感谢清华大学出版社的各位编辑在本书修改、完善和出版工作中的辛勤付出。

由于作者水平有限，书中难免存在不足之处，恳请读者批评、指正。

编　者

目 录

Chapter 1　A Brief Introduction to International Trade

Leading in

A Chinese company, the buyer, urgently needs a particular part of a machine to keep the assembly line operational and asks an American company, the seller, to rush it to China without agreeing to the price in advance.

Question: Is the buyer's proposal an offer?

1.1　Reasons for International Trade

1. Resource Acquisition

International trade, also called foreign trade, or overseas trade, in essence, is the fair and deliberate exchange of commodities and services across national boundaries. It includes import and export trade operations. It arises for many reasons.

Manufactures and distributors seek out products and services as well as components and finished goods produced in foreign countries. The different distributions of the world's resources determine the patterns of world trade. Some countries or regions are abundant in natural resources; elsewhere, reserves are scarce or nonexistent. **For example, the United States is a major consumer of coffee, yet it does not have the climate to grow any fits own. So it has to import coffee from other countries that are rich in coffee, like Brazil, the Republic of Colombia and so on. Britain possesses large reserves of coal but lacks many minerals such as copper and aluminum.** The world's raw materials are unevenly distributed, and both modern manufacturing and agriculture require many different resources. Thus, to obtain these through trading is an absolute necessity.

Climate and terrain affect the cultivation of some agricultural products, which a nation can produce and trade internationally. Some South American countries, for instance, enjoy a favorable climate for growing coffee. However, the USA almost does not grow coffee, and has to import it. On the other hand, the climate and terrain of some states of the USA are ideal for raising wheat. The wheat grown in the USA is so large that it is often exported to other countries.

2. Benefits Acquisition

With the development of manufacturing and technology, there has been another reason, i.e. economic benefit, for nation to trade. It has been found that a country benefits more from producing goods it can make most cheaply and buying those goods that other countries can make at lower costs than by producing everything it needs within its own border. This is often explained by the theory of comparative advantage, also called the comparative cost theory, which was developed by David Ricardo, John Stuart Mill, and other economists in the nineteenth century. The theory emphasizes that different countries or regions have different production possibilities. Trade among countries can be profitable for all, even if one of the countries can produce every commodity more cheaply. As long as there are minor, relative differences in the efficiency of producing a commodity, even the poor country can have a comparative advantage in producing it.

3. Comparative Advantage Acquisition

Comparative advantage has directed countries to specialize in particular products and to mass-produce. For example, the United States is relatively more efficient than Europe in producing food (using one third of the labor). Thus, while the United States has an absolute advantage in both forms of production, its efficiency in food production is greater. Consequently, a great deal of clothing is exported from Europe to the United States.

4. Diversification

Companies usually prefer to avoid wild swings in their sales and profits; so they seek out foreign markets and procurement as a means to this end. Some film companies have to smooth their yearlong sales somewhat because the summer vacation period (the main season for children's film attendance) varies between the northern and southern hemispheres. These companies have also been able to make large television contracts during different years for different countries. Many other firms take advantage of the fact that the timing of business cycles differs among countries. Thus while sales decrease in one country that is experiencing recession, they increase in another that is undergoing recovery. Finally, by depending on supplies of the same product or component from different countries, a company may be able to avoid the full impact of price swings or shortages in any country that might be brought about, for example, by a strike.

5. Expand Sales

Sales are limited by the number of people interested in a firm's products and services and by customers' capacity to make purchases. Since the number of people and the degree of their purchasing power are higher for the world as a whole than for a single country, firms may increase their sales potentials by defining markets in international terms. Ordinarily, higher sales mean higher profits.

There are still some other reasons for international trade. Some nations are unable to produce enough products of a certain item. Thus they have to import some to satisfy a large domestic demand. Moreover, the preference for innovation or style also leads to international trade, which makes available a greater variety of products and offers a wider range of consumer choice of a certain product. Finally, some nations of the world trade with others mainly for political reasons. In those cases, more considerations are given to political objectives rather than economic motivation.

1.2　Forms of International Trade

1. Dealing

Dealing refers to that the exporter (usually the supplier) and the importer (usually the dealer) signs a dealership agreement and the two sides thus establish a buying-selling relationship. Under the dealing, the importer pays for the goods, and is authorized the dealership. The importer earns the margin between the imported price and the reselling price, while he also undertakes the risk after he takes delivery of the goods. As for the exporter, he should consider the condition of the importer, including the capital, management, spot of dealing, commercial credit, influence, etc. According to the level of dealership, dealing can be divided into general dealing, exclusive dealing, special dealing and common dealing, among which the previous three ones are included in the category of franchising, in which the exporter may grant the importer some right to distribute its products, techniques, and trademarks. Under different types of dealing, the importer is authorized different rights and should also fulfill the related obligations. Generally speaking, the importer should maintain a certain sales volume, provide good after-sales service, protect the property rights and fight against illegal manufacture, etc. To be specific, general dealing refers to that the exporter grants the importer exclusive distribution right, the lowest imported price, and the priority for import in a required period and region; the other dealers in the same region must turn to the general dealer for the purchase of the named commodities. Exclusive dealing refers to that the exporter grants the importer exclusive sales right in a required period and region; the other dealers in the same region are excluded to sell the named commodities. Special dealing refers to that the exporter selects several importers as its designated dealers and grants them the authorization certificate for the named commodities; the exporter is barred from providing the named commodities to unauthorized dealers. Common dealing refers that the exporter agrees on the qualification of the importer as the common dealer without selection as long as the importer fulfills the trade obligations and settles the payment; the importer is not granted any special rights, and shoulder less obligations compared with other forms of dealing.

2. Agency

In export trade, agency is a common practice, in which the business is arranged through the agent, who, according to the power designated from the principal, introduces the potential customer to the principal or actually negotiates and concludes the contract between the two parties in return for payment on a commission basis. The difference between dealing and agency can be listed in the following: 1) Under dealing, the two sides establish a buying-selling relation, while under agency, the two sides forms a principal-agent relation; 2) Under dealing, the dealer bears the risks after he takes delivery of the commodities and is responsible for any losses, while under agency, the agent has no obligation to accept the risk, which remains with the principal; 3) Under dealing, the agent is only responsible for the introduction of potential customers and the conclusion of contract rather than the terms and conditions in the contract.

According to the level of authority granted from the principal, the agency is classified into exclusive agency, common agency, and general agency. Exclusive agency refers that the principal grants the agent exclusive rights for the promotion of the named commodities. Common agency refers that the principal selects one or several agents in a required period and region, and the agents are not granted the exclusive rights. Under general agency, the agent is authorized the exclusive rights and carries out the business activities in the required period and region on behalf of the principal.

3. Consignment

Consignment is the act of consigning, by which the consignor sends the commodities to a foreign consignee who, according to the stipulations of the consignment agreement, sells the commodities for the consignor. In the trade practice, the exporters often take consignment to expand their outlets and sales volume. The features of consignment are: 1) The relation between the two parties is that between the consignor and the consignee and not that between the buyer and the seller; 2) The consignor is retaining ownership of the commodities until they are sold to the customers; 3) The exporter is not paid until the commodities are sold out. The profit or loss belongs to the consignor only, and the consignee collects commission; 4) The consignee is not responsible for the risk and its relative expenses resulting from price fluctuation and low market.

4. Auction

An auction is a public sale in which the price is determined by bidding, and the item is sold to the highest bidder. To participate in an auction means to bid to obtain an item. An auction is most useful when the potential price of the asset to be sold is uncertain. Different auction formats exist, varying according to how prices are quoted and bids tendered. The most commonly known of these is the English Auction, which is commonly used for artworks and wine. This auction is also called the ascending price or open-outcry auction. The goods sold by auction are usually: 1) Those which are difficult to be standardized in quality and measure, such as leather, tobacco, tea, flavor, wood, etc; 2) Those which are easy to decay, such as fruits, vegetables, flowers, and ornamental fish, etc; 3) Those which are scarce or of some value in history, such as precious metal, jewellery, antiques, and works of art, etc.

5. Trade Fair

A trade fair is an exhibition organized by the local government or industry associations so that companies in a specific industry can showcase and demonstrate their latest products, study activities of rivals and examine recent trends and opportunities. By attending the trade fairs, the exporters combine the exposition and sales of their products together. Some trade fairs are open to the public, while others can only be attended by members of the trade and members of the press, therefore trade fairs are classified as either "Public" or "Trade Only". To attend trade fairs, participating companies need to invest some expenses on space rental, design and construction of trade show displays, telecommunications and networking, travel, accommodations, and promotional literature and items to give to attendees. In addition, costs are also covered at the show for services such as electrical, booth cleaning, Internet services, and material handling. As the Internet develops, online trade fairs spring up like the bamboo shoots after the spring rain. There virtual trade fairs now enjoy popularity for their low costs especially during the global financial crisis. The world's well-known trade fair, the Universal Exposition or Expo (short for "exposition"), and also known as World's Fair, which has been organized for 40 times and influenced for more than one and a half centuries. The event usually lasts three to six months. The first Expo was held in the Crystal Palace in Hyde Park, London, in 1851 under the title "Great Exhibition of the Works of Industry of All Nations".

6. Invitation to Tender and Submission of Tender

Invitation to tender, also named as "call for tender" or "call for bids", is a procedure for selecting competing offers from different tenderers expecting to win the bid. The business activities that are often conducted in this form of trade are usually construction projects and purchase of goods in large quantity. It is a game between the tenderee and the tenderer, and also a game between the tenderers. Any tenderer, when quoting the price, should consider the other tenderers' potential offers and predict the bottom line of the tenderee, while his offer cannot be too low to earn a profit. Submission to tender is giving the tender from the tenderer to the tenderee in a required time and place. In fact, invitation and submission to tender are two aspects of this form of trade. In general, there are two ways of invitation to tender:

(1) Open invitation to tender. It is open to all sellers or contractors who can guarantee performance. For most government purchase of goods, open invitation to tender is applied to ensure its competitiveness, openness, and equality;

(2) Restricted invitation to tender. It is only open to selected prequalified sellers or contractors, especially when it comes to those confidentiality issues like military contracts or sensitive technology projects. The following three concepts need to be made clear in the process of tender.

① Double envelope system. In an open bid or tender system, a double envelope system may be used. The double envelope system separates the technical proposal from the financing or cost proposal in the form of two separate and sealed envelopes. During the tender evaluation, the technical proposal would be opened and evaluated first followed by the financing proposal. The objective of this system is to ensure a fair evaluation of the proposal. The technical proposal would be evaluated purely on its technical merits and its ability to meet the requirements set forth in the invitation without being restrained by the financing proposal.

② Tender box. A tender box is a physical mailbox that is used to receive the physical tender or bid documents. When a tender or bid is being called, a tender of bid number is usually issued as a reference number for the tender box. The tender box would be open for the interested parties to submit their proposals for the duration of the bid or tender. Once the duration is over, the tender box is closed and sealed and can only be opened by either the tender or bid evaluation committee or a member of the procurement department with one witness.

③ Security deposit. Registered contractors are usually required to furnish a bond for a stipulated sum as security or earnest money deposit to be adjusted against work done.

7. Counter-trade

Counter-trade is the trade method in which the seller (the exporter) is required to accept the purchase of goods or services in equivalent or nearly equivalent value from the buyer (the importer). Counter-trade involves several types of forms, including barter trade, compensation trade, counter-purchase, buy-back, and switch trade, among which the barter trade and the compensation trade are used most often.

Barter trade is the direct exchange of goods or services without an intervention of exchange medium or money. It is either based on established rates of an exchange or by bargaining. Barter is regarded as the oldest form of commerce since the time when money does not exist in the communities. It is now widely used in modern economic world, especially for the trade of farming products. For example, Argentina and Cuba had signed an agreement on barter trade of Argentina's corn with Cuban sugar in August each year, from 1995 to 2003. Oil-for-Food Programme is established under the UN Security Council Resolution 986, with which Iraq is allowed to exchange oil with other nations for food, medicine, and other humanitarian supplies for ordinary Iraqi citizens.

Compensation trade refers that payments of imports (chiefly machinery and equipment for a factory) are to be made by products of the particular factory during certain years of its production according to the agreement. For example, in the early 1980s, foreign investors provide directly, or on the basis of credit, the machinery, equipment and technology for Chinese enterprises, who compensate the foreign investors in installments for cost of such equipment and technology with the products manufactured using the equipment and technology provided.

Counter-purchase is a reciprocal buying agreement, under which the exporter agrees to purchase goods and services back from the importer or from a company nominated by the importer within a certain period of time, and the value of the goods being purchased in future is an agreed percentage of the total price of the goods originally exported. Offset is similar to counter purchase because the exporter is required to purchase goods and services with an agreed percentage of the proceeds from the original sale. The difference is that the exporter can fulfill this obligation with any firm in the country to which the sale is being made.

The term "switch trade" refers to the use of a specialized third-party trading house in a counter-trade arrangement. When a firm enters into a counter-purchase of an offset agreement with a country, it has to fulfill the obligation of purchase within a certain period of time, which is usually called "counter-purchase credits". These should be used to purchase goods from that country. A Switch trade occurs when a third-party trading house buys the form's counter-purchase credits and sells them to another form that can make better use of them.

8. Futures

Futures, a very important financial method, which dates back to the 1700s when Japanese feudal lords collect the rents from their tenants in the form of rice, is now widely spread to almost every nation of the world. Futures markets provide manufacturers a possibility to reduce their risks in future. To illustrate this point, let's first take a look at a farmer's case. The farmer plants corn, which grows well, and the farmer has a good harvest year. But a good harvest cannot ensure him a good profit, because other farmers get the same result in this year so that abundant corns are provided in the market, leading to a drop in prices. The next year, growing conditions are getting worse, the production shrinks, and the prices therefore go up, but the farmer produces less. It seems that there is always a risk the farmer has to face up, which is known as the "farmer's dilemma". To control the risk, the farmer may enter into a standardized futures contract before the harvest time. This is the one including the agreements to sell his expected crop at a price agreed on before the harvest time by him and the buyer (people who need corn, like corn oil producers), and fulfills the delivery in future. As for the buyer, he could also reduce the uncertainty by setting a fixed cost for raw material (corn). Both the farmer and the buyer wish to establish such a contract for their price and cost certainty respectively. This kind of contract protects the farmer against price fluctuation, and to guarantee the price of the corn in the future makes the farmer clear about the expected profits. By trading the futures contract in the futures exchange the farmer can also hedge the value of his corns through the transaction with a third party. Suppose he is going to sell 100 bushel of corns to the buyer in 2 months at the spot market, on which the price is determined by the market force, and he predicts that the price will go down, he could sell a futures contract with the same amount at a current futures price. When the delivery time is due, he sells the corns at a loss, while he could buy a futures contract at a lower futures price so that the losses at the spot market are offset by the gains he received from the futures market. Similarly, the corn oil producer may hedge for the costs of corn.

1.3   Problems in International Trade

1. Cultural Difference

When dealing in international trade (exporting and importing), a businessman has to face a variety of conditions which differ from those to which he has grown accustomed in the domestic trade. The fact that the transactions are across national borders highlights the differences between domestic and international trade. **Generally, there are certain differences which justify the separate treatment of international trade and domestic trade. In particular, these differences include cultural difference, monetary conversion, and trade barriers. Foreign traders must be aware of these differences because they often bring about trade conflicts in international trade.**

There are many cultures as there are peoples on earth. When companies do business overseas, they come in contact with people from different cultures. They often speak different languages and have their own particular customs and manner. The people of all cultures are ethnocentric. This means that they judge the world from their own ways of looking at things. Therefore, in international trade, business people should be on alert against different local customs and business norms.

2. Monetary Conversion

Monetary conversion is another major problem in doing international trade. If every country in the world use the same currency, the world trade would be made much easier. But this is not the case: a Copehagen beer producer wants to be paid in Danish krone. Currencies, like other commodities such as beer, have a certain value. The only difference is that each currency's value is stated in terms of other currencies. French francs have value in the US dollars, which have a value in Britain pounds, or a value in Japanese yen. These exchange rates change every day and are constantly updated in banks and foreign exchange offices around the world.

Importing and exporting firms to whom the payment is made in foreign currency can be involved in significant foreign exchange risks because of the fluctuation in exchange rates. An importer, for example, does not receive a shipment immediately after ordering it, and is often given a short period of commercial credit. Suppose a UK importer must pay a certain amount of Deutsche Mark in 60 days to a German exporter for the import of some equipment. This transaction leaves the UK firm open to substantial exchange rate risk because during those 60 days, the pounds may depreciate relatively to the Deutsche Mark, forcing the UK firm to spend a large amount of pounds to satisfy its import commitment.

3. Trade Barriers

The third problem is trade barriers. It is generally assumed, as the famous economist David Ricardo stated in the nineteenth century, that the free flow of international trade benefits all who participate. In actual practice, however, the world has never had a completely free trading system. This is because every individual country puts controls on trade for the reasons:

a. **To correct a balanced-of payment deficit. Such a deficit occurs when the total payments leaving a country are greater than money in receipt entering from abroad. The country then tries to limit imports and increase exports.**

b. In view of national security. Nations sometimes restrict exports of critical raw materials, high technology, or equipment when such export might harm its own welfare.

c. To protect their own industries against the competition of foreign goods. This is generally on the grounds that infant industries need to be shielded from foreign competition during their start-up periods. A country usually offers protection to its domestic industries by taxing imports of similar foreign goods. The tax may be levied as a percentage of the value of the imports, which is called an ad valorem tariff. When a tariff is added to the price of a foreign product coming into a country, it raises the price of the item to the consumer.

Although tariffs have been lowered substantially by international agreements, countries continue to use other devices to limit imports or to increase exports.

Notes to the Text

I. Vocabulary and phrases.

1. foreign trade   对外贸易
2. overseas trade   海外贸易

3. international trade　国际贸易

4. to trade with　和……进行贸易

5. to do business in a moderate way　做生意稳重

6. to do business in a sincere way　做生意诚恳

7. deal　交易，经营

8. to deal in　做生意

9. to explore the possibilities of　探讨……的可能性

10. trade circles　贸易界

11. to handle　经营某商品

12. to trade in　经营某商品

13. business scope/frame　经营范围

14. trading firm/house　贸易行，商行

15. trade by commodities　商品贸易

16. visible trade　有形贸易

17. invisible trade　无形贸易

18. barter trade　易货贸易

19. bilateral trade　双边贸易

20. triangle trade　三角贸易

21. multilateral trade　多边贸易

22. counter-trade　对销贸易

23. counter-purchase　互购贸易

24. buy-back　回购贸易

25. compensation trade　补偿贸易

26. processing trade　加工贸易

27. assembling trade　装配贸易

28. leasing trade　租赁贸易

29. in exchange for　用……交换……

30. trade agreement　贸易协议

II. Sentences and paragraphs.

1. For example, the United States is a major consumer of coffee, yet it does not have the climate to grow any fits own. So it has to import coffee from other countries that are rich in coffee, like Brazil, the Republic of Colombia and so on. Britain possesses large reserves of coal but lacks many minerals such as copper and aluminum.

例如，美国是一个咖啡消费国，但由于气候的关系，它不能大量生产咖啡，因此，它不得不从其他盛产咖啡的国家，如巴西、哥伦比亚共和国等地进口咖啡。英国拥有大量的煤炭资源，却严重缺乏像铜、铝之类的矿产资源。

2. Generally, there are certain differences which justify the separate treatment of international trade and domestic trade. In particular, these differences include cultural difference, monetary conversion, and trade barriers. Foreign traders must be aware of these differences because they often bring about trade conflicts in international trade.

一般地说，有几个差异要求我们必须对国内贸易和国际贸易区别对待。这些差异主要包括文化差异、货币兑换和贸易壁垒。从事国际贸易的商人必须了解这些差异，因为这些差异经常会引起贸易摩擦。

3. Monetary conversion is another major problem in doing international trade. If every country in the world use the same currency, the world trade would be made much easier. But this is not the case: a Copenhagen beer producer wants to be paid in Danish krone.

另外一个主要问题就是货币兑换问题。如果世界上的每个国家都使用同样的货币，世界贸易将会变得容易得多。但事实并非如此，犹如一位哥本哈根啤酒商人要求用丹麦克朗来支付货款。

4. Such a deficit occurs when the total payments leaving a country are greater than money in receipt entering from abroad. The country then tries to limit imports and increase exports.

当一个国家的全部支出款项超过从国外收进的款项时，就会出现逆差。这时，该国就要限制进口，而增加出口。

Exercises

I. Match each one on the left with its correct meaning on the right.

1. motivation A. to make continual efforts to gain something

2. pursue B. the action of obtaining, esp. by efforts of careful attention

3. mark up C. which by its nature can not be known by senses, not clear and certain, not real

4. procurement D. the goods (freight) carried by a ship, plane or vehicle

5. intangible E. the amount by which a price is raised

6. cargo F. profit, interest

7. royalty G. the net value of assets or interest, invest

8. equity H. not needing other things or people, taking decisions alone

9. yield I. a share of profits

10. independent J. need or purpose

1. ( ) 2. ( ) 3. ( ) 4. ( ) 5. ( )
6. ( ) 7. ( ) 8. ( ) 9. ( ) 10. ( )

II. Decide whether the following statements are true (T) or false (F).

1. Modern manufacturing and agriculture require many different resources. Thus, to obtain these through trading is an absolute necessity. ( )

2. The climate and terrain will not affect the cultivation of wheat in a country. ( )

3. A country benefits more by producing goods it can make most cheaply and buying those goods that other countries can make at lower costs than by producing everything it needs within its own border. This is often explained by the theory of comparative advantage. ( )

4. Comparative advantage hasn't directed countries to specialize in particular products and to mass-produce. ( )

5. By depending on supplies of the same product or component from the same countries, a company may be able to avoid the full impact of price swings or shortages in any country that might be brought about. ( )

6. Firms may increase their sales potentials by defining markets in international terms. ( )

7. According to the level of authority granted from the principal, agency is classified into exclusive agency, common agency, and general agency. ( )

8. Under general agency, the agent is authorized the exclusive right and carries out the business activities in the required period and region on behalf of the principal. ( )

9. A trade fair is an exhibition organized by the local government or industry associations so that companies in a specific industry can showcase and demonstrate their latest products, study activities of rivals and examine recent trends and opportunities. ( )

10. There aren't any differences which justify the separate treatment of international trade and domestic trade. ( )

III. Answer the following questions according to the information you have got.

1. What is international trade?
2. What is the most essential motive for pursuing international trade?
3. What are the forms of international trade?
4. Set some examples of invisible trade.
5. Why do many countries impose restrictions on trade?
6. What benefits does international trade bring about?

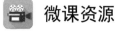

微课资源

扫一扫，获取相关微课视频。

1.1.mp4

1.2.mp4

Chapter 2　Price Terms

Leading in

China's Company A, located in Xi'an, exported 30 m/t of Liquorice Cream to Japan for USD54,000 FOB Xingang, Tianjin. Shipment should be made on or before December 25 as contracted. Company A transported the above goods to its Tianjin office in early December. Unfortunately, the goods were burnt in the warehouse the third day after arrival. Tianjin office had no choice but notify Company A to send another 30 m/t so as to catch the time of shipment.

Question: How could company A avoid the above risk?

2.1　Function and Classification of Price Terms

1. The Function of Price Terms

Price term, or trade term, is a short phrase on its English acronym to specify the price structure and the division of risks, expenses, and responsibilities. It simplifies the contents in business negotiation, shortens the period of the delivery, saves a lot of transaction expenses and makes it easy for the traders to discriminate different risks and responsibilities under different terms and conditions. For instance, according to normal practice, FOB (Free on Board) and DES (Delivered EX Ship) represent two different modes of transaction with different clear-cut risks and responsibilities taken by the two sides, who find it not necessary to spend valuable time and energy on negotiation of respective terms and conditions already included in the price terms. **It also facilitates the calculation of price and cost, because the price term underlines the price structure and the two sides have to consider different incurring expenses, including freight, insurance premium, loading and unloading charges, tariff, value added tax, cost of warehousing, etc., which is convenient for price comparison and calculation. If there is any trade disputes and the conditions on the contract that are vaguely stipulated,**

standard interpretation of price terms can be consulted to judge the disputes.

2. The Analysis of Price

Any of the trade prices constitutes the following basic components: type of currency, price per unit or total price, measurement unit, and price terms. For example, in the quoted price "$100 per dozen CIF New York", the type of currency is US dollar, the price per unit is 100, the measurement unit is dozen, and the price term is CIF New York. From the definition of price term, the price structure and terms of transaction are clearly stated. The concluded price in international trade includes the local costs, the expenses incurred abroad and the expected profits. Local costs usually constitute the manufacturing cost or purchase price, costs of commodity circulation and taxes. Expenses incurred abroad constitute transportation fees from the place of export to the place of import, insurance premium, and other relative expenses.

Different prices determine different price structures. For example, if the transaction is concluded on the basis of CIF, it is required that the exporter covers the expense of freight and insurance premium, then the price is made up of local costs, freight and insurance premium; if the transaction is based on FOB, both the expenses of freight and insurance premium are not born by the exporter, then the price is made up of local costs only. In addition to the price structure, price terms also indicate the terms of transaction, which expressly stipulate the respective responsibilities of the exporter and the importer. For example, under FOB, the importer is responsible for appointing his carrier to take delivery of cargo at the port of shipment, and the exporter is responsible for loading the cargo onto the buyer's designated ship. The point of risk transfer is at the designated ship's rail on the port of shipment, which means the exporter bears all the risks and covers any expenses before the cargo are transferred over the ship's rail on the port of shipment, while the importer bears all the risks and covers any expenses after the cargo are transferred over the ship's rail on the port of shipment. **Therefore, FOB contract is called "shipment contract" and "symbolic delivery".** Under DES, the exporter is responsible for appointing his carrier to transport the cargo to the designated port of destination, which means the exporter bears all the risks and covers any expenses before the cargo is delivered to the importer on the ship on the port of destination, and the importer bears all the risks and covers any expenses before the cargo is delivered to him on the ship on the port of destination, and the importer bears all the risks and covers any expenses after the cargo is delivered to him on the ship on the port of destination. **Therefore, DES contract is called "arrival contract" and "physical delivery".**

3. International Trade Practice Concerning Price Terms

In customary trade practice, several price terms are commonly used. However, these terms are not uniformly interpreted and often arise misunderstanding and disagreements in early 20th century. In order to give a standard and authoritative interpretation of these terms, ICC (International Chamber of Commerce) issued "Incoterms 1936", a set of international rules for the interpretation of price terms. Amendments and additions were later made in 1953, 1967, 1976,

1980, 1990 and 2000 to keep pace with the development of international trade. The latest edition is "Incoterms 2000" that has been applied for 10 years. ICC has revised "Incoterms 2000" and drafted "Incoterms 2011", which came into force on 1 January 2011. "Incoterms 2000" include 13 price terms, and each term states the exporter's and the importer's responsibilities for the obligations of transportation, loading, unloading, customs clearance, insurance premium, etc. They also specify the risk that passes from the exporter to the importer. What should be noted is that Incoterms are not laws. If there is any dispute, the first evidence to depend on is the sales contract. When the terms and conditions on the sales contract are not clear, the interpretation of Incoterms can be consulted.

4. The Classification of Price Terms

According to different standards, price terms in "Incoterms 2000" can be classified into different categories. **According to the initial letter of each abbreviation, it can be classified in the following four groups. Group E   Departure: EXW, this is the only term whereby the seller makes the goods available at his own premises to the buyer; Group F   Main Carriage Unpaid: FCA, FAS and FOB, these are the terms whereby the seller is responsible to deliver the goods to a carrier named by the buyer; Group C   Main Carriage Paid: CFR, CIF, CPT and CIP, these are the terms whereby the seller is responsible for contracting and paying for carriage of the goods, but not responsible for additional costs or risk of loss or damage to the goods once they have been shipped; Group D   Arrival: DAF, DES, DEQ, DDU and DDP, these are the terms whereby the seller is responsible for the costs and the risks associated with bringing the goods to the place of destination.**

According to the application of price terms in different modes of transportation, some terms are designed with ocean and inland waterway transportation while others are designed to be applicable to all modes. The following are two groups applicable to different modes of transportation: for maritime and inland waterway transportation: FAS, FOB, CFR, CIF, DES, DEQ; for any mode of transportation: EXW, FCA, CPT, CIP, DAF, DDU, DDP.

2.2   Commonly Used Three Price Terms to Sea and Waterway Transportation

2.2.1   FOB

1. Interprotation of FOB

FOB (Free on Board...Named Port of Shipment) means the seller delivers when the goods pass the ship's rail at the named port of shipment. This means that the buyer has to bear all costs and risks of loss or damage to the goods from that point. The FOB term

requires the seller to clear the goods for export. This term can be used only for sea or inland waterway transport. If the parties do not intend to deliver the goods across the ship's rail, the FCA term should be used. The respective obligations of the seller and the buyer can be seen in the following.

A. The seller's obligations:

1) **Provision of goods in conformity with the contract**

The seller must provide the goods and the commercial invoice, or its equivalent electronic message, in conformity with the contract of sale and any other evidence of conformity, which may be required by the contract.

2) **Licenses, authorization and formalities**

The seller must obtain at his own risk and expense any export license or other official authorization and carry out all customs formalities necessary for the export of the goods.

3) Contracts of carriage and insurance

No relevant obligation.

4) **Delivery**

The seller must deliver the goods on the date or within the agreed period at the named port of shipment and in the manner customary at the port on board the vessel nominated by the buyer.

5) **Transfer of risks**

The seller must bear all risks of loss or damage to the goods until such time as they have passed the ship's rail at the named port of shipment.

6) Division of costs

The seller must pay all costs relating to the goods until such time as they have passed the ship's rail at the named port of shipment; and the costs of customs formalities necessary for export as well as all duties, taxes and other charges payable upon export.

7) **Notice to the buyer**

The seller must give the buyer sufficient notice that the goods have been delivered.

8) **Proof of delivery, transport document or equivalent electronic message**

The seller must provide the buyer at the seller's expense with the usual proof of delivery. Unless the document referred to in the preceding paragraph is the transport document, the seller must render the buyer, at the latter's request, risk and expense, every assistance in obtaining a transport document for the contract of carriage (for example, a negotiable bill of lading, a non-negotiable sea waybill, and inland waterway document, or a multimodal transport document).

Where the seller and the buyer have agreed to communicate electronically, the document referred to in the preceding paragraph may be replaced by an equivalent electronic data interchange (EDI) message.

9) **Checking-packaging-marking**

The seller must pay the costs of those checking operations (such as checking quality, measuring, weighing, counting) which are necessary for the purpose of delivering the goods.

The seller must provide at his own expense packaging (unless it is usual for the particular trade to ship the goods of the contract description unpacked) which is required for the transport of the goods, to the extent that the circumstances relating to the transport (for example modalities, destination) are made known to the seller before the contract of sale is concluded. Packaging is to be marked appropriately.

B. The buyer's obligations:

1) Payment of the price

The buyer must pay the price as provided in the contract of sale.

2) Licenses, authorization and formalities

The buyer must obtain at his own risk and expense any import license or other official authorization and carry out all customs formalities for the import of the goods and, when necessary, for their transit through any country.

3) Contract of carriage and insurance

a) Contract of carriage: The buyer must contract at his own expense for the carriage of the goods from the named port of shipment.

b) Contract of insurance: No relerant obligation.

4) Taking delivery

The buyer must take delivery of the goods when they have been delivered.

5) **Transfer of risks**

The buyer must bear all risks of loss or damage to the goods from the time they have passed the ship's rail at the named port of shipment; and from the agreed date or the expiry date of the agreed period for delivery which arise because he fails to give notice, or because the vessel nominated by him fails to arrive on time, or is unable to take the goods, or closes for cargo earlier than the time notified, provided, however, that the goods have been duly appropriated to the contract, that is to say, clearly set aside or otherwise identified as the contract goods.

6) **Division of costs**

The buyer must pay all costs relating to the goods from the time they have passed the ship's rail at the named port of shipment; and any additional costs incurred, either because the vessel nominated by him fails to arrive on time, or is unable to take the goods, or closes for cargo earller than the time notified, or because the buyer has failed to give appropriate notice, provided, however, that the goods have been duly appropriated to the contract, that is to say, clearly set aside or otherwise identified as the contract goods; and all duties, taxes and other charges as well as the costs of carrying out customs formalities payable upon

import of the goods and for their transit through any country.

7) Notice to the seller

The buyer must give the seller sufficient notice of the vessel name, loading point and required delivery time.

8) Proof of delivery, transport document or equivalent electronic message

The buyer must accept the proof of delivery.

9) Inspection of goods

The buyer must pay the costs of any pre-shipment inspection except when such inspection is mandated by the authorities of the country of export.

2. Variants of FOB

The interpretation of FOB terms varies according to the locality where the goods are loaded, in respect of incidence of loading expense. The general idea is that the seller shall bear all the expenses, responsibility and risks before his goods are loaded on board a ship. What is meant by "the goods are loaded on board a ship"? It is open to varied interpretations. This concept is construed in some countries as the goods having effectively passed the ship's rail, and in some other countries as the goods having been placed on board of a ship, or having been put into the ship's hold. These three stages of loading work are actually linked and encompassed in one operation. Which one of the three interpretations is adopted determines the way in which the expenses, responsibility and risks are divided between the buyer and the seller. It is a matter of concern to the people engaged in foreign trade especially when they are negotiating a big business deal, say, 5,000,000 m/t of wheat, coal, mineral ore and the like. The amount of loading expenses can be a staggering sum of money.

It must be made clear at which point of time in the course of loading operation the risks shall pass from the seller to the buyer, and up to which point of time the buyer shall begin to bear the loading expenses. For instance, at some European ports, the seller shall pay all the expenses until the goods are put into the ship's hold and stowed properly according to its usual practice (or custom) of the port; but at some other ports, the seller shall pay the loading expenses except stowing expenses. Furthermore, there is such a custom (or practice) of a certain port that the seller's obligation is to send the goods to the wharf godown (shed) only; at some other ports, the entire loading expense is to be divided equally between the buyer and the seller. In view of these variants, as a foreign trade businessman he ought to be careful about the application of the FOB terms and may do well to choose one of the following FOB variants to suit his need.

1) FOB Liner Terms

It means that all the loading and unloading expenses are to be born by the party who pays the freight, i.e., the charterer of the carries vessel. Under FOB liner terms, the sellers shall not pay lading expenses, the charterer being the buyer.

2) FOB Stowed

It denotes that the seller pays the loading expenses including stowing expenses.

3) FOB Trimmed

This term signifies that the seller pays all the loading expenses including trimming expense (which actually also includes stowing expense).

4) FOB Under Tackle

This term only requires the seller to send and place the goods on the wharf within the reach of the ship's tackle.

5) FOA (FOB Airport /Free on Airport)

Under this term, goods are shipped by the air carrier. The exporter's responsibility is to supply the goods, pack and inspect the goods, prepare all the necessary documents including the export license, and pay for export taxes. The importer notifies the exporter of the air carrier and airport and all other necessary instructions and bears all risks and costs to the air carrier. The exporter's responsibility ceases only when he delivers the contracted goods to the airport authority.

6) FOR (Free on Rail)/FOT (Free on Truck)

This term is used to have the goods shipped by rail. The price quoted includes the delivery by the exporter from his premises to the railway station. The exporter fulfills his obligations by packing the goods, paying for the checking, and transportation to the station, providing usual transport documents to the importer, and notifying the importer that the goods are in position. The risk ends once the goods are in the custody of the railway authority if it is less than a car load (LCL). Full car load (FCL) cargo shall be loaded directly to the rail wagon by the exporter at his own costs. All transportation and other charges from the railway to the final destination are born by the importer, even if the shipment is arranged by the exporter.

2.2.2 CFR

1. Interpretation of CFR

CFR (Cost and Freight...Named Port of Destination) means that the seller delivers when the goods pass the ship's rail in the port of shipment. The seller must pay the costs and freight necessary to bring the goods to the named port destination. But the risk of loss or damage to the goods, as well as any additional costs due to events occurring after the time delivery, are transferred from the seller to the buyer. The CFR term requires the seller to clear the goods for export. This term can be used only for sea and inland waterway transport. If the parties do not intend to deliver the goods across the ship's rail, the CPT term should be used. The respective obligations of the seller and the buyer can be seen in the following.

A. The seller's obligations:

1) Provision of goods in conformity with the contract

The seller must provide the goods and the commercial invoice, or its equivalent electronic message, in conformity with the contract of sale and any other evidence of conformity which may be required by the contract.

2) Licenses, authorization and formalities

The seller must obtain at his own risk and expense any export license or other official authorization and carry out, where applicable, all customs formalities necessary for the export of the goods.

3) Contracts of carriage and insurance

a) Contract of carriage: The seller must contract on usual terms at his own expense for the carriage of the goods to the named port of destination by the usual route in a seagoing vessel (or inland waterway vessel as the case may be) of the type normally used for the port of goods of the contract description.

b) Contract of insurance: No relevant obligation.

4) Delivery

The seller must deliver the goods on board the vessel at the port of shipment on the date or within the agreed period.

5) Transfer of risks

The seller must bear all of risks loss or damage to the goods until such time as they have passed the ship's rail at the port of shipment.

6) Division of costs

The seller must pay all costs relating to the goods until such time as they have been delivered, the freight and all other costs including the costs of loading the goods on board and any charges for unloading at the agreed port of discharge which were for the seller's account under the contract of carriage; the costs of customs formalities necessary for export as well as all duties, taxes and other charges payable upon export, and for their transit through any country if they were for the seller's account under the contract of carriage.

7) Notice to the buyer

The seller must give the buyer sufficient notice that the goods have been delivered as well as any other notice required in order to allow the buyer to take measures which are normally necessary to enable him to take the goods.

8) Proof of delivery, transport document or equivalent electronic message

The seller must at his own expense provide the buyer without delay with the usual transport document for the agreed port of destination. This document (for example, a negotiable bill of lading, a non-negotiable sea waybill of and inland waterway document) must cover the contract goods, be dated within the period agreed for shipment, enable the buyer to claim the goods from the carrier at the port of destination and, unless otherwise agreed, enable the buyer to sell the goods in transit by the transfer of the document to a subsequent buyer (the negotiable bill of lading) or by notification to the carrier. When such a transport document is issued in several originals, a full set of originals must be presented to the buyer. Where the seller and the buyer have agreed to communicate electronically, the document referred to in the preceding paragraphs may be replaced by and equivalent electronic data interchange (EDI) message.

9) Checking-packing-marking

The seller must pay the costs of those checking operations (such as checking quality, measuring, weighing, counting) which are necessary for the purpose of delivering the goods. The seller must provide at his own expense packaging (unless it is usual for the particular trade to ship the goods of the contract description packed) which is required for the transport of the goods arranged by him. Packaging is to be marked appropriately.

B. The buyer's obligations:

1) Payment of the price

The buyer must pay the price as provided in the contract of sale.

2) Licenses, authorization and formalities

The buyer must obtain at his own risk and expense any import license or other official authorization and carry out customs formalities for the import of the goods and for their transit through any country.

3) Contracts of carriage and insurance

No obligation.

4) Taking delivery

The buyer must accept delivery of the goods when they have been delivered and receive them from the carrier at the named port of destination.

5) Transfer of risks

The buyer must bear all risks of loss or damage to the goods from the time they have passed the ship's rail at the port of shipment. The buyer must, should he fail to give notice, bear all risks of loss or damage to the goods from the agreed date or the expiry date of the period fixed for shipment provided, however, that the goods have been duly appropriated to the contract, that is to say, clearly set aside or otherwise identified as the contract goods.

6) Division of costs

The buyer must pay all costs relating to the goods from the time they have been delivered and all costs and charges relating to the goods whilst in transit until their arrival at the port of destination, unless such costs and charges were for the seller's account under the contract of carriage; and unloading costs including lighterage and wharfage charges, unless such costs and charges were for the seller's account under the contract of carriage; and all additional cost incurred if he fails to give notice for the goods from the agreed date or the expiry date of the period fixed for shipment, provided, however, that the goods have been duly appropriated to the contract that is to say, clearly set aside or otherwise identified as the contract goods; and all duties, taxes and other charges as well as the costs of carrying out customs formalities payable upon import of the goods and, where necessary, for their transit through any country less included within the cost of the contract of damage.

7) Notice to the seller

The buyer must, whenever he is entitled to determine the time for shipping the goods and/or the port of destination, give the seller sufficient notice thereof.

8) Proof of delivery, transport document or equivalent electronic message

The buyer must accept the transport document if it is in conformity with the contract.

9) Inspection of goods

The buyer must pay the costs of any pre-shipment inspection except when such inspection is mandated by the authorities of the country of export.

2. Comparison with CFR

The only difference between CIF and CFR lies in the fact that under CFR terms the buyer is responsible for the payment of insurance premium and of course, for arranging the necessary coverage with an insurance company in the buyer's country whereas under CIF terms, the buyer is not. It does not concern the seller, however, the seller must see to it that shipping advice shall be sent in time so as to enable the buyer to proceed with insurance arrangement. In case the seller fails to send the shipping advice due to oversight, he will be held responsible for any loss or damage to the goods as a result of his negligence. The variants of CFR is the same with that of CIF.

2.2.3　CIF

1. Interpretation of CIF

CIF (Cost, Insurance and Freight…Named Port of Destination) means that the seller delivers when the goods pass the ship's rail in the port of shipment. The seller must pay the costs and freight necessary to bring the goods to the named port of destination. But the risk of loss or damage to the goods, as well as any additional costs due to events occurring after the time of delivery, are transferred from the seller to the buyer. However, in CIF the seller also has to procure marine insurance against the buyer's risk of loss or damage to the goods during the carriage. Consequently, the seller contracts for insurance and pays the insurance premium. The buyer should note that under the CIF term the seller is required to obligation insurance only on minimum cover. Should the buyer wish to have the protection of greater cover, he would either need to agree as such expressly with the seller or to make his own extra insurance arrangements. The CIF term requires the seller to clear the goods for export. This term can be used only for sea and inland waterway transport. If the parties intend to deliver the goods across the ship's rail, the

CIP term should be used. The respective obligations of the seller and buyer can be seen in the following.

A. The seller's obligations:

1) Provision of goods in conformity with the contract

The seller must provide the goods and the commercial invoice, or its equivalent electronic message, in conformity with the contract of sale and any other evidence of conformity which may be required by the contract.

2) Licenses, authorization and formalities

The seller must obtain at his own risk and expense any export license or other official authorization and carry out all customs formalities necessary for the export of the goods.

3) Contracts of carriage and insurance

a) Contract of carriage: The seller must contract on usual terms at his own expense for the carriage of the goods to the named port of destination by the usual route in a seagoing vessel (or inland waterway vessel as the case may be) of the type normally used for the transport of goods of the contract description.

b) Contract of insurance: The seller must obtain at his own expense cargo insurance as agreed in the contract, such that the buyer, or any other person having an insurable interest in the goods, shall be entitled to claim directly from the insurer and provide the buyer with the insurance policy or other evidence of insurance cover. The insurance shall be contracted with underwriters or an insurance company of good repute and, failing express agreement to the contrary, be in accordance with minimum cover of the Institute Cargo Clauses (Institute of London Underwriters) or any similar clauses. When required by the buyer, the seller shall provide at the buyer's expense in the case of war, strikes, riots and civil commotion risk insurances if procurable. The minimum insurance shall cover the price provided in the contract plus 10% (i.e. 110%) and shall be provided in the currency of the contract.

4) Delivery

The seller must deliver the goods on board the vessel at the port of shipment on the date or within the agreed period.

5) Transfer of risks

The seller must bear all risks of loss or damage to the goods until such time as they have passed the ship's rail at the port of shipment.

6) Division of costs

The seller must pay all costs relating to the goods until such time as they have been delivered and the freight and all other costs, including the costs of loading the goods on board and the costs of insurance and any charges for unloading at the agreed port of discharge which were for the seller's account under the contract of carriage; and the costs of customs formalities necessary for export as well as all duties, taxes and other charges payable upon export, and for their transit through any country if they were for the seller's account under the contract of carriage.

7) Notice to the buyer

The seller must give the buyer sufficient notice that the goods have been delivered as well as any other notice required in order to allow the buyer to take measures which are normally necessary to enable him to take to goods.

8) Proof of delivery, transport document or equivalent electronic message

The seller must, at his own expense, provide the buyer without delay with the usual transport document for the agreed port of destination. This document (for example, a negotiable bill of lading, a non-negotiable sea waybill or an inland waterway document) must, covering the contract goods, be dated within the period agreed for shipment, enable the buyer to claim the goods from the carrier at the port of destination and, unless otherwise agreed, enable the buyer to sell the goods in transit by the transfer of the document to a subsequent buyer (the negotiable bill of lading) or by notification to the carrier.

When such a transport document is issued in several originals, a full set of originals must be presented to the buyer. Where the seller and the buyer have agreed to communicate electronically, the document referred to in the preceding paragraphs may be replaced by an equivalent electronic data interchange (EDI) message.

9) Checking-packaging-marking

The seller must pay the costs of those checking operations (such as checking quality, measuring, weighing, counting) which are necessary for the purpose of delivering the goods. The seller must provide at his own expense packaging (unless it is usual for the particular trade to ship the goods of the contract description packed) which is required for the transport of the goods arranged by him. Packaging is to be marked appropriately.

B. The buyer's obligations:

1) Payment of the price

The buyer must pay the price as provided in the contract of sale.

2) Licenses, authorization and formalities

The buyer must obtain at his own risk and expense any import license or other official authorization and carry out all customs formalities for the import of the goods and for their transit through any country.

3) Contracts of carriage and insurance

No relerant obligation.

4) Taking delivery

The buyer must accept delivery of the goods when they have been delivered and receive them from the carrier at the named port of destination.

5) Transfer of risks

The buyer must bear all risks of loss or damage to the goods from the time they have passed the ship's rail at the port of shipment. The buyer must, should he fail to give notice, bear all risks of loss or damage to the goods from the agreed date or the expiry date of the period fixed for shipment provide, however, that the goods have been duly appropriated to the contract, that is to say, clearly set aside or otherwise identified as the contract goods.

6) Division of costs

The buyer must pay all costs relating to the goods from the time they have been delivered and all costs and charges relating to the goods whilst in transit until their arrival at the port of destination, unless such costs and charges were for the seller's account under the contract of carriage; and unloading costs including lighterage and wharfage charges, unless such costs and charges were for the seller's account under the contract of carriage; and all additional costs incurred if he fails to give notice, for the goods from the agreed date or the expiry date of the period fixed for shipment, provided, however, that the goods have been duly appropriated to the contract, that is to say, clearly set aside or otherwise identified as the contract goods; and all duties, taxes and other charges as well as the costs of carrying out customs formalities payable upon import of the goods and, where necessary, for their transit through any country less included within the cost of the contract of carriage.

7) Notice to the seller

The buyer must, whenever he is entitled to determine the time for shipping the goods and/or the port of destination, give the seller sufficient notice thereof.

8) Proof of delivery, transport document or equivalent electronic message

The buyer must accept the transport document if it is in conformity with the contract.

9) Inspection of goods

The buyer must pay the costs of any pre-shipment inspection except when such inspection is mandated by the authorities of the country of export.

2. Important Notice

(1) Under CIF terms, the seller is obligated to arrange insurance and pay insurance premium. It is provided for in Incoterms that the goods should be covered on FPA terms at 110% of the invoice value. However, sometimes, the buyers request WPA insurance instead of FPA and occasionally demand inclusion of war risks or other special risks in insurance coverage. There are times when the buyers in some Asian countries intend to better protect their costs and profits, they require the insured value to be 150% or anywhere more than 110% of the invoice value. How to cope with such a situation? In view of the limited protection offered by FPA terms, it is deemed necessary that the CIF buyer, when the contract is made, requires the seller to get more extensive cover; but it must be made clear in the contract that the additional expenses thus incurred shall be for the buyer's account.

(2) Under CIF terms, it is the seller's responsibility to book shipping space in the case of relatively small consignment, i.e. less than a shipload, or to charter a tramp vessel in the case of shipload cargo, and pay the freight up to destination. If the buyer requests the seller to ship his goods on board of a designated vessel of certain type, nationality, class, age, etc., how does he

cope with this request? From the legal point of view, the seller has the right to decline the buyer's request provided that this arrangement is entirely feasible from the seller's point of view and does not add anything to his transportation cost. The seller may do well to advise the buyer of the date of shipment, i.e. to send shipping advice to him in order for the buyer to make arrangements for discharge.

(3) Under CIF terms, the seller shall pay the freight, but whose responsibility it is to pay unloading expenses at the port of destination is to be decided according to the custom of the port. At some ports, it is the responsibility of the shipowner to pay unloading expenses; at some others the seller has to pay the additional expenses incurred for moving the cargo from ship to wharf godown and from godown to trucks; but sometimes the situation is quite different, those expenses should be born by the buyer alone. Therefore, it is equivocal which party shall pay the unloading expense under CIF terms, the seller or the buyer. For this reason, the following CIF variants are introduced to clarify the doubtful point:

1) CIF Liner Terms

The unloading expenses will be for the account of the party who pays the freight, i.e. the seller under CIF terms.

2) CFR Landed

It means that the seller undertakes the unloading charges including the lighterage and wharfage.

3) CIF EX Ship's Hold

The buyer is to pay all unloading expenses when the goods are discharged from the ship's hold to the wharf.

4) CIF EX Tackle

It means that the seller shall undertake the charges to sling or the charges to sling the cargoes from the cabin and delivery the cargoes at the point reachable for the tackle of the ship, if the ship cannot pull in the buyer shall rent barge and undertake the charges of unloading from the barge.

These CIF variants clarify the division of expenses between the buyer and the seller. The risks pass from the seller to the buyer in the same manner as under CIF terms, i.e. at the time when the goods have effectively passed the ship's rail.

2.3 Commonly Used Three Price Terms to Any Mode of Transportation

2.3.1 Interpretation of FCA, CPT and CIP

1. FCA (Free Carrier…Named Place)

FCA means that the seller delivers the goods, cleared for export, to the carrier nominated by the buyer at the named place. It should be noted that the chosen place of delivery has an impact on the obligations of loading and unloading of the goods at that place. If delivery occurs at the seller's premises, the seller is responsible for loading. If delivery occurs at any other place, the seller is not responsible for unloading. This term may be used irrespective of the mode of transport, including multimodal transport. A carrier means any person who, in a contract of carriage, undertakes to perform or to procure the performance of transport by rail, road, air, sea, inland waterway or by a combination of such modes. If the buyer nominates a person other than a carrier to receive the goods, the seller is deemed to have fulfilled his obligation to deliver the goods when they are delivered to that person.

2. CPT (Carriage Paid to…Named Place of Destination)

CPT means that the seller delivers the goods to the carrier nominated by him, but the seller must in addition pay the cost of carriage necessary to bring the goods to the named destination. This means that the buyer bears the risks and any other costs occurring after the goods have been delivered. If subsequent carriers are used for the carriage to the agreed destination, the risk passes when the goods have been delivered to the first carrier. The CPT term requires the seller to clear the goods for export. This term may be used irrespective of the mode of transport including multimodal transport.

3. CIP (Carriage, Insurance Paid to…Named Place of Destination)

CIP means that the seller delivers the goods to carrier nominated by him but the seller must in addition pay the cost of carriage necessary to bring the goods to the named destination. This means that the buyer bears all risks and additional costs occurring after the goods have been delivered. However, in CIP the seller also has to procure insurance against the buyer's risk of loss or damage to the goods during the carriage. Consequently, the seller contracts for insurance and pays the insurance premium. The buyer should note that under the CIP term the seller is required to obtain insurance only on minimum cover. Should the buyer wish to have the protection of greater cover, he would either need to agree as such expressly with the seller or to make his own extra insurance arrangements. If subsequent carriers are used for the carriage to the agreed destination, the risk passes when the goods have been delivered to the first carrier. The CIP term requires the seller to clear the goods for export. This term may be used irrespective of the mode of transport including multimodal transport.

2.3.2　Comparison Between FOB, CIF, CFR and FCA, CIP, CPT

The difference between FOB, CIF, CFR and FCA, CIP, CPT can be seen in the following points:

(1) Modes of transportation. FOB, CIF and CFR are applied to sea and waterway transportation only, while FCA, CIP, CPT are applied to any mode of transportation.

(2) Carrier. The carriers under FOB, CIF and CFR are shipping companies, while under FCA, CIP, and CPT, the carriers can be shipping companies, railway bureau, airline companies or multimodal carriers.

(3) The place of delivery. Under FOB, CIF and CFR, goods are delivered to carrier on the designated ship on the port of shipment, while under FCA, CIP, and CPT, goods are delivered depending on different modes of transportation.

(4) Point of risk transfer. Risk is transferred when the goods pass the ship's rail under FOB, CIF and CFR, while under FCA, CIP and CPT, risk is transferred when the goods are delivered to the carrier.

(5) Transportation documents. Under FOB, CIF and CFR, the seller generally presents ocean bill of lading for bank negotiation, while under FCA, CIP and CPT, the seller may present railway bill, airway bill, or multimodal transport document, etc.

(6) The site being followed. FOB is followed by the named port of shipment. CIF and CFR are followed by the named port of destination. FCA is followed by the named place of shipment. CIP and CPT are followed by the named place of destination.

2.4　Other Price Terms

2.4.1　EXW (EX Works…Named Place)

EX Works means that the seller delivers when he places the goods at the disposal of the buyer at the seller's premise or another named place (i.e. works, factory, warehouse) not cleared for export and not loaded on any collecting vehicle. This term thus represents the minimum obligation for the seller, and the buyer has to bear all costs and risks involved in taking the goods from the seller's premises. However, if the parties wish the seller to be responsible for the loading of the goods on departure and to bear the risks and all the costs of such loading, this should be made clear by adding explicit wording to this effect in the contract of sale. This term should not be used when the buyer cannot carry out the export formalities directly or indirectly. In such circumstances, the FCA term should be used, provided the seller agrees that he will load at his cost and risk.

2.4.2　FAS (Free alongside Ship…Named Port of Shipment)

FAS means that the seller delivers when the goods are placed alongside the vessel at the named port of shipment. This means that the buyer has to bear all costs and risks of loss or damage to the goods from that moment. The FAS term requires the seller to clear the goods for export. This is a reversal from previous incoterms versions which required the buyer to arrange for export clearance. However, if the parties wish the buyer to clear the goods for export, this should be made clear by adding explicit wording to this effect in the contract of sale. This term can be used only for sea or inland waterway transport.

2.4.3   DAF (Delivered at Frontier…Named Place)

DAF means that the seller delivers when the goods are placed at the disposal of the buyer on the arriving means of transport not unloaded, cleared for export, but not cleared for import at the named point and place at the frontier, but before the customs border of the adjoining country. The term "frontier" may be used for any frontier including that of the country of export. Therefore, it is of vital importance that the frontier in question is defined precisely by always naming the point and place in the term.

However, if the parties wish the seller to be responsible for the unloading of the goods from the arriving means of transport and to bear the risks and costs of unloading, this should be made clear by adding explicit wording to this effect in the contract of sale. This term may be used irrespective of the mode of transport when the goods are to be delivered at a land frontier. When the delivery is to take place in the port of destination, on board a vessel or on the quay (wharf), the DES or DEQ terms should be used.

2.4.4   DES (Delivered EX Ship…Named Port of Destination)

DES means that the seller delivers when the goods are placed at the disposal of the buyer on board the ship not cleared for import at the named port of destination. The seller has to bear all the costs and risks involved in bringing the goods to the named port of destination before discharging. If the parties wish the seller to bear the costs and risks of discharging the goods, then the DEQ term should be used. This term can be used only when the goods are to be delivered by sea or inland waterway or multimodal transport on a vessel in the port of destination.

2.4.5   DEQ (Delivered EX Quay…Named Port of Destination)

DEQ means that the seller delivers when the goods are placed at the disposal of the buyer not cleared for import on the quay (wharf) at the named port of destination. The seller has to bear costs and risks involved in bringing the goods to the named port of destination and discharging the goods on the quay (wharf). The DEQ term requires the buyer to clear the goods for import and to pay for all formalities, duties, taxes and other charges upon import. This is a reversal from previous incoterms versions which required the seller to arrange for import clearance. If the parties wish to include in the seller's obligations all or part of the costs payable upon import of the goods, this should be made clear by adding explicit wording to this effect in the contract of sale. This term can be used only when the goods are to be delivered by sea or inland waterway or multimodal transport on discharging from a vessel onto the quay (wharf) in the port of destination. However, if the parties wish to include in the seller's obligations the risks and costs of the handling of the goods from the quay (wharf) to another place (warehouse, terminal, transport station, etc.) in or outside the port, the DDU or DDP terms should be used.

2.4.6　DDU (Delivered Duty Unpaid…Named Place of Destination)

DDU means that the seller delivers the goods to the buyer, not cleared for import, and not unloaded from any arriving means of transport at the named place of destination. The seller has to bear the costs and risks involved in bringing the goods thereto, other than any "duty" (which term includes the responsibility for and the risks of the carrying out of customs formalities, and the payment of formalities, customs duties, taxes and other charges) for import in the country of destination. Such "duty" has to be born by the buyer as well as any costs and risks caused by his failure to clear the goods for import in time. However, if the parties wish the seller to carry out customs formalities and bear the costs and risks resulting there from as well as some of the costs payable upon import of the goods, this should be made clear by adding explicit wording to this effect in the contract of sale. This term may be used irrespective of the mode of transport but when the delivery is to take place in the port of destination on board the vessel or on the quay (wharf), the DES or DEQ terms should be used.

2.4.7　DDP (Delivered Duty Paid…Named Place of Destination)

DDP means that the seller delivers the goods to the buyer, cleared for import, and not unloaded from any arriving means of transport at the named place of destination. The seller has to bear all the costs and risks involved in bringing the goods thereto including any "duty" (which term includes the responsibility for and the risks of the carrying out of customs formalities and the payment of formalities, customs duties, taxes and other charges) for import in the country of destination. Whilst the EXW term represents the minimum obligation for the seller, DDP represents the maximum obligation for the seller. This term should not be used if the seller is unable directly or indirectly to obtain the import license. However, if the parties wish to exclude the seller's obligations from some of the costs payable upon import of the goods (such as value-added tax, VAT), this should be made clear by adding explicit wording to this effect in the contract of sale. If the parties wish the buyer to bear all risks and costs of the import, the DDU term should be used. This term may be used irrespective of the mode of transport but when the delivery is to take place in the port of destination on board the vessel or on the quay (wharf), the DES or DEQ terms should be used.

2.5　"Incoterms 2010" and "Incoterms 2020"

1. "Incoterms 2010"

The new revision has taken into account the increasing volume and complexity of international trade over the past decade, to address arising security issues and ongoing changes in electronic communication. The new revision also recognizes the growth of customs-free areas. Rules of "Incoterms 2010" can be used for both international and domestic sale contracts. Incoterms rules have traditionally been used in international sale contracts where goods pass across national boarders. However, in various areas of the world many trade blocks in the world, like the European Union, have made border formalities between different countries less significant. Consequently, the 2010 rules clearly state in a number of places that the obligation to comply with export/import formalities exists only where applicable, formally recognizing that rules of "Incoterms 2010" are available for application to both international and domestic sale contracts.

"Incoterms 2010" introduce two new terms, DAP and DAT, to replace four old terms, DAF, DES, DEQ and DDU, Which decreases the number of trade terms from 13 to 11. In essence, the "D" (Delivered) terms under "Incoterms 2000" have been consolidated to reduce the number of terms that were considered to have little essential difference between them. DAT (Delivered at Terminal) replaces DEQ (Delivered EX Quay). "DAT" means that the seller delivers when the goods, having been unloaded from the arriving means of transport, are placed at the buyer's disposal at a named terminal at the named port or place of destination. It was considered that DAT would prove more useful than DEQ in the case of containers that might be unloaded and then loaded into a container stack at the terminals, awaiting shipment. There was previously no term clearly dealing with containers that were not at the buyer's premises. DAP (Delivered at place). The arriving "vehicle" under DAP could be a ship and the named place of destination could be a port. Consequently, the ICC considered that DAP could safely be used instead of DES and that it would make the Rules more "user-friendly" if they abolished terms that were fundamentally the same. Again, a seller under DAP bears all the costs (other than any import clearance costs) and risks involved in bringing the goods to the named destination.

A new concept of "string sale" is introduced in "Incoterms 2010". In international trade, goods are often sold several times during transit through a string of sale contracts. Therefore, there will be more than one seller, but only the first seller is responsible for shipping the goods. Taking this practice into account, "Incoterms 2010" allow the subsequent seller(s) to perform its obligations towards its buyer not by shipping the goods, but by procuring goods that have been shipped.

"Incoterms 2010" give electronic means of communication the same effect as paper communication, as long as the parties so agree or where customary. Though the previous revisions have admitted EDI messages as an alternative of paper documents, "Incoterms 2010" are the first edition that gives electronic messages the same effect as paper documents where agreed or customary by including the phrase "equivalent electronic record or procedure".

"Incoterms 2010" seek to avoid the buyer from potential double exposure to terminal handling charges. When contract for carriage is the seller's obligation under trade terms like CPT, CIP, CFR, CIF, DAT, DAP, and DDP, the freight (or carriage) is prepaid by the seller and later actually paid for by the buyer as part of the total selling price. The freight (or carriage) sometimes include the costs of handling and moving the goods within port or container terminal facilities at the buyer's end and the carrier or terminal operator may well charge these costs to the buyer who receives the goods, which exposes the buyer to potential double charges of the same service. To avoid this, "Incoterms 2010" clearly allocate such costs in articles A6/B6 of the relevant rules.

What's more, "Incoterms 2010" clearly allocate obligations between the buyer and the seller to obtain or assist in obtaining security-related clearances for the goods in question so as to satisfy the more restrictive security requirements cross-borders. As the first revision after the 2009 new edition of the Institute Cargo Clause, "Incoterms 2010" place information duties relating to insurance.

2. "Incoterms 2020"

"Incoterms 2020" are an internationally recognized standard for international and domestic contracts for the sale of goods, published by the International Chamber of Commerce. There are some differences between "Incoterms 2020" and "Incoterms 2010":

1. The incoterms FCA (Free Carrier) now provides the additional option to make an on-board notation on the bill of lading prior loading of the goods on a vessel.

2. The cost now appears centralized in A9/B9 of each incoterms rule.

3. CIP now requires at least an insurance with the minimum cover of the institute Cargo Clause (A) (All risk, subject to itemized exclusions).

4. CIF requires at least insurance with the minimum cover of the institute Cargo Clause (C) (Number of listed risks, subject to itemized exclusions).

5. The Incoterms rules FCA, DAP, DPU and DDP now take into account that the goods may be carried without any third-party carrier being engaged, namely by using its own means of transportation.

6. The rule DAT has been changed to DPU to clarify that the place of destination could be any place and not only a "terminal".

7. The Incoterms 2020 now explicitly shifts the responsibility of security-related requirements and ancillary costs to the seller.

Notes to the Text

I. Vocabulary and phrases.

1. price terms　价格术语

2. explicit　明确的

3. specify　指明

4. ICC (International Chamber of Commerce)　国际商会

5. Incoterms 2000 (International Commercial Terms 2000)　2000 年国际贸易术语解释通则

6. FOB (Free on Board…Named Port of Shipment)　船上交货……指定装运港

7. FOB Liner Terms　FOB 班轮条件

8. FOB Stowed　FOB 理舱

9. FOB Trimmed　FOB 平舱费在内

10. FOB Under Tackle　FOB 吊钩下交货

11. lighterage　驳运费

12. wharfage　码头费

13. CIF (Cost, Insurance and Freight…Named Port of Destination)　成本、保险费加运费……指定目的港

14. CIF Liner Terms　CIF 班轮条件

15. CIF Landed　CIF 卸至码头

16. CIF EX Ship's Hold　CIF 舱底交接

17. CIF EX Tackle　CIF 吊钩下交接

18. CFR (Cost and Freight…Named Port of Destination)　成本加运费……指定目的港

19. FCA (Free Carrier…Named Place)　货交承运人……指定地点

20. CIP (Carriage, Insurance Paid to…Named Place of Destination)　运费和保险费付至……指定目的地

21. CPT (Carriage Paid to…Named Place of Destination)　运费付至……指定目的地

22. EXW (EX Works…Named Place)　工厂交货……指定地点

23. FAS (Free Alongside Ship…Named Port of Shipment)　船边交货……指定装运港

24. DAF (Delivered at Frontier…Named Place)　边境交货……指定地点

25. DES (Delivered EX Ship…Named Port of Destination)　目的港船上交货……指定目的港

26. DEQ (Delivered EX Quay…Name Port of Destination)　目的港码头交货……指定目的港

27. DDU (Delivered Duty Unpaid…Named Place of Destination)　未完税交货……指定目的地

28. DDP (Delivered Duty Paid…Named Place of Destination)　完税后交货……指定目的地

II. Sentences and paragraphs.

1. Price term, or trade term, is a short phrase on its English acronym to specify the price structure and the division of risks, expenses, and responsibilities. It simplifies the contents in business negotiation, shortens the period of the delivery, saves a lot of transaction expenses and makes it easy for the traders to discriminate different risks and responsibilities under different terms and conditions.

价格术语或贸易术语是一种简短的词组或其英文缩写，用以说明商品价格构成和买卖双方风险、费用及责任的划分。它简化了贸易谈判的内容，缩短了交货期，节省了交易费用，便于交易双方区分不同条款下的不同风险和责任。

2. It also facilitates the calculation of price and cost, because the price term underlines the price structure and the two sides have to consider different incurring expenses, including freight, insurance premium, loading and unloading charges, tariff, value added tax, cost of warehousing, etc., which is convenient for price comparison and calculation.

它便于核算价格和成本，因为价格术语隐含了价格构成，双方必然要考虑所发生的不同费用，包括运费、保险费、装卸货费、关税、增值税、仓储费等，这便于买卖双方进行比价及核算。

3. If there is any trade disputes and the conditions on the contract that are vaguely stipulated, standard interpretation of price terms can be consulted to judge the disputes.

若合同中有关贸易纠纷及其条款表述不清，则可参考价格术语的规范解释裁定纠纷。

4. Therefore, FOB contract is called "shipment contract" and "symbolic delivery".

因此，FOB 合同被称为"装运合同"和"象征性交货"。

5. Therefore, DES contract is called "arrival contract" and "physical delivery."

因此，DES 合同被称为"到达合同"和"实际交货"。

6. According to the initial letter of each abbreviation, it can be classified in the following four groups. Group E　Departure: EXW, this is the only term whereby the seller makes the goods available at his own premises to the buyer; Group F　Main Carriage Unpaid: FCA, FAS and FOB, these are the terms whereby the seller is responsible to deliver the goods to a carrier named by the buyer; Group C　Main Carriage Paid: CFR, CIF, CPT and CIP, these are the terms whereby the

seller is responsible for contracting and paying for carriage of the goods, but not responsible for additional costs or risk of loss or damage to the goods once they have been shipped; Group D　Arrival: DAF, DES, DEQ, DDU and DDP, these are the terms whereby the seller is responsible for costs and risks associated with bringing the goods to the place of destination.

根据每个术语简称的首字母，价格术语可分为以下四组：E 组　发货：EXW, 指卖方仅在自己的地点为买方备妥货物；F 组　主要运费未付：FCA、FAS 和 FOB，指卖方须将货物交至买方指定的承运人；C 组　主要运费已付：CFR、CIF、CPT 和 CIP，指卖方须订立运输合同并支付运费，但对货物灭失或损坏的风险以及装船和启运后发生意外所产生的额外费用，卖方不承担责任；D 组　到达：DAF、DES、DEQ、DDU 和 DDP, 指卖方须承担把货物交至目的地所需的全部费用和风险。

7. FOB means the seller delivers when the goods pass the ship's rail at the named port of shipment. This means that the buyer has to bear all costs and risks of loss or damage to the goods from that point. The FOB term requires the seller to clear the goods for export. This term can be used only for sea or inland waterway transport. If the parties do not intend to deliver the goods across the ship's rail, the FCA term should be used.

FOB 是指当货物在指定的装运港越过船舷时，卖方即完成交货。这意味着买方必须从该点起承担货物灭失或损坏的一切风险。FOB 术语要求卖方办理货物出口清关手续。该术语仅适用于海运或内河运输。如当事各方无意越过船舷交货时，则应使用 FCA 术语。

8. Provision of goods in conformity with the contract. The seller must provide the goods and the commercial invoice, or its equivalent electronic message, in conformity with the contract of sale and any other evidence of conformity, which may be required by the contract.

提供符合合同规定的货物。卖方必须提供符合销售合同规定的货物和商业发票或有同等作用的电子信息，以及合同可能要求的、证明货物符合合同规定的其他任何凭证。

9. Licenses, authorization and formalities. The seller must obtain at his own risk and expense any export license or other official authorization and carry out all customs formalities necessary for the export of the goods.

许可证、其他许可和手续。卖方必须自担风险和费用，取得任何出口许可证或其他官方许可，并在需要办理海关手续时，办理货物出口所需的一切海关手续。

10. Delivery. The seller must deliver the goods on the date or within the agreed period at the named port of shipment and in the manner customary at the port on board the vessel nominated by the buyer.

交货。卖方必须在约定的日期或期限内，在指定的装运港，按照该港习惯方式，将货物交至买方指定的船只上。

11. Transfer of risks. The seller must bear all risks of loss or damage to the goods until such time as they have passed the ship's rail at the named port of shipment.

风险转移。卖方必须承担货物灭失或损坏的一切风险，直至货物在指定的装运港越过船舷时为止。

12. Division of costs. The seller must pay all costs relating to the goods until such time as they have passed the ship's rail at the named port of shipment; and the costs of customs formalities necessary for export as well as all duties, taxes and other charges payable upon export.

费用划分。卖方必须支付与货物有关的一切费用，直至货物在指定的装运港越过船舷时为止，以及货物出口需要办理的海关手续费用及出口时应缴纳的一切关税、税款和其他费用。

13. Notice to the buyer. The seller must give the buyer sufficient notice that the goods have been delivered.

通知买方。卖方必须给予买方货物已发出的充分通知。

14. Proof of delivery, transport document or equivalent electronic message. The seller must provide the buyer at the seller's expense with the usual proof of delivery. Unless the document referred to in the preceding paragraph is the transport document, the seller must render the buyer, at the latter's request, risk and expense, every assistance in obtaining a transport document for the contract of carriage (for example, a negotiable bill of lading, a non-negotiable sea waybill, and inland waterway document, or a multimodal transport document).

交货凭证、运输单据或有同等作用的电子信息。卖方必须自付费用向买方提供证明货物已交货的通常单据。除非前项所述单据是运输单据，否则卖方必须应买方要求，在承担风险和费用方面给予买方一切协助，以取得有关运输合同的运输单据 (如可转让提单、不可转让海运单、内河运输单据或多式联运单据)。

15. Checking-packaging-marking. The seller must pay the costs of those checking operations (such as checking quality, measuring, weighing, counting) which are necessary for the purpose of delivering the goods. The seller must provide at his own expense packaging (unless it is usual for the particular trade to ship the goods of the contract description unpacked) which is required for the transport of the goods, to the extent that the circumstances relating to the transport (for example modalities, destination) are made known to the seller before the contract of sale is concluded. Packaging is to be marked appropriately.

查对、包装、标记。卖方必须支付交货所需进行的查对费用(如核对货物品质、丈量、过磅、点数的费用)。卖方必须自付费用，提供按照卖方订立销售合同前已知的该货物运输(如运输方式、目的港)所要求的包装(除非按照相关行业惯例，合同所述货物无须包装发运)。包装应作适当标记。

16. Transfer of risks. The buyer must bear all risks of loss or damage to the goods from the time they have passed the ship's rail at the named port of shipment; and from the agreed date or the expiry date of the agreed period for delivery which arise because he fails to give notice, or because the vessel nominated by him fails to arrive on time, or is unable to take the goods, or closes for cargo earlier than the time notified, provided, however, that the goods have been duly appropriated to the contract, that is to say, clearly set aside or otherwise identified as the contract

goods.

风险转移。买方必须承担自在指定的装运港越过船舷时起的货物灭失或损坏的一切风险；还有自约定的交货日期或交货期限届满之日起由于买方未通知卖方，或其指定的船只未按时到达，或未接收货物，或比通知的时间提早停止装货，而引发的一切风险，但以该项货物已正式划归合同下，即清楚地划出或以其他方式确定为合同项下之货物为限。

17. Division of costs. The buyer must pay all costs relating to the goods from the time they have passed the ship's rail at the named port of shipment; and any additional costs incurred, either because the vessel nominated by him fails to arrive on time, or is unable to take the goods, or closes for cargo earlier than the time notified, or because the buyer has failed to give appropriate notice, provided, however, that the goods have been duly appropriated to the contract, that is to say, clearly set aside or otherwise identified as the contract goods; and all duties, taxes and other charges as well as the costs of carrying out customs formalities payable upon import of the goods and for their transit through any country.

费用划分。买方必须支付货物在指定的装运港越过船舷之时起与货物有关的一切费用；还有由于买方指定的船只未按时到达，或未接收上述货物，或比通知的时间提早停止装货，或买方未能给予卖方相应的通知而发生的一切额外费用，但以该项货物已正式划归合同项下，即清楚地划出或以其他方式确定为合同项下之货物为限；再是需要办理海关手续时，货物进口应缴纳的一切关税、税款和其他费用，连同办理海关手续的费用，以及货物从他国过境的费用。

Exercises

I. Match each one on the left with its correct meaning on the right.

1. FOB	A. Carriage Paid to…Named Place of Destination
2. CFR	B. Carriage, Insurance Paid to…Named Place of Destination
3. CIF	C. Free on Board…Named Port of Shipment
4. FCA	D. EX Works…Named Place
5. CPT	E. Cost, Insurance and Freight…Named Port of Destination
6. CIP	F. Delivered at Frontier…Named Place
7. DDP	G. Cost and Freight…Named Port of Destination
8. EXW	H. Free alongside Ship…Named Port of Shipment
9. FAS	I. Free Carrier…Named Place
10. DAF	J. Delivered Duty Paid…Named Place of Destination

1. (　　) 2. (　　) 3. (　　) 4. (　　) 5. (　　)
6. (　　) 7. (　　) 8. (　　) 9. (　　) 10. (　　)

II. Decide whether the following statements are true (T) or false (F).

1. Visible trade is the exchange of services, while invisible trade is the exchange of goods.

(   )

2. Absolute advantage theory and comparative advantage theory are proposed by Adam Smith.

(   )

3. Agency is a common practice, in which the business is arranged through the agent, who, according to the power designated from the principal, introduces the potential customer to the principal or actually negotiates and concludes the contract between the two parties in return for payment on a commission basis.

(   )

4. The consignee has the ownership of the commodities when they are sent from the consignor.

(   )

5. Under consignment, the exporter must be paid when the commodities are transferred to the importers.

(   )

6. Guangzhou Import and Export Trade Fair is held once a year.

(   )

7. The tenderers are usually required to furnish security deposit.

(   )

8. Compensation trade refers that payments of imports are to be made by products of the particular factory during certain years of its production according to the agreement.

(   )

9. MFN is a status given by one nation to another in international trade, with which the receiving nation will be granted all trade advantages that the other nations don't enjoy.

(   )

10. Import licensing is one type of non-quantitative NTBs.

(   )

III. Questions & discussions.

1. What is absolute advantage theory?

2. Elaborate comparative advantage theory.

3. How many forms of international trade are there? What are they?

4. What are the differences between dealing and agency?

5. What is counter-trade? Tell the forms of counter-trade in practice.

6. Tell the types of tariff barriers and non-tariff barriers.

 微课资源

扫一扫，获取相关微课视频。

2.1.mp4

2.2.mp4

2.3.mp4

Chapter 3　Name, Quality, Quantity and Packing of Commodity

Leading in

ABC company signed a contract to export red dates. The contract specified that the dates should be "Grade 3". But at the time of shipment, there were not enough third-grade dates on hand for delivery. As a result, dates of higher quality, Grade 2, were used as substitutes. The seller proudly marked the invoice, "Dates of Grade 2 sold at the price of Grade 3".

Question: In such a case, could the buyer refuse to accept the goods? Why? And if you were the seller, would you do differently?

3.1　Name of Commodity

When conducting business negotiations and making contracts, both the buyer and the seller should first reach an agreement concerning what commodities or goods are under transaction and describe the goods in the sales contract exactly. The name of a commodity is essential to a sales contract. In most cases, it may be simply put under the contract item "Name of Commodity", for example, Name of Commodity: China Black Tea. However, many goods under the same name are of different kinds. It is necessary to provide further description such as specifications, grades, etc. Hence, the name and the quality description are often merged into one, e.g. Description of Commodity: China Black tea, Grade One. In such a case, the name of commodity may constitute part of the "Description of Commodity" or "Description of Goods" in the contract.

Name of commodity, as a basis for the delivery of goods, has a bearing on the interests and rights of both importers and exporters. Therefore, the name should be clearly and properly specified in a sales contract and the name of the goods delivered should exactly

conform to the contract. To avoid subsequent disputes, the following three issues need to be considered.

1. Being clear, specific and precise

The expression of the commodity name must be clear, specific and precise, avoiding vagueness and ambiguity. For example, the name "rice" is too general as there are different kinds of rice in the market. In addition, the same type of rice produced in different places may be of different quality. Proper description of commodities like rice should also include details such as type, name of origin and some necessary specifications.

2. Being practical

The wording of name of the commodity should avoid unnecessary modifiers, especially those restrictive ones adding to the difficulty in the execution of the contract. Take "pure cotton T-shirts" for example. The word "pure" is an unnecessary modifier which may make it extremely difficult for the seller to fulfill the contract unless he has the intention and capability to deliver T-shirts which are of 100% cotton, or the buyer and the seller have reached an agreement concerning the definition of "pure cotton". See a case about misunderstanding caused by the name of the commodity in Case 3-1.

[Case 3-1] Misunderstanding caused by the name of the commodity

One Chinese company signed a sales contract with a Vietnamese trading company to export 1, 000 boxes of writing paper. Name of commodity in the sales contract is "Handmade Writing Paper". While all the documents indicating "Handmade", the end-user found part of the manufacturing process was mechanical operation when checking the goods. According to the Vietnam domestic law, such practice belongs to misinterpretation or over-promotion, so the end-user rejected the goods. The importer suffered huge losses and file a claim against the exporter. However, the Chinese company argued that the production process was by large manual operation, and the key process was accomplished entirely by hand, so they couldn't entertain the importer's claim.

Question: Was the importer entitled to compensation? Did the Chinese company make any mistakes?

---

3. Adopting widely accepted names

Sometimes a product is named differently in different countries and regions. As a result, different names may refer to the same commodity or the same name may mean different products. For example, "Coke" may refer to the soft drink Coca-Cola, or coke. To protect the interests of both parties, commodity names used on contracts should bear common interpretation by the seller and the buyer. Possible disputes can be further avoided by adopting internationally standardized and widely accepted names such as those listed in the HS Code. (See Note 3-1)

[Note 3-1] Harmonized System of Commodity Description and Coding

The Harmonized Commodity Description and Coding System (HS Code) was introduced by the World Customs Organization to harmonize international trade by creating a standard commodity classification and coding system which is globally acceptable. The HS Code is used as a basis for custom tariffs and for the collection of international trade statistics.

Country-specific product codes consist of at least 8 digits, of which, the first 6 digits will be the same for a given product produced anywhere in the world. For example, the HS Code for Basmati rice is "1006. 3010". The first 2 digits signify the chapter to which the product belongs. Here rice comes under Chapter "10", which is "Cereals"; the next 2 digits "06" denote the heading in the chapter associated with the product (In this example "1006" refers to the heading "Rice"); the 2 digits "30" denote the product subcategory, referring "semi-milled or wholly milled rice, whether or not polished or glazed"; the final 2 digits "10" are country specific and are assigned by individual countries. Hence the HS Code for Basmati rice is "1006. 3010".

There is very often, at the last column of the book of HS Code, a customs duty rate applicable on the product. From which the exporter would know the customs duty applicable on Basmati rice in Pakistan is 10%, while in China, there is no customs duty for exporting rice.

There are websites offering HS Code consulting service like:

http:www.hsbianma.com;

http:www.china-customs.com/customs-tax/10/06;

http:www.hscodelist.com.

In some cases, the appropriate choice of commodity names may facilitate the flow of import and export and reduce costs of transaction in terms of reducing customs tariff, avoiding non-tariff trade barriers and lowering transportation costs. It happens that when the same product is imported or exported under different names or categories of commodities, differential tariff rates or freight rates and trade policies may apply. Traders, therefore, should give some consideration to the tactical employment of the commodity names so as to benefit the most.

3.2   Quality of Commodity

Quality refers to the intrinsic elements of commodities including the internal properties or ingredients as well as the external appearance. Hence description of the quality may provide information related to the shape, structure, form, color, flavor, chemical composition, physical and mechanical properties, biological features and other aspects of the product.

The importance of quality is self-evident. It is the core element of the whole business and also determines the price value of the goods. According to the United Nations Convention on

Contracts for the International Safe of Goods (CISG), if the quality of the goods received does not conform to the contract, the buyer has the right to lodge a claim or even to declare the contract null and/or avoid. No matter if the quality is higher or lower than that stipulated in the contract, it is considered to be breach of contract. Consequently, the task of defining the quality details on a business contract becomes critical as it involves the fundamental interests of both parties. The seller depends on it for setting production or purchase standards; and the buyer uses it as the criteria for accepting the goods. If quality requirements are not presented properly, disputes are likely to occur. See a case about trouble caused by the method of production in Case 3-2.

[Case 3-2]

A Guangxi Import & Export Company exported to Saudi Arabia 500 boxes of frozen Zhanjiang chickens. The contract provided that the approach slaughtering chickens with a knife should be according to the Islamic practice. When the goods were arrived in Saudi, the frozen chickens were found with no knife trace on the necks. The importing authorities concluded that the way to use the knife violated the practice of Islam, so they rejected the goods and called for the Guangxi Import & Export Company to refund.

Question: In this case does the importer have the right to reject the goods and request a refund? Why?

Owing to the fact that large portions of international commodity transactions are conducted for goods normally unavailable at the time of contracting, two major ways have been developed to describe the quality of goods in a contract: sale by description and sale by sample. In some rare cases, a third way may also be adopted for the deal of ready goods-sale by actual commodity or sale by actual quality. Table 3-1 shows different methods of specifying quality of commodities.

Table 3-1　Methods of specifying quality

Categories	Types
Sale by sample	Sale by the seller's sample
	Sale by the buyer's sample
	Sale by counter sample
Sale by description	Sale by specification
	Sale by grade
	Sale by standard
	Sale by brand or trade mark
	Sale by place of origin
	Sale by description or illustration

3.2.1　Sale by Sample

A sample refers to a single item of a consignment of goods or a part of a whole product, possibly selected from a whole consignment or specially designed or processed. It is a usual practice that a sample can be regarded as the representative of the whole shipment to be delivered. In trading, samples are frequently offered to potential buyers as the evidence of quality.

A sale is made by sample if the seller and the buyer agree that samples are used as reference of quality and condition of the goods to be delivered (refer to Note 3-2). This method is used when it is difficult to describe quality of the commodity by words. Some products contain some properties or features that are far beyond the scope of any scientific or technical description. When words are futile, the product can talk. A lot of light industrial products, agricultural native produce, arts and crafts, and garments rely on samples for quality confirmation. In the case of a sale by sample, the reference number and the date of sampling should be indicated. Typical expression on the contract may read as "Plush Toy Bear, Size 24", "Quality as per Sample ST001".

Samples can be provided by either the seller or the buyer. According to the supplier of the sample, there are three cases under sale by sample: sale by the seller's sample, sale by the buyer's sample and sale by counter sample.

[Note 3-2] Duplicate sample, sealed sample and reference sample

When a transaction is made by sample, the seller should keep one or more equivalent samples for himself when delivering a sample to the buyer. The sample kept by the seller is called a duplicate sample. If necessary, the seller may also, before sending samples or delivering goods to the buyer, ask a third party, for example a notary party or a local commercial inspection institution to keep one additional copy of the sample. The sample is sealed by sealing wax, and the seller and the buyer will sign or stamp the sample. The sample kept by the third party is called a sealed sample. A sealed sample may serve as proof of quality in disputes over the quality of goods.

In addition, when sale is made by description sometimes, either the seller or the buyer may send a sample to his counterpart as a material reference. Samples provided for this purpose should carry marks clearly showing "for reference only". A reference sample is not considered as the basis of delivery and a transaction using reference sample does not belong to sale by sample.

1. Sale by the seller's sample

When a sale is made based on the sample provided by the seller, it is a sale by the seller's sample. In international trade it often happens that the seller presents collection of samples and the buyer makes his selection. Since the buyer's purchasing decision is based on the samples presented by the seller, it is rather natural to stick to the same samples for the purpose of quality specification. This is the most common one among the three.

If this method is used, it should be clearly stipulated in the contract that quality is "as per Seller's Sample" and the quality of the actual goods should conform to that of the sample.

2. Sale by the buyer's sample

Sometimes buyers may provide samples to sellers, requesting supply of the same goods. In this case, samples from buyers are referred to as the benchmark of quality requirement. It is called as a sale by the buyer's sample.

Under such circumstances, wording like "quality as per Buyer's Sample" should be clearly stipulated in the contract and the seller should provide goods of the same quality as that of the buyer's sample.

In case of a sale by the buyer's sample, the seller has to study the samples thoroughly, ensuring that all details are covered. A frequent mistake that sellers may make is that they are able to identify the external features, but ignore the intrinsic characteristics of the sample. In addition, he might need to pay special attention to factors such as raw material supply, processing techniques and equipment available, managing to achieve the equivalent quality of the samples. Considering the probability of miscomprehension of product properties and the limitation of local conditions sometimes, sellers are not encouraged to use this approach.

3. Sale by counter sample

A counter sample is a replica made by the seller of the sample provided, normally by the buyer. As the buyer is usually required to return the sample back to the seller with his confirmation if he approves of the sample, a counter sample is also called a returned sample or a confirmed sample.

This method is a good substitute to the sale by the buyer's sample because it removes the risk that sellers have to bear under other approaches. By sending a replica to the buyer, the seller is free from the uncertainty of getting the right picture of the product. If the counter sample is not in conformity with the original one, it will be disapproved by the buyer. The seller hence greatly lowers the risk of providing large batch of unqualified products due to his misunderstanding. On the other hand, once the counter sample is confirmed by the buyer, it will replace the original sample and become the final standard of quality of the transaction. The seller would be more confident to supply the whole batch of products according to a sample provided by himself. Even in the worst scenario that the buyer later finds the counter sample does not match with the original, the seller doesn't assume any responsibility as the counter sample has been confirmed by the buyer.

3.2.2 Sale by Description

In fact, in most cases, sale by description is a way to express quality of goods. Sale by description may take the form of sale by specification, sale by grade, sale by standard sale by brand name or trade mark, sale by origin and sale by descriptions or illustrations. **Different forms may be chosen depending on the attributes nature, and characteristics of a commodity. Generally speaking, sale by description is applicable to commodities of which quality can be expressed by some scientific indices.**

1. Sale by specification

The specifications of a commodity comprise some important indicators such as composition, content, purity, length and size. Defining quality by specification is simple and accurate, therefore is widely used in international trade. See Example 3-1.

[Example 3-1]

Plain Satin Silk

Width (inch): 55; Length (yds): 38/42; Weight (m/m): 16.5; Composition: 100% Silk

Printed Shirting "Jumping Monkey"

Yarn (counts): 30 × 36; No. of Threads (per inch): 72 × 69; Width (inch): 35/36

2. Sale by grade

Based on some industry customary practice or traditions, some products are classified into different grades, such as Grade A, B, C; or Grade 1, 2, 3. Under a sale by grade, the quality of a product may be indicated simply by stating its grade, presumably the seller and the buyer have reached a consensus on the implication of grades. To avoid misunderstanding and subsequent disputes, however, it is recommended to lay down some major specifications apart from the use of grade. See Example 3-2.

[Example 3-2]

Fresh Hen Eggs, shell light brown and clean even in size

Grade AA　60-65 gm per egg

Grade A　55-60 gm per egg

Grade B　50-55 gm per egg

Grade C　45-50 gm per egg

3. Sale by standard

When specifications or grades are laid down and proclaimed in a unified way, they become standards. Standards are formulated either by governments or by commercial organizations. Some apply to individual countries; others are used internationally. Many countries have their own standards, for example, BS in Britain, ANSI in the USA, JIS in Japan and GB in China. The typical international standard is ISO[①] standard. As standards of commodities are subject to changes or amendments over time, it is important to mark the year in which the standard is created to avoid ambiguities.

Different categories of products have different standards. Some special standards are designed for particular reasons. Fair Average Quality (FAQ) and Good Merchantable Quality (GMQ) are good examples of this type. Generally speaking, it is difficult to establish fixed quality standards for agricultural products since they can be easily affected by all sorts of external factors. **Thus FAQ is used to indicate that the quality of the product offered is about equal to the average quality level of the same crop within a certain period of time (e.g. a year). GMQ, on the other hand, means that the goods offered are of quality sufficiently good to satisfy the purpose of use or consumption which are mutually understood by both the buyer and the seller. It is used sometimes as the bottom-line of quality requirement.**

Similar as using sale by grade, standards are usually supplemented by some detailed specifications for clearer presentation of information. See Example 3-3.

[Example 3-3]

Tetracycline HCL Tablets (Sugar Coated) 250 mg. BP 1993

(Note: BP refers to British Pharmacopoeia)

Chinese Tung Oil, FAQ, FAA 4% max.

Cassava piece 2020, FAQ, 10% moisture max.

4. Sale by brand name or trademark

It is possible to define the quality of some products by simply referring to their brand names or trademarks. Many consumption products adopt this approach. Typical examples include Sony Television, Haier Refrigerator, Tiger Head Battery and Triangle Tire. A brand name is a company-specific name for a particular product or a group of products, usually used to differentiate that product from competitor offerings. It usually forms a part of an easily recognizable design on packing or advertising material. A trademark, on the other hand, refers to a name or a symbol that is unique to one product, representing a commercial enterprise. Trademarks are often officially registered and therefore protected. Both are signs for distinguishing the products from other competing goods of the same line.

---

① ISO: International Standard Organization, ISO is the biggest and most authoritative organization in the field of international standard. It was established on 14th, October, 1946 when 64 representatives from 25 countries including China, UK, France, and the Soviet Union gathered in London and approved to establish an organization. ISO was formally established on 23rd, February, 1947 after the charter of ISO got 15 governmental approvals. Today, ISO offers service to some related department in the United Nations and is closely related to more than 600 international organizations.

This approach, however, can only apply to those widely recognized brands or trademarks. Only if a brand name or a trademark is established in the market successfully, it can be considered as the indication of certain level of quality. It is also believed that in most cases goods of the same brand or trademark are of unified and stable quality. Therefore, other products of the same company may benefit from the spillover effect of the brand as well. With the importance of branding increasingly highlighted, more and more enterprises are taking proactive measures to build up their brands in the international market.

In practice, due to the varieties and complexities of some brand products, some detailed quality particulars must be specially and legibly stated in the contract as well, like "Skyworth Television, 55S8".

5. Sale by name of origin

Sale by origin refers to the sale of goods by using the name of the place of origin as the indication of quality. It is more suitable for agricultural products or by-products. Owing to the unique and favorable natural conditions or traditional production techniques in some areas, the native products are renowned for their specialty and excellence in quality.

Sale by origin usually used by companies with other necessary quality indices such as specifications, grades or brands. For example, specify the tea as "West-lake Longjing Tea, Grade 1, Zhejiang Origin" specify the vinegar as "Zhenjiang Gold Plum Brand Vinegar 6 Years Aged".

6. Sale by descriptions or illustration

Sale by descriptions or illustrations is especially applicable to full sets of equipment or instruments. These commodities are usually complicated in property and structure. It is difficult to use simple indicator such as data or parameters to describe the quality. In addition, the installation, usage and maintenance of such equipment or instruments shall follow certain procedures. Therefore, specific descriptions, sometimes with illustrations, are necessary for specifying the quality.

In the case of sale by descriptions or illustrations, clauses such as "quality and technical data to be strictly in conformity with the description submitted by the seller" are to be stipulated in the contract and relevant technical manuals, booklets of directions, drawings or diagrams will be attached as well to serve the purpose. See Example 3-4.

[Example 3-4]

Skyworth Television, 55S8, quality and technical data to be strictly in conformity with the instruction attached,

Haier Refrigerator, BCD-329WDVL, quality and technical data to be strictly in conformity with the descriptions submitted by the seller.

It should be noted that all approaches discussed above are not independent of each other. If necessary, two or more ways can be used simultaneously in order to specify the quality with clarity. In the meantime, traders, especially sellers, should also be aware of the problem of "double standard". When one specifying method is sufficient to serve the purpose; it is advisable not to employ any others because sellers are obliged to provide goods in strict conformity with the requirements contracted. As CISG Article 35 states, if a transaction is made both by description and by sample, the seller must deliver goods not only conforming to quality descriptions in the contract but also possessing the equivalent quality of the sample. The more criteria included the greater the difficulties would be for the sellers to fulfill their obligations. See a case about disputes over the quality in Case 3-3.

[Case 3-3] Disputes over the quality

One Chinese company exported to a British company a batch of soybean with the contract stipulated that: "Moisture not more than 14%, impurity not more than 2%." Before the deal, the exporting company sent the sample to the buyer and advised the buyer that the delivery was similar to the sample after signing the contract. When the goods arrived, the buyer found the goods were not in conformity with the sample, and presented them to the local inspection institutions for examination. The inspection result showed that the quality of the goods was inferior to that of the sample by 7%. On the basis of the inspection certificates, the buyer filed a claim against the seller for 25, 000 pounds without mentioning whether the quality conform to the provisions of the contract or not.

Question: Should the export company compensate the importer?

3.3   Other Quality Clauses

Apart from defining the basic quality criteria, quality clauses in a sales contract usually include some other elements as well, which constitute the condition to apply the quality standards formerly identified. One of them is the statement of quality latitude or quality tolerance. If it is a sale by the buyer's sample or a sale by counter sample, a safeguard clause is also inserted.

1. Quality latitude or quality tolerance

Absolute equivalence of quality is not practically feasible in most cases. Therefore, the quality latitude or quality tolerance clause is introduced to address the issue.

Quality latitude means the permissible range within which the quality of the goods delivered by the seller may be flexibly controlled. Quality tolerance refers to the quality deviation recognized which allows the quality of the goods delivered to have certain difference within a range. According to international practice quality with some deviation within a certain range is still considered to meet the quality stipulation in a contract.

Evidently a quality latitude or tolerance clause is necessary in the contract. It is normally set by stating the flexible quality range or scope, the maximum or minimum requirements, or a deviation allowance for certain quality indices. See Example 3-5.

[Example 3-5]

To stipulate a certain scope e.g. Yarn - dyed Gingham, Width 41/42

To stipulate "max." or "min." e.g. Fish Meal, Protein 55% min., Fat 9% max.

When a sale is made by sample, it is also impossible for the seller to deliver goods of quality identical to that of the sample. Therefore, wording such as "about" should be added to the quality clause to allow quality flexibility. See Example 3-6.

[Example 3-6]

Quality shall be about equal to the sample.

Quality is nearly the same as the sample.

The quality of the goods shipped to be about equal to the sample.

Shipment shall be similar to the sample.

In most cases, prices of the commodities remain unchanged when the quality varies within the tolerance or latitude unless otherwise specified in the contract. However, when the difference in quality is big enough to constitute fundamental change to the quality of goods, prices are to be adjusted accordingly and it should be explicitly stipulated in the contract. See Example 3-7.

[Example 3-7]

Soybean, if the oil content of the goods shipped is 1% higher, the price will be accordingly increased by 2%.

China sesame seed, Moisture (max.)8%; Admixture (max.)2%; Oil content (wet basis ethylether extract) 52% basis. Should the oil content of the goods actually shipped be 1% higher or lower, the price will be accordingly increased or decreased by 1%, and any fraction will be proportionally calculated.

2. Safeguard clause

According to CISG Article 42, the seller must deliver goods that are free from any right or claim of a third party based on industrial property or other intellectual property. In the case of a sale by the buyer's sample or a sale by counter sample however, there exists the possibility that the seller might provide goods alleged to have infringed the copy right of a third party without this privity. Therefore, a safeguard clause is usually stipulated in the contract. It can protect the seller from any undeserved liabilities. See Example 3-8.

[Example 3-8]

For any goods produced with designs, trademarks, brands and/or stampings provided by the buyer, should there be any dispute arising from infringement upon the third party's industrial property or other intellectual property right, it is the buyer to be held responsible for it.

In case the buyer's sample results in any disputes of infringement of industrial property, the seller will have nothing to do with it.

3.4　Quantity of Commodity

Quantity of commodity is another indispensable clause in a sales contract. It is always shown as a specific amount in number, weight, length, width, area, volume and capacity, etc. in international trade. It is obligatory for sellers to deliver the quantity of goods that is identical to that called for in the contract. According to Article 52 of CISG, "if the seller delivers a quantity of goods greater than that provided for in the contract, the buyer may take delivery or refuse to take delivery of the excess quantity. If the buyer takes delivery of all or part of the excess quantity, he must pay for it at the contract rate".

3.4.1　System of Measurement

In international trade, four systems of measurement are used: the Metric System, the British System, the US System and the International System of Units (SI).

1. Metric system[①]

The main units are kilogram (kg), meter (m), square meter (sq. m), liter (l). Other derived units include metric ton (m/t), kilometer (km) and so on. This system is widely used around the world. But the UK's official system is still pound-based and the USA is using its own system together with metric system in parallel.

2. British system

Under this system, primary units are pound and yard. It is adopted by the British Commonwealth. However, announcement of abandoning this system has been made by Britain

---

① There are two categories of metric units, which are used to show the quantity of commodity in international trade. One is the metric unit, including weight, length, area, volume and capacity. The other is numbers, including some customary units such as dozen, gross, great gross, ream, and some packing units like barrel, bale (cotton), etc.

since it has been a member of EU. It presently uses the metric system.

3. US system

The primary units are the same as the British system, that is, pound and yard. But there are differences in some derived units. For example, while the British system's long ton (l/t) equals to 2,240 pounds, the US system's short ton (s/t) equals to 2,000 pounds. Besides, some capacity units like gallon and bushel are of the same names under the British system and the US system, but the actual capacities are different.

4. International system

International system is published by the International Standard Metrical Organization, and is based on metric system, its primary units include kilogram, meter, second, and so on. This is also China's legal metrical system. Table 3-2 shows different measurements in practical use.

Table 3-2　Units of measurement

Measurement	Units of measurement	Measurement	Units of measurement
weight	1 metric ton = 1,000 kilograms 1 long ton = 1,016 kilograms 1 short ton = 907 kilograms 1 avoirdupois ounce = 28.350 grams 1 troy ounce = 31.103 grams 1 carat = 200 milligrams	area	1 square yard = 0.836 square meters 1 square inch = 6.452 square centimeters
number	1 dozen = 12 1 gross = 12 dozen 1 ream = 480-500 pieces	volume	1 cubic meter = 1.308 cubic yards = 35.315 cubic feet
length	1 meter = 100 centimeter 1 foot = 12 inches 1 inch = 2.54 centimeters 1 yard = 3 feet 1 mile = 1,760 yards	capacity	1 British gallon = 4.546 liters 1 US gallon = 3.785 liters 1 British barrel = 163.659 liters 1 US barrel [oil] = 158.987 liters 1 US barrel [liquid] = 119. 240 liters 1 bushel = 36 liters

When adopting a particular measurement unit to define the quantity, traders need to be aware of the consistency of system. Currently, among different measurement systems, the metric system and SI units are universally accepted and adopted in all countries. A notable fact is that some units in different systems carry the same name though they are indicating standards of measurement with significant differences. In addition, it is true that due to the local background and customary practice, different countries adopt different systems of measurement. As a result, traders, while having their business communications, need to clarify the use of unit and measurement system to avoid unnecessary disputes.

3.4.2　Interpretation of Weight

Weight is a very important concept in international trade. Besides serving as the most frequently used unit for defining quantity of commodity in transaction, it constitutes an indispensable part of information about each consignment frequently demanded by different parties with different intentions. Moreover, when used in various occasions, the data would be treated differently, resulting in a series of different names. Being able to interpret the concepts properly will add value to the operational proficiency of the practitioners.

1. Gross weight

Gross weight is the total weight of the commodity and the tare, that is, the packing weight. It is applicable to commodities of comparatively low value.

2. Net weight

Net weight is the weight of the commodity excluding the tare. According to CISG Article 56, the weight of a commodity is calculated by its net weight unless otherwise stated in the contract.

However, some products can be weighted only when they are packed. If net weight is used, the weight of packing, i.e. the tare, must be deducted. Thus the relationship between net weight and gross weight is as follows:

$$\text{Net weight} = \text{Gross weight} - \text{Tare weight}$$

In international trade, tare weight can be calculated by actual/real tare, by average tare, by customary tare or by computed tare. Actual/real tare refers to the actual weight of the packing of the commodities. In order to get the actual tare of the goods, each packing of goods has to be weighted in order to get a total.

By average tare, the weight of the packing is calculated on the basis of the average. The average tare can be calculated by weighing a part of the packing of the commodities and working out the average when the packing materials are uniform and the specifications of goods are standardized.

The packing of some commodities are unified and standardized and the weight of the packing is known and accepted by everyone. In this case, the recognized weight of the packing, which is called the customary tare, can be used in calculating the net weight.

Computed tare is the weight of the packing agreed upon by the parties concerned. In this case, the net weight is calculated by deducting the tare previously agreed upon from the gross weight of the commodity.

Sometimes the packing may become an indivisible part of the product, such as tobacco flakes; or the packing material is almost of the same value as that of the goods, like grain and fodder. If it is inconvenient to measure the net weight of the commodity, the "gross for net" practice will be adopted. In the case of "gross for net", the goods are priced by their gross weight instead of the net.

3. Conditioned weight

Some commodities like wool, cotton and raw silk, not usually packed in a vacuum container, tend to absorb moisture. The weight of these commodities is likely to be unstable due to the fluctuation of their actual moisture content, which varies greatly from time to time, and from place to place. When these products are of high value, it becomes important for the buyer and the seller to reach an agreement on the concept of weight. Without prior agreement, the difference between "dry goods" (i.e. goods with little moisture) and "wet goods" (i. e. goods with much moisture) could be great and the slightest difference may cause considerable difference in the price. In that case, conditioned weight is used. Conditioned weight equals to the dry weight of a commodity plus the standard moisture content. It can be calculated by first deducting the actual moisture from the actual weight of the commodity and then adding the standard moisture. The formula of calculating the conditioned weight is explained as below:

$$\text{Conditioned weight} = \text{Dried weight} \times (1 + \text{Standard regain weight})$$

$$= \frac{\text{Actual weight}}{1 + \text{Actual regain rate}} \times (1 + \text{Standard regain rate})$$

$$= \text{Actual weight} \times \frac{(1 + \text{Standard regain rate})}{(1 + \text{Actual regain rate})}$$

4. Theoretical weight

Theoretical weight is the weight in theory. If the weight of each item, such as galvanized iron, tin plate and steel plate is approximately the same, the total weight of the product is calculated by multiplying the total quantity and the unit weight, rather than measured actually. The weight got in this way is called the theoretical weight.

5. Legal weight

Legal weight is the weight of merchandise itself plus that of its immediate, inner or direct wrapping material but not of the outside shipping container. According to the customs laws and regulations in some Latin American countries, legal weight is usually used for the purpose of assessing import duties.

3.4.3 Quantity Allowance

In practice, sometimes it is hard to strictly control the quantity of goods supplied, especially bulk cargoes like agricultural products and mineral products, owing to contingencies in goods preparation. Besides, the differences in transport facilities may also lead to the inconsistency between the actual shippable quantity and the contracted quantity that might be the result of estimation. **For the sake of efficient shipment and less complexity in contract execution it is common to allow the seller to deliver the goods with a certain percentage of more or less in quantity accordingly.** This kind of stipulation on the contract is usually referred to as the "more or less clause".

When drafting the more or less clause the following issues are to be concerned: how much more or less should be allowed; which party is entitled to make the decision; and how the more or less portion of the goods should be priced.

1. How much "more or less" should be allowed

There is no fixed rule to decide how much the range of quantity difference should be. Traders normally make their decisions based on customs or result of negotiation. The ratio also varies among different lines of products. Most traders prefer to express the flexible portion by percentage: and the common range for the ratio is between 3% and 10%. An example may read as "1,000 metric tons, with 5% more or less". Other traders, on the other hand, would like to set an absolute number as the tolerable quantity disparity. Whatever way is chosen, the stipulation should be clear and specific. Ambiguous terms like "about", "circa" or "approximately" should be avoided, as they are easy to be interpreted differently.

In order to reduce disputes, UCP 600 Articles stipulate that the words "about", "approximately", "circa" or similar expressions used in connection with the amount of the credit or the quantity or the unit price stated in the credit are to be construed as allowing a difference not to exceed 10% more or 10% less than the amount or the quantity or the unit price to which they "refer". **In absence of any more or less specifying the quantity a tolerance not exceeding 5% more or 5% less is allowed, provided the quantity is not stipulated by number (of package units or individual items) and provided that the total amount of the goods does not exceed the amount of the credit.**

2. Which party is to make the decision

Who can determine how much more or less would be allowed? This should also be legibly stipulated in the contract to avoid possible disputes. In practice, as the quantity of goods delivered may be influenced by the natural condition of goods, the packing patterns, and the actual handling of shipment, it is practical to allow the party in charge of shipment to decide the quantity.

3. How should the more or less portion be priced

Under a "more or less" clause, the payment for the over-load or under-load portion will be made either according to contract price or at the market price at the time of shipment. According to CISG, unless otherwise stipulated in the contract, the payment for the more or less portion of the goods shall be calculated at the contract rate.

However, if the parties are concerned about the possible great change in price at the time of delivery, they can further include statements in the contract that settlement for this more or less part is based on the market price at the time when the goods are doing so. The method of calculation should also be set forth in Example 3-9.

[Example 3-9]

1, 000 metric tons, 5% more or less at the seller's option.

20, 000 metric tons, the sellers are allowed to load 5% more or less, the price shall be calculated according to the unit price in the contract.

80, 000 metric tons, 5% more or less at the buyer's option with more or less portion priced at the market price at the time of shipment.

The quantity clause in a sales contract is the legal basis for the seller to effect shipment and for the buyer to take delivery and make payment later on. Considering the various measurement units and systems, it is crucial to stipulate the quantity clause in a manner, which is clear, specific, and reasonable at the same time, to make the fulfillment of the contract flexible and smooth. See a case about a quantity clause with "about" in Case 3-4.

[Case 3-4] A quantity clause with "about"

A Bank in Mumbai, India opened an L/C to import 48,000 yards of cotton print cloth from China, partial shipment not allowed. There was a word "about" before the quantity of 48,000 yards.

Owing to insufficient stock, the beneficiary/exporter only shipped 45,600 yards of print cloth. According to international practice, the word "about" used in connection with the quantity stated in the credit is to be construed as allowing a difference not to exceed 10% more or less than the quantity to which they refer. The delivery of 45,600 yards was within this range (48,000−48,000 × 10% = 43,200). The beneficiary presented the documents for negotiation and the negotiating bank sent these documents to the issuing bank after finding no mistakes in them.

After receiving the documents, the issuing bank claimed that the applicant/importer refused to take up the documents because of the shortage. The applicant would not accept the documents and make the payment unless the beneficiary could ship the short-delivered goods, i.e. 2,400 yards of print cloth within three weeks. The beneficiary insisted that according to UCP 600 the documents had been made out in accordance with the L/C.

Question: Did the importer have the right to reject the documents and not to make the payment?

3.5   Packing and Marking of Commodity

Most internationally traded goods have to travel long distance to reach the final consumers. In the course of transit, goods are vulnerable to all sorts of unexpected events. To protect the safety of cargo to the fullest extent possible, usually exporters have to take every necessary step from the design of packaging to the choice of transport.

However, some exceptions do exist. For a special category of products, packing is neither necessary nor viable. These kinds of goods normally have a primitive and stable nature hence not apt to be easily damaged unless accidents out of the ordinary range happen. Raw material or industry products like rolled steel, lead ingots, rubber and timber fall into this category. According to the extent of encapsulation they are called nude cargo. Some finished products like complete automobiles are also considered nude cargo. There is another type of goods which shares the similar features of not easily being influenced by outside circumstances and hereby bearing no packing. These goods are addressed as bulk cargo. The differences are only that while nude cargo usually are in a solid state? Bulk cargo are more of a liquid-like existence and normally of low value. Ore, coal, grain and liquid chemicals not sold with individual container all belong to this category.

In international trade, most goods demand proper packing or packaging for protection against all kinds of hazards, so they belong to packed cargo. **Actually, packing not only serves as a form of protection but also facilitates loading, unloading and stowage, and prevents pilferage.** Furthermore it can promote sales. The packing of goods should meet requirements by foreign customers, relative regulation, laws or customs. According to Article 35 (d) in CISG, it says "Except where the parties have agreed otherwise, the goods do not conform to the contract unless they are contained or packaged in the manner usual for such goods or, where there is no such manner, in a manner adequate to preserve and protect the goods." This section is mainly about packed cargoes, see Figure 3-1.

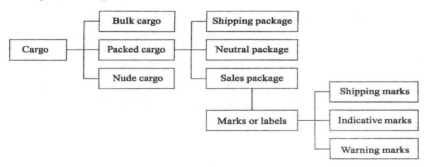

Figure 3-1   Cargo and packing

3.5.1   Functions and Determinants of Packing

Packing of commodity has become increasingly important in international trade. Increasingly fierce competition in the market space and the gradually diversified and particular demand of end consumers bring great challenges to the traders. New products, new ways of selling must be created promptly to meet the market needs. Packing in many cases has become an essential element of the product. More and more attention has been put on the design, use of material and technique for packing purpose. The functions of packing for export goods these days are multifaceted. The major ones can be briefly summarized as follows: ①Protecting goods. Packing can be used to protect the goods and keep them good and complete in the circulation field. Usually, strong packing can prevent the goods from being stolen or damaged; ②Facilitating delivery. Packing makes it convenient to store, transport, load, unload and count the goods; ③Reducing cost. Reasonable packing can optimize the use of shipping space and thus lower transportation costs; ④Promoting sales. Sales packaging provides retailers easier distribution and end customers convenient purchase and delivery. In addition, unique and attractive packaging can help create product image, build up brand, and ultimately promote sales.

In order to maximize the function of packing, decision has to be made with careful consideration for different factors. Some variables are key to the choice of packing.

1. Properties of cargo

Cargoes of different properties may require different methods of packing. Typical characteristics such as nature, value and fragility have great impact on packing of goods. For example, apples can be consigned in cases, boxes, cartons or pallet boxes while cement may be shipped in five-ply or six-ply paper bags, in containers or in bulk. Generally speaking, consignment of high value normally requires more expensive packing than low value commodities; and the more fragile the cargo is, the higher the packing requirement would be.

2. Mode of transport

The use of different transportation modes may have some implication for the packing of cargo. For instance, air transport encourages palletized consignments with cargo strapped to it throughout the transit, and packing materials light in weight such as fiberboard cartons will be preferred. For ocean freight, however strong and durable packing are always the first choice.

3. Customs or statutory requirements

Customs or statutory requirements are another affecting factor for packing. While using certain kind of packing, exporters must be sure that the material and pattern of packing used strictly comply with the regulatory requirements of the importing country. For example, in some countries, straw, rice husks and wood products are unacceptable packing materials due to the risk of insects being imported.

4. Weather

Packing must take into account the weather condition in transit. For instance, if great variation in temperature is expected during the course of the transit, packing must be designed to permit the cargo to breathe and avoid excessive sweating.

5. Ease of handling and stowage

Awkwardly shaped cargoes are usually packed in regular shape containers such as carton, cases to facilitate cargo stowage and handling.

6. Insurance

When cargoes are to be covered by insurance, there are likely to be some conditions imposed on the packing. For example, cargoes which are particularly fragile or which are more likely to be subject to damage or pilferage may have to conform to a prescribed packing specification.

7. Transportation cost

To minimize transportation cost, size, shape and strength are the three main considerations in proper packing. In addition, a shipper needs to consult his shipping agent in order to ascertain the mode of packing and to secure a favorable rate of freight. It can be noted from the above discussion that proper packing is important for most of the goods traded internationally; and packing may serve different purposes. Taking a closer look at those functions covered in previous sections of this chapter, we can conclude that packing in general can be put into two categories: One is used for transportation purpose, and the other is designed for marketing intention. They are named as transport packing and sales packaging respectively. In the following section transport packing is the focus of discussion, and only some typical issues related to sales packaging in international trade will be touched on.

3.5.2　Transport Packing

Transport packing, also called shipping packing, outer packing or big packing, is mainly adopted to facilitate cargo transportation. In international trade transport packing can be categorized according to different criteria, typical ones including container and method of packing.

There are various containers that can be used for packing, such as cases, drums, bags, bales or crate, etc.

Cases include wooden cases, crates, cartons, corrugated cartons, etc. This type of packing gives complete protection and lessens pilferage plus an aid to handling. It is particularly prominent with surface transport and is used for goods that cannot be compressed tightly, such as machinery and other items of expensive equipment. However, it is becoming less popular as the cost of timber has risen sharply in recent years and containerization has lessened the need for such strong packing in certain trades.

Drums/Casks/Hogsheads/Barrels include wooden drum, iron drum and plastic cask, etc. They are used for the conveyance of liquid or greasy and powdered or granular goods. The main problems associated are the likelihood of leakage if the unit is not properly sealed, and the ability of the drums becoming rusty during transit.

Bags include gunny bags, cloth bags and paper bags, etc. They are ideal for a wide variety of powdered, granular or bulk goods such as cement, fertilizer, flour, oil cakes, animal feeding products, chemicals and many consumer products. Bags can pile up on pallets to facilitate handling but they subject to damage by water, sweat, leakage or breakage.

Bales or bundles are suitable for wool, cotton, feather, silk and piece goods, etc. These goods are to be compressed into bales first and then packed with cotton cloth and gunny cloth strengthened by metal or plastic straps outside.

Crates or skeleton cases are a form of container halfway between a bale and a case. They are of wooden construction. Light weight goods of larger cubic capacity, such as machinery, domestic appliances, refrigerators, cycles, and certain foods tuffs, for instance, oranges are suitable for this form of packing.

According to the method of packing, transport packing can be categorized into unit packing and collective packing. Unit packing is used on the smallest shippable unit of cargo. It can be in different forms of containers used for packing such as cases, cartons, drums, bags, bales, bundles, etc. Collective packing is also called "group shipping packing". By means of collective packing, a certain number of units of cargo are grouped together to form a large collection. Pallet, flexible container, and container are the commonly used equipment for collective packing in international trade (see Figure 3-2).

pallet   flexible container   container

Figure 3-2   Collective packing

Pallet is a large tray or platform allowing a number of units of cargoes to be grouped together. Pallets can move cargoes in loads instead of single pieces from one vehicle to another, e.g. from a lorry into a train or onto a ship. **Flexible container** is a big bag of different sizes facilitating the carrying of large quantities of cargo. **Container** is a large metal case, of standard shape and size, for carrying goods by specially built road vehicles, railway wagons and ships. Some views argue that a container is only part of the transport vehicle rather than a way of collective packing.

Apart from protecting the cargoes, collective packing also facilitates and speeds up the loading and unloading operation. At present, in order to improve the speed of operation and utility of ports and docks, some countries enforce regulations stipulating that cargoes shall be transported in collective packing.

3.5.3　Marking

Marking refers to different diagrams, words and figures which are written, printed, or brushed on the outside of the shipping packing. When goods are well wrapped by the packing, there is no clue to identify them. People need certain kind of indicator to guide their handling of the cargo along the flow logistics. Marking plays an important role in the use of transport packing. According to its function, marking can be classified into four types: shipping marks, indicative marks, warning marks and supplementary marks.

1. Shipping marks

Shipping marks are a type of marking on the shipping packing. It quickens the identification and transportation of the goods and helps avoid shipping errors. Therefore, the design of shipping marks should be simple, clear and easily identifiable. For instance, the position of the shipping marks should be proper; the color of the marks should be durable. Besides, no advertizing words and pictures are allowed to be inserted into the shipping marks (see Figure 3-3).

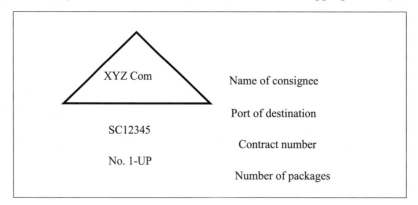

Figure 3-3　Example of shipping marks

International standard shipping marks recommended by the International Organization for Standardization are made up of the following four parts:

(1) Consignee's code: usually the initials or abbreviation of a consignee;

(2) Destination: the name of the port or place of destination;

(3) Reference No.: the number of the relevant contract, order invoice, etc;

(4) Number of packages: the consecutive number of each package.

Adopting standard shipping marks can not only make it easy to identify and transport the goods, but also simplify the process of checking the relative documents and certificates. See a case about compensation for discrepant packing in Case 3-5.

[Case 3-5]

A Chinese export company exported some goods to Canada, valued at USD 800,000. The contract stated that it should be packed in biodegradable PCL plastic bags each labeled in French and English. However, when delivering the goods the export company employed PP plastic bags labeled only in English. In order to meet the sales requirement of the local market the importer had to hire people to change all the packages and labels. Then the importer lodged a claim against the exporter.

Question: Was the importer's claim justified or not?

2. Indicative marks

Indicative marks are diagrams and simple words used to draw different parties' attention when they handle the goods in the process of loading, unloading, carrying and storing. Indicative marks, if necessary, are also painted or stenciled on the outer packing of the commodities.

3. Warning marks

To ensure safe carriage of dangerous goods in international transportation, warning marks, also called dangerous marks, are used to indicate dangerous cargoes such as explosive, corrosive, inflammable and radioactive products. Since different countries have different regulations regarding hazard classification and labeling, the need to comply with multiple regulations is costly and time consuming, and the transport worker, consumers and emergency responders are often confused about the specific hazard, or even sometimes injured without taking the required protective measures. To ensure the information on physical hazards and toxicity from chemicals available and enhance the protection of human health and the environment during the handling, transport and use of hazards. The Globally Harmonized System of Classification and Labeling of Chemicals (GHS) was set up to replace the assortment of hazardous material classification and labeling schemes previously used around the world. This new system has been enacted to significant extents in most major countries as of 2007. The GHS provides appropriate labeling tools to convey information about each of the hazard classes and categories. See some examples in Figure 3-4.

Figure 3-4　Examples of warning marks under GHS system

4. Supplementary marks

Sometimes, in accordance with the rules and regulations laid down by the importing and exporting countries, or the agreement entered into by the parties concerned, some supplementary marks are inserted such as the mark of weight or volume and the mark of origin. See Figure 3-5.

① Mark of weight or volume.

Marks of weight or volume are marks indicating the volume or the gross/net weight of the package to facilitate loading/unloading or booking shipping space.

② Mark of origin.

Marks of origin are required by many exporting or importing countries for customs statistics and taxation. In some countries, mark of origin is compulsory for imported goods. While some other countries may require marks of origin to avoid confusion over the real origin of the goods.

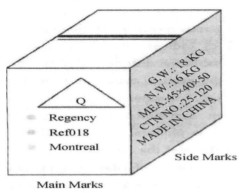

Figure 3-5   Examples of supplementary marks

The mark of origin must be legible, indelible and clearly visible. In addition, each country has relevant regulations governing the way of marking for imported goods, including language and marks to be used and even the size of the letters of marking. Therefore, the way of marking depends on the requirements of the specific country. Usually, exporters, who put on the mark of origin, should look into the importing country's marking regulations before packing and marking their goods for export shipment.

3.5.4   Sales Packaging

Sales packaging is also called inner packaging, small packaging, immediate packaging or marketing packaging. The main purpose of such packaging is for sales promotion.

To facilitate sales, different packages are designed to match with various kinds of goods: carrying packaging, hang-up packaging, easy-open packaging, spraying packaging, pilling-up packaging, gift packaging, and so on.

Instead of exploring the variety and novelty of the design of sales packaging, a topic probably more appropriate in the field of marketing we will address several issues that are related to the sales packaging and relevant to the practice of international trade at the same time.

1) Neutral packing

Neutral Packing is a special type of marking rather than a type of packing as its name may indicate. While neutral packing is required, no marking of origin or name of the manufacturer should appear on the product, on the shipping packing or sales packaging.

There are two cases for neutral packing: neutral packing with designated brand and neutral packing without designated brand. In the case of neutral packing without designated brand, neither brand or mark nor the country of origin is indicated on the packing. There are cases when the exporter is required to use a specified brand or trade designated by its importer, it becomes neutral packing with designated brand.

Neutral packing is generally adopted as a means to promote export sales. By means of neutral packing, exporters may break down the high customs duties or unreasonable import quota levied on the imports by the importing countries. However, in recent years neutral packing has been restricted by many countries. For instance, as mentioned in the previous section, the mark of origin is compulsory for imported goods in some countries. Goods, packed in neutral packing in absence of marking of origin, are not allowed to enter into these countries. Therefore, cautions must be taken while exporters agree to adopt neutral.

2) OEM

OEM is the short form of Original Equipment Manufacturer. It refers to a kind of international trade practice that sellers use the brand name or trade mark designated by buyers on their manufactured goods. Supermarkets, large department stores and monopolized-commodity stores in many countries adopt OEM for the goods sold to secure a rise both in their reputation and price.

To large and regular orders, exporters are also willing to accept OEM. By means of OEM, sellers can make good use of buyers' well established brand names or trade marks, good reputations and status to expand sales and increase competitiveness in the world market.

In case of neutral marking with trade marks or brands designated by the buyer, or OEM, close attention should be paid to issues concerning infringement on a third party. Usually, the buyers are required to produce certificates evidencing their right in using the brand name or trade mark they designate. Still, it is advisable for sellers to insert a safeguard clause or similar stipulations in the contract to that effect. See Example 3-10.

[Example 3-10]

As to the trade marks designated by the buyer, if the seller is charged with the infringement by any third party, the buyer shall take up the matter with the plaintiff and it has nothing to do with the seller. Any losses thus sustained shall be compensated by the buyer.

3) Labeling

Labels refer to the tags on the sales packaging of goods, which usually consist of words, diagrams and figures. There are special requirements for labeling goods such as prepared goods, beverages, pharmaceuticals and toys.

Usually, regulations require that the label should show the name and address of the manufacturer, a list of ingredients, the weight or volume of the contents, and all other relevant information in the language and weight and measuring systems of the importing country. Thus exporters should ensure that their export goods comply with the labeling requirements of the importing country.

4) Barcode

Barcode is an optical, machine-readable representation of data, which provides the information of the product in international trade, such as the name, specifications, origin and price. Traditional barcodes systematically represent data by varying the widths and spacings of parallel lines, and may be referred to as linear or one-dimensional (1D). Later, two-dimensional (2D) variants were developed, using rectangles, dots, hexagons and other geometric patterns called matrix codes or 2D bar codes, although they do not use bars as such. Initially, barcodes were only scanned by special optical scanners called barcode readers. Later application software became available for devices that could read images, such as smart phones with cameras.

Several barcode systems exist at the same time. The Universal Product Code (UPC), compiled by the Universal Code Council (UCC), is the universal bar coding system. There are five versions of UPC from A to E, among which Version A, the basic version, is the most common and usually seen on store items and UPC Version E is the second most common one used on packaging. Another universally used coding system is the European Article Numbering System (EAN) compiled by European Article Number Association (EANA). There are two principal EAN versions. One is the Standard EAN (also called EAN-13) which has ten numeric characters, two or three characters, and a check digit. The other is the EAN-8, EAN-8 consists of eight digits, which is actually the short form of EAN-13, only used if the article is too small for an EAN-13 when an EAN-13 may use more than 25% of the front space of the article.

3.5.5　Packing Clause in the Sales Contract

A sales contract should expressly indicate the packing method (e.g. the material 9 dimensions, weight of every single piece, filling material used and reinforcement conditions, etc.), the packing cost and the shipping marks.

Details of the packing methods must be clear in the packing clause and shall include such details as shape, size, material used, etc. For example, 30 cm × 40 cm × 50 cm cartons, new iron drums containing 190 kg net weight or four-ply Kraft paper bags containing 25 kg. In addition, reinforcement conditions or filling material, if applicable, must also be properly stipulated. For instance, "packed in wooden drum or reinforced with iron band"; "packed in cartons, 10 cartons to a plastic pallet"; "packed in iron drums, 80 drums to a container. Ambiguous expressions such as "sea worthy packing", "customary packing" should be avoided in the contract. When the buyer is required to supply the packing material, wholly or partly, the seller should also stipulate in the contract the time limit within which the packing material shall arrive.

Shipping cost division must be specified in the packing clause. Packing expense can be included in the price of the commodity; in this case, it is the seller who bears the packing cost. However, it can also be excluded from the price with packing cost born wholly or partly by the buyer. In the latter case, the seller should specify in the contract the expense to be paid by the buyer and the method of payment as well. See Example 3-11.

[Example 3-11]

Packing: In new iron drums of 175 kg each, net.

Packing: Each pair of nylon socks is packed in a polybag and 12 pairs to a box.

Packing: In new single jute bags 5,100 kg net each.

Shipping Marks: At the seller's option.

Shipping Marks: At the buyer's option, the relevant shipping marks should reach the seller ×× days before the time of shipment.

Shipping marks are usually to be supplied by the buyer. Occasionally they are at the seller's option. When the buyer designates the shipping marks, it is advisable for the seller to stipulate the arrival time of the marks.

In trade practice, unless otherwise stipulated in the contract, the cost of packing are included in the contract price and the design of the shipping marks are at the seller's option.

Notes to the Text

I. Vocabulary and phrases.

1. counter sample   对等样品

2. reference sample   参考样品；成交样品

3. sale by actual commodity   凭实际商品买卖

4. sale by sample   凭样品买卖

5. sale by standard/grade   凭标准/等级买卖

6. sale by trade mark/brand name   凭商标/品牌买卖

7. sale by specifications/descriptions/illustrations   凭规格/说明书/图样买卖

8. quantity latitude   品质公差

9. quality tolerance   品质机动幅度

10. gross weight   毛重

11. tare   皮重

12. net weight   净重

13. gross for net   以毛计净

14. more or less clause   溢短装条款

15. metric system   公制

16. conditioned weight   公量

17. shipping package   运输包装

18. indicative mark   指示标志

19. bulk cargo   散装货

20. nude cargo 裸装货

21. packed cargo 包装货

22. customs or statutory requirements 海关或法定要求

23. shipping mark 唛头

24. warning mark 警示标志

25. labeling 标识

26. neutral packing 中性包装

27. barcode 条形码

28. OEM 贴牌生产

II. Sentences and paragraphs.

1. Name of commodity, as a basis for the delivery of goods, has a bearing on the interests and rights of both importers and exporters. Therefore, the name should be clearly and properly specified in a sales contract and the name of the goods delivered should exactly conform to the contract.

作为商品交付依据的商品名称(品名)关系到进出口双方的权益。因此,在外贸合同中应当明确、正确地写明商品名称,而且交付的商品名称应与合同相符。

2. Quality refers to the intrinsic elements of commodities including the internal properties or ingredients as well as the external appearance. Hence description of the quality may provide information related to the shape, structure, form, color, flavor, chemical composition, physical and mechanical property, biological features and other aspects of the product.

品质是指商品的内在要素,包括内在的属性或成分以及外在外观。因此,对品质的描述可以提供与产品的形状、结构、形式、颜色、风味、化学成分、物理机械性能、生物特性及其他方面有关信息。

3. Different forms may be chosen depending on the attributes nature, and characteristics of a commodity. Generally speaking, sale by description is applicable to commodities of which quality can be expressed by some scientific indices.

不同形式的选择取决于商品属性、性质和特性。一般而言,凭文字说明买卖常用于可用一些科学指标表示品质的商品。

4. Thus FAQ is used to indicate that the quality of the product offered is about equal to the average quality level of the same crop within a certain period of time (e.g. a year). GMQ, on the other hand, means that the goods offered are of quality sufficiently good to satisfy the purpose of use or consumption which are mutually understood by both the buyer and the seller. It is used sometimes as the bottom-line of quality requirement.

因此,FAQ (良好平均品质)用来表示所提供产品品质大约等于在某一特定时期内(例如一年)同类产品的平均质量水平。另外,GMQ (良好可售品质)是指所提供的货物品质足以满足买卖双方相互理解的使用和消费目的。它有时被用作品质要求的底线。

5. Quality latitude means the permissible range within which the quality of the goods delivered by the seller may be flexibly controlled. Quality tolerance refers to the quality deviation recognized which allows the quality of the goods delivered to have certain difference within a range.

品质公差意为卖方交付的货物品质有在公认的一定范围内的差异。品质机动幅度是指允许所交付货物的品质在一定幅度内的品质偏离。

6. For the sake of efficient shipment and less complexity in contract execution it is common to allow the seller to deliver the goods with a certain percentage of more or less in quantity accordingly.

为了有效装运和降低合同执行的复杂性，通常允许卖方以相应的一定百分比的数量交付货物。

7. In absence of any more or less specifying the quantity a tolerance not exceeding 5% more or 5% less is allowed, provided the quantity is not stipulated by number (of package units or individual items) and provided that the total amount of the goods does not exceed the amount of the credit.

如果没有对溢短装具体规定的，则增减幅度小于等于 5%是允许的。如果未以包装单位件数或货物自身件数方式规定货物数量的，货物数量允许有 5%以内的增减幅度，但总金额不超过信用证金额。

8. Actually, packing not only serves as a form of protection but also facilitates loading unloading and stowage, and prevents pilferage.

事实上，包装不仅仅是起到保护的作用，而且便利装卸，易于储存，防止偷窃。

9. Shipping marks are a type of marking on the shipping packing. It quickens the identification and transportation of the goods and helps avoid shipping errors.

唛头是在运输包装上的一种标记，可起到快速辨认与运输货物并可避免运输错误的作用。

10. Neutral Packing is a special type of marking rather than a type of packing as its name may indicate. While neutral packing is required, no marking of origin or name of the manufacturer should appear on the product, on the shipping packing or sales packaging.

中性包装是一种特殊类型的标志，而非如其名称所表明的包装种类。当要求采用中性包装时，产品、运输包装或销售包装上不应出现原产地或制造商名称的标记。

Exercises

I. Finish the multiple choice questions.

1. The sample made by the seller according to the buyer's, and then sent to and confirmed by

the buyer is called _____.

  A. duplicate sample   B. returning sample

  C. original sample   D. counter sample

 2. _____ are usually sold by trade mark or brand name.

  A. Manufactured goods with steady quality B. Raw materials

  C. Machine and instrument   D. Goods with special shape

 3. The methods commonly used to express the quality include the followings except _____.

  A. sale by sample   B. sale by materials

  C. sale by description   D. sale by trade mark or brand name

 4. In international trade, the goods that are demanded on special shape or the characteristics of color and taste should be sold _____.

  A. by sample   B. by specification   C. by grade   D. by name of origin

 5. Quality standard of FAQ means that _____.

  A. the goods are suitable for sales   B. the goods are merchantable

  C. the goods have bad quality   D. the goods have fair average quality

 6. If there is a quality tolerance clause in a contract, within the range of the tolerance, the buyer _____.

  A. can't refuse to accept the goods

  B. can refuse to accept the goods

  C. can demand the price to be adjusted

  D. can refuse to accept the goods or demand the price to be adjusted

 7. The more or less clause is normally used for _____.

  A. bulk goods   B. packed units

  C. individual items   D. containerized goods

 8. _____ are marks of simple designs, some letters, numbers and simple words of packages, often stenciled, that serve as an identification of the consignment to which they belong.

  A. Shipping marks   B. Supplementary marks

  C. Indicative marks   D. Warning marks

II. Decide whether the following statements are true (T) or false (F).

 1. The grade of the same products are always the same in different countries.   ( )

 2. "Gross for Net" is often stipulated in the contract to indicate that the weight of the less valued products is calculated by gross weight.   ( )

 3. Quality tolerance will be stipulated in the contract to indicate that so long as both parties agree, quality difference can be tolerated.   ( )

 4. Packing can only serve as a form of protection.   ( )

 5. Neutral packing is adopted to break tariff and non-tariff barriers of some importing countries, and tends to be widely adopted by many countries.   ( )

III. Answer the following questions according to the information you have got.

1. If a seller has to take one product from a consignment of goods as a sample for sale, should he select the best quality product? Why or why not?

2. If a contract says "the quality of the goods delivered is the same as the quality of the sample", should the seller accept the condition?

3. The following is a quality clause in a sales contract: "Chinese groundnut kernel: Moisture 13%, broken grains 5%, oil content 44%". Is this acceptable? Why?

4. If the seller delivers a quantity of goods greater than stipulated in the contract, how can the buyer cope with the situation?

5. What are the advantages and disadvantages of the neutral packing? What are the issues to be concerned when adopting this practice?

 微课资源

扫一扫，获取相关微课视频。

3.1.mp4

3.2.mp4

3.3.mp4

Chapter 4 International Cargo Transport

Leading in

A Chinese company (Company A) signed a sales contract with a Brazilian company (Company C). Company A entrusted a shipping company (Company B) to ship the 10,000 sacks of coffee beans from Shanghai Port to a port in Brazil. Company B issued a clean B/L evidencing that shipment of 10,000 sacks of coffee beans, each weighing 60kg, are in apparent good condition. When the goods arrived at the destination, Company C found that the weight of 600 sacks of goods was 25% less in quantity than contracted and the packages were loosened.

Therefore, Company C sued Company B for the quantity discrepancy between the delivered goods and the descriptions on the B/L, and asked Company B to compensate for the loss. Company B later provided evidence to prove that the loosened packages and the short weight had existed when the goods were loaded on board, and the company issued the clean B/L because of failure in checking every package. Since the discrepancy in delivered quantity was not caused by Company B, the company should not compensate for the loss. Investigation also confirmed that the short weight of 600 sacks of goods was not caused by the carrier but by the shipper, Company A.

Question: In the case, which party should compensate Company C? Give your reasons.

4.1 Parties Involved in Transport

Organizing and executing the movement of goods can sometimes be very complex and involve a large number of parties or stakeholders (for example, consignor, consignee, carrier, freight forwarder), who need to communicate and exchange relevant information among each other and fulfill contractual obligations as well as comply with official procedures and documentary requirements from a range of authorities including, but not limited to customs, transport authorities and security agencies.

The main parties involved in ship chartering are as follows.

Consigner, or the shipper. A consigner is a party without a cargo who takes a vessel on charter for a specified period from the owner and then trades the ship to carry cargoes at a profit above the hire rate. A shipper is a person or company that sends or transports goods.

Freight agent. As a common practice, the importer and the exporter may entrust an agent with the work of handling ship chartering or space booking. Sometimes the freight agent may even arrange warehousing and clear customs for the importer or the exporter.

Chartering broker, also called chartering agent, whose main business is, according to the instruction of the client (ship owner or charter), to look for suitable means of transportation for clients and collect commission from it.

Transport company, sometimes called ship-owner or shipping company. It is the real carrier of the goods. In reality, the consigner may directly contact the ship owner without using freight agent or chartering broker as a middleman. Some freight agents themselves also serve as chartering agents.

4.2　Modes of Transport

In the business of international trade, goods are transferred from the seller to the buyer through international cargo transport operations. Before a shipment is made, the exporter has to consider many different factors influencing the transport considerations such as cost, safety, speed and convenience. Carriage of goods can take place by sea, rail, air, road, inland waterway, parcel post, container and multimodal transport.

4.2.1　Marine Transportation

Marine transportation, also called ocean transportation, is the most widely used mode of transportation in international trade. It is cheap for delivering large quantities of goods over long distances. About 2/3 of the world trade volume are transported by sea.

It has the following advantages, such as easy passage since about 70% of the earth is covered by water, a large capacity, relatively low-cost way to transport goods. However, compared with road or air transportation, marine transportation is slow, vulnerable to bad weather and less punctual.

In accordance with the different ways of ship operation, maritime transport can be divided into liner transport and charter transport, which can be divided into voyage charter, time charter and demise charter.

1. Liner transport

Liner is a kind of vessel which sails between specified ports regularly, and liner shipping is a shipping service that operates within a schedule and has a fixed port rotation with published dates of calls at the advertized ports. A liner shipping generally fulfills the schedule unless in cases where a call at one of the ports has been unduly delayed due to natural or manmade disasters.

1) Main features

The liner has a regular line, port, timetable (or sailing schedule) and comparatively fixed freight. The carrier is responsible for loading and unloading operations, i.e., gross terms, and the loading and unloading charges are included in the freight. The two parties don't calculate demurrage and dispatch money, since the ship owner usually leases part of shipping space instead of the whole ship. The B/L drawn by the shipping company is the shipping contract between the carrier and the consignor. The rights and obligations of the carrier and the consignor are based on the B/L drawn by the shipping company.

2) Freight of liner

Liner freight consists of two parts: basic freight and additional freight (or called surcharges).

$$\text{total liner freight} = \text{basic freight} + \text{additional freight}$$

Basic freight is the major and requisite part of the total liner freight. And the basic freight rate is usually listed in a liner tariff quoted by the carrier or freight conference and unchanged in a rather long time.

The basic standards for calculating basic freight are stipulated as follows.

Gross weight (i.e. weight ton), which is indicated by "W" in the tariff. The freight is to be calculated per metric ton or long ton which is decided by liner companies. Heavy cargoes are usually charged on this basis.

Volume (i.e. measurement ton), which is indicated by "M" in the tariff. The freight is to be calculated per meter or 40 cubic feet. Often light cargoes are charged on the basis.

Gross weight or volume, means choosing the higher rate between the two, which is indicated by "W/M" in the tariff.

The value of the cargo, i.e., a certain percentage of FOB prices which is indicated by AV (Ad Val) in the tariff. Usually a percentage between 1% and 4% is charged on the value of goods such as gold, silver, precious stones, and valuable drawings and paintings.

Gross weight or volume or AV, i.e., choosing the highest rate of the three, which is indicated by W/M or AV.

Gross weight or volume, and then plus a certain percentage of AV indicated by W/M plus AV.

The number of the cargo, the freight is to be calculated according to the number of the cargo carried, which is indicated by "unit". For example, a freight of so much is for one trunk or one head of live animal.

The special agreement, the freight is to be calculated according to temporary or special agreement between the carrier and the consignor. Principally, shipment of grains, ores, coal, etc. in large quantity is subject to a special freight fixed in an interim agreement between the carrier and the shipper.

The basic freight is generally based on the basic route for transport between ports and the average level of fees charged to general cargo. In fact, there are some goods that require special handling, which may lead to differences in the transportation costs. In order to get some additional compensation expense, the liner shipping company may collect some additional freight.

Common types of additional freight are:

Fuel surcharge, such as FAF (Fuel Adjustment Factor), BAF (Bunker Adjustment Factor), BRC (Bunker Recovery Charge), EBS (Emergency Bunker Surcharge), or EBA (Emergency Bunker Adjustment).

Fuel cost in shipping companies accounts for a large proportion of the transporting costs. If the fuel price increases suddenly, the operating costs of the liner company will increase directly. Therefore, the fuel surcharge is generally used by the liner shipping company to deal with short-term changes in fuel prices and costs. When fuel prices decline, the fuel surcharge will be adjusted or even be canceled.

CAF (Currency Adjustment Factor). The freight currency depreciation will reduce the real income of the carrier and the liner shipping may charge CAF.

Port surcharge, such as SPS (Shanghai Port Surcharge), ORC (Origin Receipt Charge), THC (Terminal Handling Charge), or PCS (Port Congestion Surcharge). Inefficient port handling or the port charges are too high, or the existence of the special charges will increase the operating costs of the carrier. So the carrier may charge the Port Surcharge.

Extra Charges on Over Length (or Over-length Surcharge) discharging of goods whose length exceeds a certain length, usually 9 meters, will be more difficult and increase the cost of the liner company. So the Extra Charges on Over Lengthy may be charged.

Extra Charges on Heavy Lifts (or Over-weight Surcharge). Loading and discharging of goods whose single unit weight exceeds a certain weight will be more difficult and increase the cost of the liner company. So the Extra Charges on Heavy Lifts may be charged.

Direct Additional. If the consignor asks the liner company to transport the goods directly to a port which is not the fixed ports of call advertized by the liner company, the liner company may charge the Direct Additional.

Transshipment Surcharge. If the consignor asks the line company to transship the goods to a port which is not the fixed ports of call advertised by company, the liner company may charge the Transshipment Surcharge.

In order to calculate the freight, it should start with conformity to the English name of the commodity, find out the freight standard for calculating the freight grade; then find out the basic freight rate in the route freight tariff according to the grades and purpose sea route; moreover, decide the relative surcharges for the suitable route and basic port; finally, the basic freight rate plus various additional surcharges is the freight per freight ton.

The formulas for calculating the freight are as follows:

Freight per freight ton = Basic freight rate + $\sum$ Rate of surcharge

Total freight amount = The freight ton of the goods × Freight per freight ton

See Example 4-1.

[Example 4-1]

Company A exports 1,000 cases of goods ×××to London. The volume per case is 40 cm × 30 cm × 20 cm, and the gross weight is 30 kg. On the list of Classification of Commodities, goods ×××falls within the scope of class 10, and the freight is based on W/M. On the Freight Tariff (China-London), the basic freight rate for class 10 is USD222, with 10% port surcharges.

Question: How much is the total freight?

Calculation:

Total weight: 0.03 m/t × 1,000 =30 m/t

Total volume: 0.4 × 0.3 × 0.2 × 100 =2.4 m^3

Since Total weight > Total volume, "W" is the basis for calculating freight.

Total freight = Total weight × (Basic freight rate + Surcharge)

　　　　=30 × (USD222 + USD222 × 10%)

　　　　=USD7,326

2. Charter transport

Charter transport is also called tramp, which doesn't sail on firm schedule and regular routes, but goes all over the world in search of cargoes, primarily bulk shipments, like grain timber, steel, coal, ores, fertilizers, etc., which are carried in complete shiploads. Tramp vessels are engaged under chartering on a time and voyage basis, and occasionally are chartered to supplement existing liner services to meet peak cargo shipment demands. Generally, there are three kinds of chartering: voyage charter, time charter and demise charter.

1) Modes of charter transport

A voyage charter is the hire of a ship for a particular trip, which might be for one single or consecutive single voyage or for one return or consecutive return voyages. The charterer should pay the freight for his shipment of cargoes on an agreed rate.

A time charter is the hire of a ship for a specified period of time, from a few months up to several years. During the time of chartering, the business of the ship is under the management of the charterer.

There are some differences between voyage charter and time charter. For voyage charter, the charterer charters the ship to transport a stated quantity and type of cargoes between named ports. The ship owner is responsible not only for the management of the ship, but also for the driving, sailing and transportation of the goods. The freight is charged according to the quantities of the shipment and the contract shall stipulate time of shipment or rate of shipment. For time charter, the charterer charters the ship for a limited agreed period of time. Their contracts are also different. The ship owner is responsible for the ship's maintenance, repair and crew's wages, but transportation of the goods loading and unloading the goods is born by charterer. The freight is charged to according to the period of time and the contract doesn't have to stipulate time of shipment.

Demise charter is also called bare boat charter. Under demise charter, the ship owner only rents the charterer the boat, while the charterer is responsible for crewing, provisioning and fueling, and the boat is under complete control of the charterer. To some extent, it is a form of time charter.

2) Freight of charter

In the case of voyage charter, the ship owner and the charterer shall reach an agreement on the loading and unloading cost and put it clearly in the charter party. There are four methods for stipulating the expenses of loading and unloading:

Liner terms/Gross terms: the ship owner shall be responsible for loading and unloading cost.

Free in (F.I.): the ship owner bears the unloading cost, not loading cost.

Free out (F.O.): the ship owner bears the loading cost, not the unloading cost.

Free in and out (F.I.O.): the ship owner does not bear unloading and loading cost.

Free in and out and stowed and trimmed (F.I.O.S.T.): the ship owner is responsible neither for loading and unloading nor for stowed and trimmed cost. When adopting this method, the interested parties should indicate who will bear the expenses of stowing and trimming.

4.2.2   Railway Transportation

Rail transport is a major mode of transport in terms of capacity, only second to ocean transport. It is capable of achieving relatively high speed and is most economical, especially if it provides the complete trainload for a shipper on regular basis. Besides, it is less prone to interruption by poor weather. But it is confined to railroad and therefore less flexible.

In China, there are mainly two types: international combined rail transport and railway transport to Hong Kong and Macao. International combined rail transport of goods are carriage under a single contract and through a consignment note made out for the whole route over the territories of at least two countries i.e., the point of departure of the consignment and the planned point of delivery of the goods are in different countries.

China is a contracting country of Agreement Concerning International Carriage of Goods by Rail (CMIC), which has 22 contracting states, including China, Vietnam, Mongolia, Democratic People's Republic of Korea, Iran, Bulgaria, Poland, Albania and 14 CIS (Commonwealth of Independent States) countries (except Armenia). So the goods can be transported from China to these contracting countries by international combined rail transport.

4.2.3 Air Transport

Air transport is one of the youngest forms of distribution. The most obvious advantage of air freight is quick transit. Quick, reliable transits eliminate need for extensive warehouse accommodation and reduce the risk of stockpiling, obsolescence, deterioration and capital tied up in transit. Low risk of damage and pilferage with consequent competitive insurance premium is another advantage. However, air transport is subject to a high operating cost and initial cost of aircraft when compared to overall capacity. Air transport is ideal for the goods that are in small quantity, light and precious, and need to be urgently transported.

Air transport includes four types: scheduled airlines, chartered carriers, consolidated consignment and air express.

Scheduled airlines: operating on a scheduled service, over a fixed airline and between fixed airports, suitable for conveying fresh, emergent and seasonal goods.

Chartered carriers: the hire of an aircraft by a shipper or several shippers to deliver cargoes, ideal for carrying cargoes of large quantities or carrying cargoes of different shippers to the same destination.

Consolidated consignments: the air freight forwarder usually assembles a number of individual shipments into one consignment and dispatches them on one air waybill. A consolidated shipment made up by several shipments can be dispatched to one common destination. Many shippers prefer this kind of shipment as the freight rate is 7% ~ 10% lower than that of a scheduled airline.

Air express service: the express service is provided by air freight forwarders specializing in this line of business between consignors, airports and users, suitable for urgently needed articles and important documents.

Table 4-1 shows the names and codes of major China airline.

Table 4-1　Names and codes of major China airline

Code	Chinese name	English name
CA	中国国际航空(集团)公司	Air China
MU	中国东方航空(集团)公司	China Eastern Airlines

continued

Code	Chinese name	English name
CZ	中国南方航空(集团)公司	China Southern Airlines
4G	深圳航空公司	Shenzhen Airlines
3U	四川航空股份有限公司	Sichuan Airlines
MF	厦门航空有限公司	Xiamen Airlines
SC	山东航空公司	Shandong Airlines

4.2.4　International Multimodal Transport

1. The definition of international multimodal transport

International multimodal transport (international combined transport) means the carriage of cargo by at least two modes of transport on the basis of a Multimodal Transport Contract (MTC) from a place at which the cargoes are collected in one country to a place designated for delivery in another country by Multimodal Transport Operator (MTO). Although different modes of transport are combined, only one MTO is responsible for taking the cargo from the consignor and delivering them to the consignee. Multimodal Transport Document (MTD) is the only document used.

2. The basic conditions of international multimodal transport

The basic conditions of international multimodal transport are as follows:

① There must be an MTC to stipulate the right, responsibility, obligations and exemption of the parties;

② It includes two or more different modes of successive transportation;

③ Transport documents, i.e. combined transport documents shall cover the whole journey;

④ It shall be international transportation;

⑤ The MTO shall be responsible for the whole journey;

⑥ The whole journey shall use a single factor rate.

The use of containers in multimodal transport means high efficiency, better quality of transport, lower cost and less time being required for cargo movement between the point of origin and the place of delivery. MTD is the only document used, which also adds to the economy and simplicity of the documentation process.

3. The MTO

The MTO means any person who on his own behalf or through another person acting on his behalf concludes an MTC and who acts as a principal, not as an agent or on behalf of the consignor or of the carriers participating in the multimodal transport operations, and who assumes responsibility for the performance of the contract.

An MTO accepts an order from the shipper for carriage of his cargo from a port or place as designated by him or by concluding an MTC between them. Pursuant to the terms of the contract, he undertakes to provide for different modes of transport and other services required for the conveyance of the cargo under the contract to the designated destination and charges the freight on a through rate basis.

4.2.5 Container Transport

With the rapid development of containerization, containers as a very special form of transportation are widely used in different modes of transportation. Containerization is a method of distributing merchandise in a unitized form adopting an intermodal system which provides a possible combination of sea, road and other modes of transportation.

To transport goods by container transportation, the carrier shall first stow large quantity of cargoes into standard-sized and reusable vans at the manufacturer's plant inland, or at Container Yard (CY) or the Container Freight Station (CFS), and then ship them in unit loads to its destination. During transit, containers are loaded and unloaded by mechanical devices. From the moment a container is locked and sealed, the cargo inside is kept intact until it reaches the final destination.

1. Descriptions of container

Containerization is a method of distributing merchandise in a unitized form, suitable for ocean, rail and multinational transport. It is the most modern form of physical international distribution and overall is highly efficient in terms of reliability, cost, quality of service, advanced technology and so on. Today, nearly 90% of non-bulk cargo is handled by containers. And one fourth of world's total containers originate from China. Containerization is a system of intermodal freight transport using standard ISO (International Standards Organization) containers that can be loaded and sealed intact onto container ships, railroad cars, planes, and trucks.

ISO Technical Committee defines the container as Article of Transport Equipment which is:

- Of a permanent character and accordingly strong enough to be suitable for repeated use;
- Specially designed to facilitate the carriage of goods, by one or more modes of transport, without intermediate reloading;
- Fitted with devices permitting its ready handling, particularly its modes of transport, transferring from one mode of transport to another;
- So designed as to be easy to fill and empty;
- Stackable;
- Having an internal volume of one cubic meter or more.

On the recommendation of the International Organization for Standardization, the following standardized dimensions in Table 4-2 are now universally accepted.

Table 4-2　Standardized dimension of main containers

Type	Dimension			Maximum weight	Remarks
	Height	Width	Length		
1A	2.438m (8′)	2.438m (8′)	12.191m (40′)	30.48 m/t	40 f/t
1AA	2.591m (8′6″)	2.438m (8′)	12.191m (40′)	30.48 m/t	40 f/t
1B	2.438m (8′)	2.438m (8′)	9.125m (30′)	24.50 m/t	30 f/t
1C	2.438m (8′)	2.438m (8′)	6.058m (20′)	20.32 m/t	20 f/t

Notes: m refers to meters; m/t refers to metric ton; f/t refers to freight ton.

Sizes of container also vary to a certain degree, but the most widely adopted sizes are twenty-foot equivalent unit (TEU) and forty-foot equivalent unit (FEU).

2. Features of container transportation

Containers are constructed of metal and of standard length, mostly ranging from ten to forty feet. The use of containers provides a highly efficient form for transport by road, rail and air. Container transportation is highly efficient in terms of reliability, cost, quality of service and advanced technology. Features of container transportation are follows:

- **It offers a door-to-door service under FCL/FCL, door to Container Freight Station (CFS) service under FCL/LCL, CFS to CFS service under LCL/LCL, or CFS to door service under LCL/FCL.**

The terms FCL, LCL, CFS and CY stand for: FCL—full container load; LCL—less than container load; CFS—container freight station; CY—container yard.

- It can be handled quickly and easily by standardized equipment and thus save labor and loading and unloading charges.
- The low risk of cargo damage and pilferage enables more favorable cargo premiums to obtained compared with break-bulk cargo shipments.
- Less packing is required for containerized consignments.
- Faster transit, coupled with more reliable maritime schedules, and ultimately increased service frequency, produces savings in warehouse accommodation needs, lessen risks of obsolescent stock and speed up capital turn over.

3. Types of container

There are many kinds of container to serve the different needs for cargo transportation. Containers can be classified into dry cargo container refrigerated/reefer container, tanker container (designed for liquid cargo in bulk) and car container (designed for carriage of cars). Different types of containers are variational to suit different needs. They chiefly comprise:

- **Dry cargo container**. It is Used for carrying general cargoes.
- **Refrigerated container/Reefer container**. There is freezing equipment in the container. The temperature can be adjusted from −28℃ to +26℃.
- **Open top container**. The open top container does not have the top part. Cargoes can be loaded or unloaded through the top of the container by elevating equipment. It is suitable for carrying extra-big cargoes.
- **Frame container/flat rack container**. There is no top part and two flank walls on the container. Cargoes can be loaded into or lifted out of the container through the two side-frames.
- **Pen container**. The two sides of this kind of container are covered by metal nets, which makes it convenient to feed the live-stock and ventilate the container.
- **Tank container**. The tank container is suitable for carrying liquid cargoes such as oil, etc.
- **Platform container**. Suitable for carrying extra-long and extra-heavy cargoes. The length can reach more than 6 meters and the weight more than 40 m/t.
- **Bulk containe**r. There are two or three openings on the top of this kind of container, which makes it convenient to load the cargo. There are elevating frames at the bottom of the container that can elevate at a sloping angle of 40 degrees, which makes it convenient to unload the cargo.

4. CY and CFS services

Container transportation provides various services as well. According to the capacity container load, FCL service shall be adopted if the goods are of small quantity. FCL is suitable as the freight is calculated based on container capacity and the origin and destination of the goods, not on the quantity of the goods involved. In such cases, LCL service is preferred as it enables the shipper to have his goods shipped at reasonable freight rate. As far as cargo in small quantity is concerned, total freight under LCL is much less than that under FCL service because LCL allows the carrier to ship the goods at lower cost by consolidating them with consignments of different shippers, which are to be delivered to the same destination.

According to the place of shipment and destination, container transportation service can be mainly divided into following services, details which are summarized in Table 4-3.

Table 4-3   Types of international cargo transported by container

Type of service	Conditions of delivery/receipt	Place of packing the container	Place of unpacking the container	Meaning
CY/CY	FCL/FCL	Shippers or forwarder' premises	Consignee's premises	Door-to-door container service
CY/CFS	FCL/LCL	Shippers or forwarder' premises	Carrier's CFS at the place (port) of destination	Door to CFS service
CFS/CY	LCL/FCL	Carrier's CFS at the place (port) of origin	Consignee's premises	CFS to Door container service
CFS/CFS	LCL/LCL	Carrie's CFS at the place (port) of origin	Carrier's CFS at the place (port) of destination	CFS to CFS service

1) CY/CY container service

The CY/CY container service, also called FCL/FCL service, is a door-to-door container service or house-to-house container service, whill broadly means that the whole container received by the carrier is packed at the shipper's or the forwarder's premises, and the delivery of that same whole container to the consignee's premises.

2) CY/CFS container service

The CY/CFS container service broadly means that the whole container received by the carrier is packed at the shipper's or the forwarder's premises, and that same whole container is emptied at the carrier's container freight station at the port of destination. The consignee arranges the delivery of the loose cargo from the container freight station to his/her premises.

3) CFS/CY container service

The CFS/CY container service broadly means that the delivery of the loose cargo to the carrier's container freight station at the port of origin is packed into the whole container, and the delivery of that same whole container to the consignee's premises.

4) CFS/CFS container service

The CFS/CFS container service broadly means that the delivery of the loose cargo to the carrier's container freight station at the port of origin is packed into the whole container, and that same whole container is emptied at the carrier's container freight station at the port of destination. The consignee arranges the delivery of the loose cargo from the container freight station to his/her premises.

5. Calculation of container freight

The container freight can be calculated by the freight rate of bulk-cargo or by box rate.

Freight rate. If the goods are transported by LCL, the freight is usually calculated by a freight rate of bulk-cargo. It is almost the same as the calculation of liner shipping freight.

Box rate. If the goods are transported by FCL, the freight is usually calculated by a box rate. There are three kinds of box rate:

FAK rate (Freight for All Kinds). It is irrespective of the commodity inside the container and generally formulated based on container capacity and the origin and destination of the merchandise.

FCS rate (Freight for Class). A further type of container rate is based on the class of commodity inside the container. Hence the rate will vary with the commodity in the container (FCL).

FCB rate (Freight for Class or Basis). It is based on the class of commodity and the freight basis.

Besides the basic and container freight, there are some surcharges, such as Inland Transport Charges, LCL Service Charges, Terminal Handling Charges (THC), Fee for use container and other shipments.

See Example 4-2.

[Example 4-2]

Company A exports 600 PCS of wrench to Kobe, Japan. The total gross weight is 16.2 m/t and the measurement is 23.316M^3. The goods is packed into a container of 20' GP for Wrench, the freight rate is W/M, and the Freight Tariff (Shanghai—Kobe) for 20' GP is USD870/M or USD 850/W. The packing charge is USD120/205 GP.

Question: How much is the total freight?

Calculation:

Measurement > Weight, "M" is the freight calculation basis, that is USD 870/M per 20' GP

Total freight = Total measurement (Basic freight + surcharge)

Total freight = 23.316 × (USD870 + USD120) = USD23,082. 84

4.2.6   Road Transport

The road transport is used between countries connected by roads, very flexible in its operation. It has a high distributive ability of offering door-to-door service without intermediate handling. However, road transport has limited capacity and relatively high operating cost. There is also a high risk of pilferage and damage throughout the transit. One of the problems facing road transport is the complication, in relation to customs examination and possible duty payments when the vehicle is involved in crossing several frontiers. Road transport is ideal for general merchandise and selective bulk cargoes in small quantities.

4.2.7　Land Bridge Transport

Land bridge transport is a mode of transport that connects the ocean transport on the two sides of the land by the railway and land which runs across the continent, i.e., ship-train-ship. Land bridge transport uses the container as a medium, so it has advantages of container transport.

There are three main land bridges in the world: American land bridge; Siberian land bridge and the New European-Asia land bridge.

4.2.8　Postal Transport

According to international trade practice, the seller fulfills the duty of delivery only if he delivers the parcel to the post office pays off the postage, and gets the receipt. The post office is responsible for the delivery of the goods to the destination, and the consignee goes to the post office for picking up his goods. Postal transport falls into two kinds: regular mail and air mail.

4.2.9　Pipelines Transport

Pipelines are used for transporting commodities, such as crude oil and gases etc., long distances over land and under the sea. Rising fuel costs make pipelines an attractive economic alternative to other forms of transport in certain circumstances. Safety in transferring flammable commodities is another important consideration.

4.3　Transportation Documents

Shipping documents are critical to all forms of international payment. As all transactions involve money and payments, the form and content of these documents are of great importance for the international traders. Subtle differences between forms and subtle changes in wording can lead to considerably different results. The documents required by a certain form of payment usually vary according to the goods being transacted and the countries involved in the transaction.

4.3.1   Bill of Lading

Bill of lading (B/L) is a document which is issued by a carrier to a shipper with whom the earner has entered into a contract for the carriage of goods.

1. Main functions of B/L

The B/L in the international sale and movement of goods is probably the most important document. It has been relied upon by the commercial community for hundreds of years. When issued by the carrier it has three distinct functions:

1) Evidence of a contract of carriage

A B/L is the evidence of the contract of carriage between the consignor and the carrier. Listed on the B/L are the rights and liabilities of the carrier and the consignor under a charter party, the rights and liabilities are to be decided by the charter party.

2) A receipt for goods

A B/L is a cargo receipt. It is a receipt issued by a carrier evidencing that a consignment of goods has been received at his disposal for shipment, or actually loaded on board the ship. Thus a B/L will show the quantity and apparent condition of the cargo loaded.

In international trade practice, the information about goods is normally provided by the shipper and confirmed by the earner as the goods are transferred to him or loaded responsible only for the apparent compliance rather than the contents packed inside, i.e, a carrier simply makes sure that the labels comply with the goods listed and that the packages are in good condition.

3) A document of title to the goods

A B/L is a document of title to the goods i.e., the legal owner of a B/L holds legal possession of the goods described in it. The legal holder of the B/L is given the right to take delivery of the goods at the port of destination. For this function, the goods still in transit can be transferred from one owner to another by means of selling and buying of a B/L.

The legal responsibilities and liabilities of the parties involved in the carriage are set out in the Legal Issues Document but what needs to be considered in this document is the commercial role of the B/L in relation to the transfer of title of goods and their payment. In effect, the only party able to take delivery of the goods at destination is the one who is the legitimate holder of the consigned or endorsed B/L.

Safe is the knowledge that a contract of carriage exists and that goods have been received by the carrier, the B/L shows the buyer and the buyers bank that dispatch of goods according to the contract of sale is under way. For the exporter, holding a B/L as title to the goods may control when the buyer takes delivery by choosing the point at which it is transferred. Increasingly, ocean earners will request the data for the B/L to be submitted electronically in order to save them re-keying the information, thereby reducing the scope for transcription errors.

As a negotiable document, which allows the title of goods to be transferred by endorsements and delivery one or other parties to the transaction may control the title to the goods. For this reason, letters of credit often specify certain types of B/L in order for this control to be exercised, and there are different types available to exporters depending on the type of service being used. There are also various clauses applicable. A "clean" bill is one that does not bear any clause or notation that expressly mentions a defective condition of the goods or packaging. Sometimes called for under a letter of credit when it is sufficient to prove that the goods have passed into the hands of the carrier responsible for shipping the goods. It does not show that actual shipment has taken place.

2. Types of B/L

Bill of lading can be classified into various types according to different criteria.

1) Shipped (on board) B/L and received for shipment B/L

On board B/L refers to the one that shall be issued after the cargo has been actually shipped on board vessel. It will be marked the name of vessel, voyage number, date of shipment and "shipped on board" on its face. This kind of B/L is a shipped (on board) B/L.

Received for shipment B/L is the one that acknowledges that goods have been received for shipment but not been loaded on board the carrying vessel yet, and usually is marked "received" on its face. It is issued when the goods have been placed in the custody of the carrier awaiting shipment. Such a bill does not show the name of the carrying vessel and the date of shipment. The absence of date of shipment makes it difficult to anticipate the date of the goods. Therefore it is generally not favored by the buyer, and usually the L/C will require the seller to present on board B/L for negotiation at the bank. But it can become a shipped on board B/L by adding an on board notation and signed by the carrier or agent on the received B/L.

2) Clean B/L and unclean B/L

Clean B/L is an on board B/L that does not show any defects on the goods' exteriors after shipment at the port of shipment. This type of B/L is favored by the buyer and its banks.

Unclean B/L is also named a dirty B/L. If defects are found on the exteriors of the goods after they are shipped on board the vessel, the on board B/L will be marked as "unclean" or "… packages in damaged condition" or other statements evidencing the goods are not in apparent good order or condition. Unclean B/L is usually unacceptable to the buyer and its banks.

A contract of sale may stipulate that an exporter must produce "clean shipped on board" B/L and a letter of credit (commonly referred to as a "Documentary Credit" by the banking sector) will almost certainly require this. **In any case, this type of B/L is clearly the most useful due to its prima facie evidence that goods are actually a route to the port of destination on a named vessel on a specified date and that the goods are in the condition stated on the bill at the time** of shipment. See case 4-1.

[Case 4-1]

In January of 2004, Chinese Garments Export Co. and a Mexican importer signed a S/C for sport shirts. As the seller, Chinese Garments Export Co. exported 50,000 PCs of sport shirts to the Mexican importer, on FOB Shanghai terms. Both parties agreed that this batch of goods should be delivered to the carrier appointed by the Mexican importer by the end of Mar. 15th.

On Mar. 9th, Chinese Garments Export Co. packed the 50,000 PCs in 1, 000 cartons, handed over the good to the carrier appointed by the Mexican importer—Hongkong Ocean Shipping Company. The caption of SS. "Fuxing" issued a clean B/L after preliminary inspection of the goods. With the clean B/L, the Chinese Garments Export Co. negotiated the payment with the bank.

When the goods arrived in Mexico, the importer inspected the shirts and found the quantity is less than 50,000 pieces. About 100 of the 1,000 cartons are short delivered with the shortage ranging from several pieces to dozens. The importer then employed a professional inspection agency to issue a certificate of shortage, and file a claim against the seller.

However, since the bank had already negotiated the payment, the Chinese exporter refused to compensate the buyer's loss with the arguments that the carrier issued the Clean B/L while the inspection was conducted after the arrival of the goods. Finally, both parties submit the case for arbitration to the China International Economic and Trade Arbitration Commission and file for arbitration.

Question: If you were an arbitrator, how would you make the judgment?

3) Straight B/L, blank B/L and order B/L

Straight B/L is made out so that only the named consignee at the destination is entitled to take delivery of the goods under the bill. This kind of B/L is not transferable, so it is not commonly used in international trade and normally applies to high-value shipments or goods for special purposes.

Blank B/L (bearer B/L or open B/L) refers to the bill in which the name of a definite consignee is not mentioned. There usually appears in the box of consignee words like "To the bearer", which means that anyone who holds this kind of bill is entitled to the goods. And no endorsement is needed for the transfer of the blank B/L, so this kind of B/L is highly risky and rarely used in international trade.

Order B/L refers to the one that is made out in such a way that it is consigned or destined to the order of a named person instead of a definite consignee. In the box of consignee of order B/L, "To order", "To order of the shipper", or "To order of ×××" is marked. It means that the goods are consigned or destined to the order of a named person. It can be transferred only after endorsement is made. Moreover, if the B/L is made out "To order" or "To order of the XXX", the XXX will endorse the B/L to transfer it. A blank endorsement is usually required for a "To order" B/L.

There are two types of endorsement: special endorsement and blank endorsement. In the case of special endorsement an order B/L must be signed by the shipper (endorser or transferor) showing both the names of the endorser and the endorsee. While in the case of a blank endorsement, only the "signature of the shipper (endorser or transferor)" is required (without indicating the endorsee of transferee). An order B/L with blank endorsement serves the purpose of the further transfer of the B/L from one to another.

4) Direct B/L, transshipment B/L and through B/L

Direct B/L refers to the B/L which states that the goods will be transported directly to the port of destination and won't be transshipped while transshipment B/L refers to the B/L which states that the goods need to be transshipped at an intermediate port.

Through B/L means a B/L that is covering origin place, transshipment port, port of destination, final place and the journey of the goods which are usually to be transported with more than one vessel. In international trade it is sometimes necessary to employ two or more carriers to get the goods to their final destination. In this case, if the first transportation is sea transport, the carrier will usually sign and issue a through B/L. Furthermore, it shall be emphasized that the carrier who issues a through B/L is usually not responsible for the whole journey of the goods from place of origin to final place and is usually responsible for the sea transport only.

5) Long form B/L and short form B/L

Long form B/L refers to the B/L on the back of which all the detail terms and conditions about the rights and obligations of the carrier and the consignor are listed as an integral part of the bill.

Short form B/L is a document which omits the items and conditions on the back of the B/L.

6) Original B/L and copy B/L

Original B/L refers to one that is signed and dated by either the shipping company or by a duly authorized agent. The B/L must show how many signed originals were issued, the originals are marked "Original" on their face and they become valid only after being signed by the carrier. The original B/L is a piece of evidence showing the ownership of goods, one of which must be presented to the carrier at the destination in exchange for the goods.

In some cases, a "full set" of rather than just one original B/L is required to be presented. In practice, the B/L is normally made out in a set of three originals and if a full set is required, all three originals are to be delivered to the buyer or the consignee. When one of the originals is used, the others automatically become null and void.

Copy B/L is marked "Copy", "Duplicate" or "Non-negotiable" instead of "Original". For easy distinction, copy and original B/L are usually designed and printed in two different colors.

Copy B/L are mainly used for reference or for records.

7) Freight prepaid B/L and freight to be collected B/L

Freight prepaid B/L indicates that the freight has been paid by the consignor. This type of B/L is usually issued only after the freight has been paid. Freight to be collected B/L refers to the B/L on which "freight payable at destination" or "freight be collected at destination" is indicated.

8) Liner B/L, house B/L and charter Party B/L

Liner B/L is issued by a liner company for shipment on scheduled ports of call through scheduled routes, while house B/L is a B/L issued by a freight forwarder before he gets one set of B/L from the ship owner. Charter party B/L means a B/L which indicates that it is subject to a charter party. According to UCP 600, this kind of B/L is not acceptable.

9) Deck B/L, stale B/L and advanced B/L

Deck B/L is issued when the cargo is loaded on the ship's deck. It applies to goods like livestock, plants, dangerous cargo, or awkwardly-shaped goods that can't fit into the ship's hold. In this case, the goods are exposed to greater risks and therefore usually specific insurance must be taken out against additional risks.

Stale B/L is presented to the consignee or the buyer or his bank after the goods are due at the port of destination. In practice, it is important the B/L is available at the port of destination before the goods arrive. As a cargo cannot be collected by the buyer without the B/L. The late arrival of the B/L may have undesirable consequences such as warehouse rent, etc. and therefore should be avoided. Sometimes especially in the case of short sea voyages it is necessary to add a clause of "Stale B/L is acceptable".

Advanced B/L refers to the kind of on board B/L issued before the goods have been shipped on board, and on which the date of shipment is a date earlier than the actual shipment date. In practice, if the seller couldn't ship the goods during the shipment period stipulated in the sales contract or L/C, the seller may ask the carrier to issue an ante-dated B/L or an advanced B/L, which is fraudulent conduct. Once the buyer finds these, he/she can reject the goods and claim for damages.

3. Main contents of B/L

Although there are various forms of B/L, to perform the above mentioned functions, a B/L shall contain essential information about the consignment, the carriage of goods and the rights and obligations of the parties involved. The basic terms are usually shown on the lace of the bill while some general terms and conditions are printed on the back. The items on the face of a B/L are usually the information concerning the following contents (as shown in Figure 4-1).

- Shipper or consignor. It is usually the exporter.
- Consignee. If it is stipulated in L/C such as ① "to ×× Co", or ②"Full set of B/L made out to order", or ③ "B/L issued to order of ××"; then the consignee should be

made out respectively: ① "Consigned to ×× Co", ② "To order", ③ "To order of ××".

- B/L No. It is given by the shipping company or its agent.

- Notify party, addressed to. If it belongs to straight B/L, the consignee's address is written in details; if it states otherwise, fill in the blank as the requirement in the sales contract and/or L/C.

- Ocean vessel and voyage No. If transshipment is allowed, the second ship's name is filled in here. If transshipment is not allowed the first ship's name is filled in.

- Port of loading. Fill in the name of port, e.g. "Tianjin", "Qingdao", it should not be written as "Chinese port" on CIF or CFR basis.

- Port of discharge. If the ship arrives at the destination port directly fill the port of destination; if transshipment is allowed, fill in the port that the cargo is unloaded after the first voyage.

- Place of delivery. It should be subject to the stipulations of the contract and L/C. If there is no L/C, it should be in conformity with the terms of the contract and the invoice.

- Marks and Nos. According to the requirements of the sales contract and L/C; if there are no marks, fill in "N/M".

- No. of packages. Fill in the number of package in figures.

- Description of goods. Fill in the name and specifications of the commodity, which can be in general.

- Gross weight and measurement. Fill in the gross weight in kilogram as calculating weight unit. If there is no package or in bulk, you can write "Gross for Net". Fill in the cargoes volume, keep three decimal fraction.

- Total number of packages in words. Fill in the number in words.

- Freight and charges. If the trade term is CIF, or CFR, fill in "Freight Prepaid"; if the trade term is FOB, fill in "Freight Collect" or "Freight Payable at Destination".

- No. of original B(s)/L. Fill in "THREE" or "TWO" or "ONE", etc. according to the actual number of the original B/L and indicating "ORIGINAL" usually.

- Place and date of issue. The place is the port of loading; date of issue refers to the date of shipment and the date should be earlier than the validity of L/C.

- Signed for the carrier. The B/L shall be signed by the carrier (or a named agent for or on behalf of the carrier), or the master (or a named agent for or on behalf of the master). And any signature by the carrier, master or agent must be identified as that of the carrier, master or agent. Any signature by an agent must indicate whether the agent has signed for or on behalf of the carrier or the master.

Shipper (Insert Name, Address and Phone)	B/L No.

Consignee (Insert Name, Address and Phone)	ORIGINAL

BILL OF LADING

Notify Party (Insert Name, Address and Phone)

Pre - carriage by	Place of Receipt
Ocean Vessel Voy. No.	Port of Loading
Port of Discharge	Place of Delivery

Marks & Nos. Container / Seal No.	No. of Containers or Packages	Description of Goods	Gross Weight	Measurement

Total Number of Containers and/or Packages (in words)

Freight & Charges	Revenue Tons	Rate	Per	Prepaid	Collect

Ex. Rate:	Prepaid at	Payable at	Place and date of issue
	Total Prepaid	No. of Original B(s)/L	

LADEN ON BOARD THE VESSEL
DATE   BY

Figure 4-1   Sample of B/L

4.3.2   Sea Waybill

A sea waybill is a transport document issued by a shipping company as an alternative to a B/L. It only performs as a receipt of goods and a contract of carriage. Like the ocean B/L, the sea waybill acts as a receipt for the goods and evidence of contract of carriage but there the similarity ends. The sea waybill does not generally mirror the B/L as a negotiable document conferring title to the goods. However, where the ability to transfer title is not required, the sea waybill does offer a simple alternative to the B/L. It has particular application in situations where a company might be moving goods between its own international locations, and payment for exports is not as issued. It might also suit the needs of a forwarder as a document to control consolidated (groupage) cargo, with the waybill sent forward with the goods, allowing the consignee to take immediate delivery. The legal protection offered to a shipper using the sea waybill has often been regarded as inferior to that of a B/L but it still has its place in commercial trading practice.

4.3.3　Rail Waybill

The rail waybill is the transportation contract and binding upon the consignee, the consignor and the railway department. The railway bill together with the goods is transported from the place of dispatch to the place of destination and then is delivered to the consignee after he has paid off the freight and other charges. The consignor may make exchange settlement with the bank against the duplicate of the railway bill.

A duplicate is given to the shipper as a receipt of the goods. Unlike B/L, it is not a document of title and not negotiable. In international combined rail transport, the rail waybill is subject to the Berne Convention Concerning International Carriage by Rail (COTIF) or Agreement Concerning International Carriage of Goods by Rail (CMIC).

4.3.4　Air Waybill

The air waybill, or consignment note, is issued by the carrying airline or a duly appointed agent on its behalf. It is a document of carriage and proof of receipt of goods for shipment. It also provides evidence of the contract of carriage between a single exporter (or consignor) and the airline. However, unlike the Bill of Lading used for similar purposes in the maritime environment, it is not a document of title (to the goods) and is therefore a non-negotiable document.

The reverse of the air waybill contains the airlines' conditions of carriage. These relate to the limited liability of the carrier in the event of the loss, damage or delay to a given consignment as provided for in the Warsaw and Montreal Conventions that govern liability for the international movement of cargo. Air waybills can either be completed using pre-printed sets with specific issuing airline identification, or more commonly by agents using so-called "neutral" air waybills without any pre-printed identification specific to a named airline. Air waybills can also be produced using a combination of plain paper and a laser printer.

The air waybill contains data fields that must be completed that include information relating to the exporter and overseas consignee, number of packages, weight and description of the goods and instructions to the airline as to which of the above two parties is responsible for payment of the freight and ancillary charges.

There are two types of air waybills: Master Air Waybill that is issued by airlines and House

Air Waybill that is issued by freight forwarders.

1) Master air waybill

A master air waybill is identical in all respects to the generic air waybill document described above. The difference is that a master air waybill is routinely completed by an agent on behalf of two or more exporters moving goods by air on the same airline flight to the same airport of destination. This type of movement is known as a consolidation or groupage.

2) House air waybill

When cargo is required to be uplifted as part of a consolidated movement, each individual shipment must be able to be uniquely identified when en-route to its final place of destination. Therefore, each one is issued with a house air waybill. The information contained on the house air waybill mirrors that shown on the airline air waybill.

4.3.5　Container Bill of Lading

It is a B/L issued under container transportation, most of the items of the B/L is similar to that of a normal B/L except: the B/L usually contains container No., seal No., the place and modes of delivery of the goods (such as CY/CY or CFS TO CFS, 1 x 20' GP).

Container B/L usually contains the "shipper's load and count (SLAC)" clause. The "SLAC" clause is a manifest clause used when containerized cargo is loaded and sealed by the shipper, and the piece count in the container is not checked or otherwise verified by the carrier.

4.3.6　Multimodal Transport Bill

A multimodal transport document, also called combined transport document, evidences the contract of carriage of goods by at least two modes of transport, such as shipping by rail and by sea, issued by a multimodal transport operator under a multimodal transport contract.

The FIATA Multimodal Transport Bill is designed by the International Federation of Freight Forwarding Agents' Associations (FIATA) and based on UNCTAD/ICC rules. The FIATA Multimodal Transport Bill of Lading (FBL) is designated as a negotiable status document for use in a multimodal transport or as a single transport document for port-to-port shipments. It is now used in more than 60 countries and is acceptable as a marine ocean bill of lading under the ICC UCP 600 rules. As an international transport document the FBL is well suited, functioning as a forwarder house bill or as a multimodal transport document. It is issued under the same conditions throughout the world and each issuer is required to have the carrier's liability insurance. Consequently, the FBL offers a substantial degree of protection to customers of forwarders. As such it is recommended by BIFA to its members. FIATA also has a non-negotiable multimodal transport waybill (Sea waybill). A number of FIATA exclusive documents are available from members of BIFA.

4.3.7　Parcel Post Receipt

Postal receipt is a transport document which isn't issued by a postal authority. It relates to the posting of goods only. It is not a document of title to the goods nor is it an evidence contract of carriage.

4.4　Procedures of Booking Space

Generally, there are two ways of getting ships chartered: One is to find a freight agent/ shipping agent and fill out shipping orders and shippers export declaration form; the other is to make orders online. Big shipping agents usually have their own websites and ships can be chartered by simply clicking the mouse. For example, one can send out his message of chartering vessels on the website *www.shipping.com.cn* in Shenzhen. After the reservation is done successfully, the exporting company will be contacted to prepare all the invoices and fill out the consignment agency agreement.

The exporter should arrange shipment in accordance with the importers shipping instructions specified in the L/C. When chartering shipping space and preparing for shipment, time needed for the transport, market conditions of the goods and availability of the transport vehicles should be taken into careful consideration. Usually, the exporter should contact the ship's agent or the shipping company for chartering ships a few days before the date of shipment of the L/C so as to allow time to deal with accidents. If the foreign trade company is capable of handling shipping issues on its own, it can simply fill out a B/N (booking note). For companies not engaged in such business they can entrust a freight agent to chartering ships from the shipping company.

① The exporter sends a shipping note enclosed with commercial invoices, packing lists and other documents to the freight agent to book space for him. Sometimes the freight agent is also entrusted to clear customs, arrange storage and transport of the goods besides booking trailers from trucking companies.

② The freight agent entrusted sends the container shipping note along with the commercial invoices and other documents to the shipping company to book space.

③ Upon receipt of the shipping note, the shipping company will check the shipping lines, ports of call, and the shipping space before issuing booking confirmation. The shipping company then marks the B/L number on the shipping note and fills in the name of the ship to be employed, the booking number to confirm acceptance of booking. Then the shipping company ends the

Shipping Order (S/O), cargo receipt, and equipment interchange receipt back to the consigner.

④ The consigner fills the Customs Export Declaration Form and presents S/O, the commercial invoices packing lists and other documents required by the customs administration to clear customs.

⑤ After the documents and goods are checked and approved by the customs, the customs will stamp the S/O and return it to the consigner.

⑥ With the sealed S/O at hand, the consigner instructs the captain to load goods. After loading, the captain releases the Mate's Receipt (M/R) to the consigner.

⑦ The consigner pays for the freight to the shipping company after receiving the M/R.

⑧ The shipping company issues an original clean shipped on board B/L to the consigner.

⑨ During the process, the exporter and the freight agent are in the principal-agent relationship. As such, the consigner refers to both the exporter and the freight agent. For an exporting company that operates its own transportation business, consigner refers only to company. The procedures involved in chartering ships are the same as described above. Nowadays, along with the rapid development of logistics, fewer international traders choose to contact the shipping companies or carriers directly; instead, they prefer to find freight agents or other transport intermediaries, whose expertise and professionalism are important guarantee for the smooth shipment of goods across national boundaries.

4.5　Shipment Clause in International Trade Contract

The clause of shipment specifies all the details regarding the shipment of the goods in the contract. The details include time of shipment, port (place) of shipment, port (place) of destination, advice of shipment, partial shipment and transshipment, etc. The buyer and the seller should reach an agreement on these issues and specify them legibly in the contract. Clear stipulation of the shipment clause is an important condition for the smooth execution of the contract.

4.5.1　Time of Shipment and Delivery

Time of shipment is the deadline by which the seller makes shipment of the contracted goods. Time of delivery is the deadline during which the seller shall deliver the goods to the buyer at the agreed place. Time of shipment is a very important clause in a contract as any delay or advance of delivery constitutes a violation of the contract.

1. Time of shipment and time of delivery

Time of delivery refers to the time limit during which the seller shall deliver the goods to the buyer at the agreed place.

For all shipment contracts time of shipment is time of delivery and they can be used interchangeably in the contract. According to Incoterms 2020, contracts concluded on the basis of such terms as FOB, CFR, CIF, FCA, CPT, CIP are shipment contracts. Under shipment contracts, the seller fulfills his obligation of delivery when the goods are shipped on board the vessel or delivered to the carrier and the seller only bears all risks prior to shipment. The delivery of goods under a shipment contract implies a symbolic delivery. After the seller loads the goods on board the vessel and presents the whole qualified documents which include certificates of title to the goods, the seller is said to have finished delivery of the goods. It is unnecessary for the seller to guarantee the goods to be received by the buyer actually.

For all arrival contracts, time of shipment and time of delivery are two completely different concepts and the time of delivery should be stipulated in the contract. According to Incoterms 2020, contracts concluded on the basis of terms such as DAT, DAP and DDP are arrival contracts. The seller delivers the goods into the actual possession of the buyer. Arrival contracts differ from shipment contract in that the seller should be responsible for all risks of bringing the goods to the named destination. Arrival contracts usually suggest actual delivery. Actual delivery is made when the goods are actually delivered from the seller to the buyer. In the actual delivery contract, there are two different time limits, one is the time of shipment, the other is the time of delivery.

In the contract under F and C groups of trade terms, the time of shipment and the time of delivery belong to the same concept while in the contract under D terms, they are different.

2. Ways of stipulating the time of shipment/delivery

Time of shipment is the deadline by which the seller makes shipment of the contacted goods. There are basically two ways to setting the time of shipment. One is specifying clearly a time period or the definite deadline. For example, "Shipment on or before Sept. 15th"; "Shipment not later than July 31st"; "Delivery or shipment during June 2020". The other is setting the time of shipment/delivery based on the time of receiving L/C or other payment guarantee. For example, "Shipment is to be made within 30 days after receipt of the L/C"; the relevant L/C must reach the seller not later than 30 June, 2020". By doing so, the seller is able to reduce his risks of losses resulted from the buyer's failure in opening the L/C required.

When stipulating the time of shipment, both parties should consider the availability of goods, ships and shipping spaces, the issuing date of L/C and the nature of the cargo. It is very abnormal to stipulate a fixed time since the shipping space could be unavailable, and normally, L/C should arrive at least 15 days before the time of the shipment to permit sufficient time to check the L/C and make necessary shipping arrangements. It is not advisable to use ambiguous phrase, such as "Immediate shipment", "Prompt shipment" or "The goods shall be shipped in the near future", since there are could be different understandings of those expressions in different countries.

4.5.2 Port of Shipment and Port of Destination

As the place of shipment concerns the handling of formalities, payment of charges and transfer of risks, it is very important to stipulate it clearly in the contract. The port of shipment or the place of departure is the port where goods are shipped and depart, while the port of destination is at the port where goods are ultimately discharged. Both terms should be specified when the contract is signed. Generally, a specific port of shipment and a specific port of destination are stipulated. But sometimes two or more of each are stated to meet special requirements. In case a decision cannot be made, several alternatives should be listed, such as "One port out of Dalian / Qingdao/Shanghai as the port of destination at the buyer's location" or perhaps a general clause like "China ports" may be used. When choosing the port of shipment and the port of destination, try to make them as clear as possible; provide some flexibility by allowing optional ports. Optional ports are set forth in the contract such as "Liverpool optional Hamburg/Rotterdam".

When determining the port of shipment and the port of destination, sellers should pay attention to the following:

① The port of shipment should be close to the origin of the goods. For instance, when the goods are manufactured in Shandong Province, it is not a wise idea to stipulate "Guangzhou, China" as the port of shipment.

② Port facilities, regulations, specific transportation conditions, charges and possible sanctions should be taken into consideration. For example, if a consignment is intended to be shipped by a container liner, only a port with a container yard or container station can be considered as the port of shipment in the contract.

③ The stipulation of the port of destination should be definite and specific. Ambiguous terms, such as "European Main Ports", "Japanese Ports" shall be avoided. Without a definite stipulation for the port of shipment, the seller will find it difficult to book shipping space and arrange shipment thus difficult to fulfill the contract.

④ In addition, the name of the country and the place should be put in front of the name of the port for fear of the possibility of different ports having the same name. For example, there are 12 "Victoria" ports in the world. There are examples of port of shipment/destination clause shown in Example 4-3.

[Example 4-3]

Port of shipment: Guangzhou and Shanghai

Port of shipment: Shanghai /Guangzhou/Shenzhen

Port of destination: London/Liverpool/Manchester

CIF London/Hamburg/Rotterdam optional

CIF London, optional Hamburg/Rotterdam. Optional and additional for the buyer's account

4.5.3　Partial Shipment and Transshipment

1. Partial shipment

Partial shipment means shipping the commodity under one contract in more than one lot. **In case of an export covering a large amount of goods, it is necessary to make shipment in several lots by several carriers sailing on different dates. This is done because of the limitation of shipping space available, poor unloading facilities at the port of destination, dull market season, or possible delay in the process of manufacturing the goods, etc.** And this is allowable only if the clause "Partial shipment to be allowed" is agreed upon in the sales contract. If partial shipment is not allowed, the clause "No partial shipment" or the like should be given in the contract.

There are some disagreements about whether a shipment is considered partial or not in cargo transportation practice. In such cases traders in international trade are suggested to refer to UCP 600 Article 31 for resolution:

① Partial drawings or shipments are allowed.

② A presentation consisting of more than one set of transport documents evidencing shipment commencing on the same means of conveyance and for the same journey, provided they indicate the same destination will not be regarded as covering a partial shipment even if they indicate different dates of shipment or different ports of loading, places of taking in charge or dispatch. If the presentation consists of more than one set of transport documents, the latest date of shipment as evidenced on any of the sets of transport documents will be regarded as the date of shipment.

A presentation consisting of one or more sets of transport documents evidencing shipment on more than one means of conveyance within the same mode of transport will be regarded as covering a partial shipment, even if the means of conveyance leave on the same day for the same destination.

③ A presentation consisting of more than one courier receipt, post receipt or certificate of posting will not be regarded as a partial shipment if the courier receipts, post receipts certificates of posting appear to have been stamped or signed by the same courier or postal service at the same place and date and for the same destination.

And Article 32 of UCP 600 stipulates: "If a drawing or shipment by installments within given periods is stipulated in the credit and any installment is not drawn or shipped within the period allowed for that installment, the credit ceases to be available for that and any subsequent installment."

[Case 4-2]

A Shandong company exported 500 m/t of peanuts overseas. The foreign importer opened an irrevocable L/C, with the clause of shipment stipulated as follow: "Shipment from Chinese port to Singapore in May/June. Partial shipment prohibited." Due to the shortage of supply, the exporter first loaded 200 m/t of peanuts at the port of Qingdao by S. S. "Dongfeng" on May 29th, and obtained the first B/L; then they got another supply in Yantai, and arranged for the same ship to sail to Yantai Port and take the remaining 300 m/t of peanuts. On June 3rd, the exporter got the second B/L. After that exporter submitted two sets of B/L to the bank for negotiation within the presentation period, the bank dishonored on the grounds of partial shipment being not allowed according to the L/C.

Question: Is the bank's action reasonable? Why?

2. Transshipment

Transshipment in maritime transport is the movement of goods in transit from one carrier to another at the ports of transshipment before the goods reach the port of destination. Transshipment is necessary when ships going directly to the port of destination are not available, or the port of destination does not lie along the sailing route of the liner. Transshipment is allowed when the sales contract has a clause like "transshipment to be allowed".

If transshipment is carried out in order to reach the agreed destination, the seller would have to pay the cost of transshipment. However, if the carrier exercised his rights under a transshipment or similar clause in order to avoid unexpected hindrances (such as ice, congestion, labor disturbances, government orders, war or warlike operations), then any additional cost would be on the buyer's account.

4.5.4   Shipping Advice

The shipping advice is a notice to the importer on summary of the shipment. The buyer is to arrange the cargo insurance on time based on the shipping advice (if the buyer is to arrange the insurance). Moreover, the buyer may know when to receive the goods and arrange with a customs broker for the cargo clearance.

On FOB term, the seller usually sends out the shipping advice before the agreed time of shipment, saying 30~45 days, telling the buyer that the goods have been prepared for shipment. After receiving such advice, the buyer then takes note of the seller vessel name, time of arrival and so on to let the seller prepare for shipment in time. After having shipped the goods, the seller should send out the shipping advice to the buyer covering contract number, name of commodity, number of package, weight, voice value, vessel name and time of shipment to enable the buyer to effect insurance and prepare for receiving goods and customs declaration (See Example 4-4).

[Example 4-4]

Date

Dear Sir,

We are pleased to inform your esteemed company that the following mentioned goods will be shipped out on Jan.18, 2005, full details were shown as follows:

1. invoice No.:

2. bill of lading No.:

3. ocean vessel:

4. port of loading:

5. date of shipment:

6. port of destination:

7. description of goods:

8. marks and number on B/L:

9. L/C No.:

4.5.5　Lay Days, Demurrage and Dispatch

The time of loading and unloading will affect the turn-over rate of the ship, and this will affect the interests of the ship owner. Therefore, it is the main clause specified in the charter party. Lay time is the time allowed for the completion of loading and unloading, and it is usually expressed by days or hours. There are several ways of stipulating lay time:

- Days or running days: including bad weather days, Sundays or any other holidays, unfavorable to the shipper;
- Weather working days of 24 hours: excluding Sunday, holidays and rainy days, favorable for shipper but unfavorable for ship owner;
- Weather working days of 24 consecutive hours: excluding the bad weather time period, suitable for ports that operate day and night.

As lay time concerns the interests of the ship owner, consignor or consignee it is important to make it clear in the contract. Vague phrase as "to load/discharge in customary quick dispatch" should be avoided. If loading and unloading are not completed within the agreed lay time, demurrage should be paid at an agreed rate by the party that charters ships to the ship owner to compensate for the cost sustained. Demurrage is an extra charge that a shipper pays for detaining a freight car or ship beyond time permitted for loading or unloading. On the other hand, if loading and unloading are completed in advance, the ship owner will pay dispatch money as a reward to the party who charters ships. Dispatch is an amount paid by a vessel's operator to a charterer if loading or unloading is completed in less time than stipulated in the charter agreement, demurrage and dispatch are considered as a way of encouraging timely shipment and are sometimes specified in the shipment clause. See an Example in Example 4-5.

[Example 4-5]

- Shipment during Oct. /Nov. /Dec. 20××, with partial shipments and transshipment allowed.
- Shipment during Jan./Feb. 20×× in about two equal lots.
- Shipment during Jan./Feb. 20×× in two equal monthly lots (in two equal monthly shipments), transshipment to be allowed.
- During Mar./Apr. in two shipments, transshipment is prohibited.
- During Mar./Apr. in two equal monthly shipments, to be transshipped at Hong Kong.
- Shipment during May from London to Guangzhou, the sellers shall advise the buyers 30 days before the month of shipment of the time the goods will be ready for shipment. Partial shipments and transshipment are allowed.

Notes to the Text

I. Vocabulary and phrases.

1. marine transport　海洋运输
2. consigner　发货人
3. the shipper　托运人
4. liners transportation　班轮运输
5. freight of liner　班轮运费
6. weight ton　重量吨
7. measurement ton　尺码吨
8. fuel surcharge　燃油附加费
9. CAF (currency adjustment factor)　货币贬值附加费
10. Extra Charges on Over Length (Over-length Surcharge)　超长附加费
11. charterer　租船人
12. charter transport　租船运输
13. timer charter　定期租船
14. tramp　(航线不定的)货船
15. voyage charter　航程(航次)租船，程租
16. demise charter　光船租赁
17. container　集装箱

18. Container Yard (CY)　集装箱堆场

19. Container Freight Station　集装箱(货)运站

20. FCL (full container load)　整箱装

21. LCL (less than container load)　拼箱装

22. box rate　箱费

23. freight for all kinds rate (FAK rate)　均一包箱费率

24. international multimodal transport　国际多式联运

25. land bridge transport　大陆桥运输

26. bill of lading　海运提单

27. combined transport B/L　多式联运提单

28. consignment note　发货通知单

29. booking note　托运单，订舱委托书

30. clean B/L　清洁提单

31. order B/L　指示提单

32. blank endorsement　空白背书

33. on board B/L　已装船提单

34. received for shipment B/L　备运提单

35. original B/L　正本提单

36. copy B/L　副本提单

37. deck B/L　甲板提单

38. stale B/L　过期提单

39. advanced B/L　预借提单

40. sea waybill　海运运单

41. master air waybill　主运单

42. house air waybill　分运单

43. manifest　货单

44. procedures of booking space　订舱流程

45. mate's receipt and M/R　大副收据

46. parcel post receipt　邮政凭据

47. time of shipment　装运时间

48. partial shipment　分批运输

49. transshipment　转运

50. shipping advice　装运通知

II. Sentences and paragraphs.

1. In accordance with the different ways of ship operation, maritime transport can be divided into liner transport and charter transport which can be divided into voyage charter, time charter

and demise charter.

根据船舶经营方式不同，海上运输可分为班轮运输和租船运输，租船运输分为航次租船、定期租船和光船租船。

2. The special agreement, the freight is to be calculated according to temporary or special agreement between the carrier and the consignor. Principally, shipment of grains, ores, coal, etc. in large quantity is subject to a special freight fixed in an interim agreement between the carrier and the shipper.

特别协议中，运费按照承运人与托运人之间的临时或者特别约定计算。原则上，装运谷物、矿石、煤炭等数量较大商品的运费，可根据承运人和托运人之间的临时协议规定的具体固定运费率计算。

3. In order to calculate the freight, it should start with confirming to the English name of the commodity, find out the freight standard for calculating the freight grade; then find out the basic freight rate in the route freight tariff according to the grades and purpose sea route; moreover, decide the relative surcharges for the suitable route and basic port; finally, the basic freight rate plus various additional surcharges is the freight per freight ton.

关于海运费计算，首先要确定商品的英文名称，找出计算的运费费率标准或费率等级，然后根据等级和目的航线，在航线运价表中找出基本运费率，并确定适合航线和基本港口的相对附加费。最后，海运费就是每吨运费的基本运价加上各种附加费。

4. International multimodal transport (international combined transport) means the carriage of cargo by at least two modes of transport on the basis of a Multimodal Transport Contract (MTC) from a place at which the cargoes are collected in one country to a place designated for delivery in another country by Multimodal Transport Operator (MTO).

国际多式联运(国际联运)是指根据多式联运合同，多式联运经营人将货物从一国收货地运至另一国指定交货地的至少两种运输方式的运输。

5. It offers a door-to-door service under FCL/FCL, door to Container Freight Station (CFS) service under FCL/LCL, CFS to CFS service under LCL/LCL, or CFS to door service under LCL/FCL.

集装箱运输可提供 FCL/FCL 下的门到门，FCL/LCL 下的门到集装箱堆场，LCL/LCL 下的堆场到堆场，以及 LCL/FCL 下的堆场到门的服务功能。

6. In any case, this type of B/L is clearly the most useful due to its prima facie evidence that goods are actually a route to the port of destination on a named vessel on a specified date and that the goods are in the condition stated on the bill at the time of shipment.

无论如何，提单作为初始凭证确实有用，它证明在特定的日期，货物通过指定的船只运到指定的目的地，它也能表明符合要求的货物已装运。

7. Order B/L refers to the one that is made out in such a way that it is consigned or destined to the order of a named person instead of a definite consignee.

指示提单是指凭指定人而不是确定签发人的指示进行接收或交付而签发的一种提单。

8. Original B/L refers to the one that is signed and dated by either the shipping company or by a duly authorized agent. The B/L must show how many signed originals were issued, the originals are marked "Original" on their face and they become valid only after being signed by the carrier.

正本提单是指由船运公司或经正式授权的代理人签发并注明日期的提单。提单上必须注明签发的正本提单数量，有"正本"字样，且经承运人签字后方可有效。

9. When stipulating the time of shipment, both parties should consider the availability of goods, ships and shipping spaces, the issuing date of L/C and the nature of the cargo.

在规定装运时间时，贸易双方应该考虑货物、运输订舱的可得性及舱位空间大小，以及信用证的签发日和货物的本身属性。

10. In case of an export covering a large amount of goods, it is necessary to make shipment in several lots by several carriers sailing on different dates. This is done because of the limitation of shipping space available, poor unloading facilities at the port of destination, dull market season, or possible delay in the process of manufacturing the goods, etc.

当出口货物数量较大时，必须考虑应在不同日期由承运人分批装运，之所以分批运输是由于运输舱位可获取性、目的港卸货设施可用性、市场淡季或者生产制造过程的延迟性等原因造成的。

Exercises

I. Finish the multiple choice questions.

1. The characteristics of liner transport are that _____.

    A. its freight is determined by the market

    B. the line, the port, the time and the freight rate are fixed

    C. the variety and quantity of goods shipped are more flexible

    D. the obligations and rights of both the seller and the buyer are stipulated in the B/L

2. According to general international trade practice, only _____ B/Ls are accepted by banks for payment under a letter of credit.

    A. received and clean   B. shipped and clean

    C. transshipment and order   D. straight and direct

3. The operator who signs the multimodal transport document is _____.

    A. only responsible for the first stage of the transportation

    B. must be responsible for the whole transportation

    C. not responsible for transportation

    D. only responsible for the last stage of the transportation

4. Which of following is right about the stipulation of the port of shipment and the port of destination clauses in the international trade contract? _____

    A. To stipulate two ports roughly.

    B. Only one port of shipment and one port of destination can be stipulated in the contract.

    C. More than one port is contracted to be the port of loading or more than one port is contracted to be the port of destination in case it is difficult to decide.

    D. To stipulate two ports of shipment or two ports of destination.

5. Which stipulation of the date of shipment is often used in a contract? _____

    A. one day, such as 1st July

    B. prompt shipment

    C. within several days after the L/C has been received

    D. a time period such as during June

6. Transshipment may be necessary when _____.

    A. direct liners are not available   B. the amount of the cargo is very small

    C. the shipping date is very close   D. the export covers a large amount of goods

7. If a B/L can be transferable, it must be a _____.

    A. clean B/L   B. transshipment B/L   C. order B/L   D. On board B/L

8. _____ is issued by the shipping company after the goods are actually shipped on board the designated vessel.

    A. Shipped B/L   B. Clean B/L

    C. Received for shipment B/L   D. Liner B/L

9. _____ means that there is no definite consignee of the goods.

    A. Blank B/L   B. Order B/L   C. Direct B/L   D. Straight B/L

10. Air waybill differs from B/L in that _____.

    A. air waybill is not a negotiable title to goods

    B. air waybill is a receipt of goods

    C. it is evidence of dispatch

    D. both A and B

II. Decide whether the following statements are true (T) or false (F).

1. The consignee can take delivery of the goods by using originals of B/L or copies of B/L signed by the carrier.   (   )

2. Consignment note is used not only for road or rail transport, but also for multimodal transport.   (   )

3. The freight of liners is relatively fixed, while the freight of tramps is mainly determined by the market.   (   )

4. Time of shipment in a contract can only be a fixed period of time.   (   )

5. Partial shipment means that the goods under one contract are shipped in different terms or by different lots. ( )

III. Answer the following questions according to the information you have got.

1. What is a marine B/L? What are the three basic functions of a marine B/L?

2. Discuss the differences between order B/L and blank B/L.

3. State the main purposes of B/L and explain why it is the most important document in foreign transactions.

4. What should be considered when choosing a port of shipment and a port of destination?

5. Could you list the document used in cargo transportation?

6. What are the main responsibilities of a multimodal transport operator?

7. What are the main stipulations of "UCP 600" in connection with partial shipments?

8. Can the shipment advice coordinate the responsibilities of the exporter and the importer?

9. Why is container transportation popular in today's international trade?

10. Briefly describe the procedures of chartering and booking.

 微课资源

扫一扫,获取相关微课视频。

4.1.mp4

4.2.mp4

Chapter 5   International Cargo Insurance

Leading in

In September 2019, a technology import and export company imported a set of equipment at the price of FOB Ottawa, Canada. The contract total value was $850,000. After the contract has been signed and the transportation of the goods has been arranged, the company signed a Notice of Departure of International Transportation Open Deposit Insurance[①] with an insurance company in November. The company paid the premium to the insurance company and received a receipt. Unfortunately, the insured cargo was stolen from the carrier's warehouse in Ottawa. In December, the company informed the accident situation, and meanwhile lodged a claim to the insurance company. The insurance company claimed that the company didn't have the insurable interest, and the contract was invalid and refused to accept the claim. So the technology import and export company sued the court.

Question: What is the commencement and termination of Ocean Marine Insurance under the FOB contracts?

5.1   The Coverage of Marine Cargo Insurance

The marine cargo insurance is also the first used insurance and so has the longest history among the all. **Marine cargo insurance is defined as a contract of insurance whereby the**

---

① Notice of Departure of International Transportation Open Deposit Insurance (《国际运输预约保险起运通知书》).

insurance in return for premium collected undertakes to indemnify the insured in a manner and to the extent thereby agreed, against marine losses, that is to say, the losses incidental to marine adventure. Such insurance involving the marine conveyance of cargo from one country to another is, then, marine cargo insurance, which is seen as an indispensable adjunct to foreign trade.

The scope of marine cargo insurance usually covers insured risks, losses and expenses. They are closely related to one another (See Table 5-1).

Table 5-1　The scope of marine cargo insurance

Risks	Perils of the sea	a. Natural calamities
		b. Fortuitous accidents
	Extraneous risks	a. General extraneous risks
		b. Special extraneous risks
Losses	Total loss	a. Actual total loss
		b. Constructive total loss
	Partial loss	a. General average
		b. Particular average
Expenses	Sue and labor expenses	
	Salvage charges	

1. Risks

Marine risks in connection with cargo in transit can be classified into two types: perils of the sea and extraneous risks.

1) Perils of the sea

a. Natural calamities: bad weather, thunder and lightening, earthquake, volcanic eruption, flood and so on.

b. Fortuitous accidents: fire, grounded, stranded, collision, explosion, sunk, ship missing, etc.

2) Extraneous risks

a. General extraneous risks: theft, breakage, leakage, contamination, sweating and/or heating, taint of odor, rusting, hook damage, fresh and/or rain water damage, shortage in weight, clashing and so on.

b. Special extraneous risks: war, strike, failure to delivery, rejection, etc.

2. Losses

Marine losses refer to the damages or losses of the insured goods incurred by perils of sea. According to the extent of damage, losses in marine insurance fall into two types: total loss and partial loss.

1) Total loss

a. Actual total loss: the complete loss of the insured cargo in value. It includes total loss of the subject matter, the total loss of the value, theft and arrest, the ship being lost for more than half a year.

b. Constructive total loss: it means the cargo is not totally lost, but the actual total loss shall be unavoidable or the cost to be incurred in recovering or reconditioning the goods together with the forwarding cost to the destination named in the policy would exceed their value on arrival.

2) Partial loss

a. General Average (GA): a partial and deliberate sacrifice of the ship, freight, cargo, or the additional expense has to be incurred, in order to avoid some threat to the whole venture; or some loss or damage is deliberately inflicted, in order to save the ship and some of the cargo. According to maritime law, those interests, whose property was saved, must contribute proportionally to cover the losses of the one whose property was voluntarily sacrificed.

GA can be established under four conditions:

① The peril must be existent or unavoidable;

② The sacrifice made should be reasonable and conscious;

③ The sacrifice or expenditure must be extraordinary in nature but not a direct result of the peril;

④ The action of the ship's master shall be successful in saving the voyage.

b. Particular Average (PA): it means a partial loss suffered by part of the cargo. An example of a PA occurs when a storm or fire damages part of the shipper's cargo and no one else's cargo has to be sacrificed to save the voyage. The cargo owner whose goods were damaged looks to his insurance company for payment, provided, of course, his policy covers the specific type of loss suffered.

The differences between GA and PA are:

(1) GA is manmade loss in order to remove or alleviate risks; PA is caused directly by risks.

(2) The loss of sacrifice as well as the expenses incurred in a GA shall be shared among all parties; the damaged party is responsible for losses incurred in a PA.

See Case 5-1.

[Case 5-1]

A vessel with Compartment 1 and Compartment 2 caught a fire during the trip and Compartment 1 was on fire. However, the captain mistakenly thought both compartments were on fire and ordered the crew to put out the fire with water cannons. Losses are:

(1) the main engine was damaged;

(2) Compartment 1 was burned down partially;

(3) Compartment 2 was water logging.

Which belongs to PA and which belongs to GA?

3. Expenses

Marine cargo insurance covers the expenses incurred to avoid or reduce the damage to or loss of the subject matter insured. There are mainly two types：

1) Sue and labor expenses

Sue and labor expenses are extraordinary expenditures made in time of peril to avert or minimize any loss or damage to the goods insured.

2) Salvage charges

Salvage charges are expenses resulting from measures properly taken by a third party other than the insured, his agent, or any person employed by them to preserve maritime property from perils at sea.

5.2 Ocean Marine Cargo Clauses of CIC

Insurance coverage refers to the risks and losses covered by the insurer. It is the basis of not only performing rights and obligations, but also the basis of collecting insurance premium. The most commonly used terms in cargo insurance in China is the China Insurance Clauses (CIC). There are mainly two types of insurance coverage:basic coverage and additional coverage (See Table 5-2).

Table 5-2　Insurance coverage of CIC

Basic Coverage	FPA
	WPA
	All Risks Insurance
Additional Coverage	General Additional Coverage
	Special Additional Coverage

1. Basic Coverage

Basic coverage mainly includes Free from Particular Average (FPA), With Particular Average (WPA) and All Risks Insurance.

1) FPA

FPA means the compensation does not cover PA. Under the FPA, the insurance company should be liable for:

① Actual total loss or constructive total loss of the whole consignment hereby insured caused in the course of transit by natural calamities such as heavy weather, thunder and lightening, tsunami, earthquake, flood, etc.;

② Total or partial loss caused by accidents such as stranding, striking upon the rocks, collision, fire and explosion;

③ Partial loss of the insured cargo attributable to heavy weather, lightning, and/or tsunami, where the conveyance has been grounded, stranded, sunk or burnt irrespective of whether the event or events took place before or after such accidents;

④ Partial or total loss resulting from the falling of entire package or packages into sea during loading, transshipment or discharge;

⑤ Reasonable cost incurred by the insured in salvaging the goods or averting or minimizing a loss recoverable under the Policy, provided that the cost shall not exceed the sum insured of the consignment to be saved;

⑥ **Losses attributable to discharge of the insured goods at a port of distress following a sea peril as well as special charges arising from loading, warehousing and forwarding of the goods at an intermediate port of call or refuge;**

⑦ Sacrifice and contribution to general average and salvage charges;

⑧ Such proportion of losses sustained by the ship owners as is to be reimbursed by the cargo owner under the Contract of Affreightment "Both to Blame Collision" clause.

See Case 5-2.

[Case 5-2]

A vessel was caught in a storm during the trip and water came into the compartments, resulting in USD6,000 of losses. The goods valued at USD18,000 was covered with FPA. Three days later, the vessel caught a fire.

Question: Shall USD6,000 of losses be indemnified by the insurance company?

---

2) With Particular Average (WPA)

This insurance covers wider than FPA. Aside from the risks covered under FPA conditions as above, this insurance also covers partial losses of the insured goods caused by heavy weather, lightning, tsunami, earthquake and/or flood and so on.

3) All Risks Insurance

All Risks Insurance is the most comprehensive of the three basic coverages. A side from the risks covered under FPA and WPA, this insurance also covers all risks of loss or damage to the insured goods whether partial or total, arising from external causes in the course of transit. It covers all risks of physical loss or damage from an external cause, but does not include war, strikes, riots, seizure of detention, unless endorsed by a special clause or separate policy.

4) Exclusions from the Basic Coverage

Under basic coverage, insurer is not liable for:

① Loss or damage caused by the intentional act or fault of the insured;

② Loss of damage falling under the liability of the consignor;

③ Loss or damage arising from the inferior quality or shortage of the insured goods prior to attachment of this insurance;

④ Loss or damage arising from normal loss, inherent vice or nature of the insured goods, loss of market and/or delay in transit and any expenses arising therefrom;

⑤ Risks and liabilities covered and excluded by the Marine Cargo War Risks Clauses and Strike, Riot and Civil Commotion Clauses.

2. Additional Coverage

Additional coverage includes general additional coverage and special additional coverage. Additional coverage can not be purchased to insure goods independently. Since the scope of cover of general additional coverage is already included in that of All Risks Insurance, it is not necessary for the goods to be insured by general additional coverage if it is insured by All Risks Insurance.

1) General Additional Coverage

There are eleven types of general additional coverage:

① Theft, pilferage and non-delivery clause.

To cover loss or damage to the insured goods on the insured value caused by theft and/or pilferage; non-delivery or entire package; loss or damage for which the liability of the ship owner or other party concerned is exempted by the Contract of Carriage.

② Fresh water and/or rain damage clause.

To cover loss or damage to the insured goods directly caused by rain and/or fresh water.

③ Shortage clause.

To cover risks of shortage occurring during the course of transit due to breakage of outer packing, or loss of quantity and actual shortage in weight in the case of bulk cargo, but excluding normal lost.

④ Intermixture and contamination clause.

To cover risks of intermixture and contamination occurring during the course of transit.

⑤ Leakage clause.

To cover risks of leakage occurring during the course of transit caused by damage to the container, or deterioration of the insured goods resulting from leakage of liquid in which the insured goods are stored.

⑥ Clash and breakage clause.

To cover risks of breakage and clash occurring during the course of transit caused by shock, collision or press of the insured goods.

⑦ Taint of odor clause.

To cover risks of taint of odor of the insured edible, Chinese medicine, toilet material, etc. occurring during the course of transit effected by other goods.

⑧ Sweat and heating clause.

To cover risks of sweat, heating and wetting occurring during the course of transit arising from sudden change of temperature or breakdown of ventilation of the carrying vessel.

⑨ Hook damage clause.

To cover hook damage to the insured goods occurring during loading or unloading including expenses of reconditioning or change of packing, if any.

⑩ Breakage of packing clause.

To cover loss or damage occurring during the course of transit caused by breakage of packing resulting from rough handling, loading and unloading including expenses of reconditioning and change of packages, if any, for the safe prosecution of transportation.

⑪ Rust clause.

To cover risks of rust occurring during the course of transit.

2) Special Additional Coverage

Special additional coverage differs from general additional coverage in that the former covers loss or damage caused by some special extraneous reasons such as politics, law, regulations and war. Special additional coverage is not in the coverage of All Risks Insurance Like general additional coverage, special additional coverage can not be insured alone. There are eight types of special additional coverage, among which War Risk and Strike Risk are the main ones.

① War Risk;

② Strike Risk;

③ On Deck Risk;

④ Import Duty Risk Clause;

⑤ Rejection Risk;

⑥ Alfatoxin Risk;

⑦ Failure to Delivery Clause;

⑧ Fire Risk Extension Clause for storage of cargo at the destination of Hong Kong, including Kowloon or Macao.

3. Commencement and Termination of Ocean Marine Insurance

1) Commencement and Termination of Basic Coverage

The Warehouse to Warehouse Clause (W-W Clause) is adopted in stipulating the terms of commencement and termination of basic coverage. **In the W-W Clause, the insurance company undertakes an insurance liability over the insured cargo from the warehouse or the place of storage of the shipper named in policy until the cargo has arrived at the warehouse or the place of storage of the receiver named in the policy**. The insurance liability terminates once the cargo arrives at the warehouse of the receiver. The insurance shall be limited to 60 days after completion of discharge of the insured goods at the final port of discharge before they reach the above mentioned warehouse of storage.

In the international insurance business, the insurance company does not hold the W-W Clause in the insurance contract. Under the FOB, CFR contracts, the seller delivers the cargo at the port of shipment. Thus, their insurance liability is from ship to warehouse.

2) Commencement and Termination of War Risk

It is based on "ocean" clauses and limited to ocean risks, which is totally different from the W-W Clause. It is used to cover the cargo from the exporter's sea coast to the sea coast of the importer with a time limit. The cargo has to be loaded from the board of the ship within 15 days after discharge or the policy will no longer cover the cargo.

3) Commencement and Termination of Strike Risk

Commencement and termination of strike risk fits the W-W Clause which is the same as that of basic coverage.

5.3　London Insurance Institute Cargo Clauses

The Institute Cargo Clauses (ICC) were initially published by the Institute of London Underwriters in 1912 and were revised in 1981 and the newest clauses came into effect on Jan. 1st, 1982. There are six types of coverage:

(1) Institute Cargo Clauses A (ICC(A));

(2) Institute Cargo Clauses B (ICC(B)) ;

(3) Institute Cargo Clauses C (ICC(C));

(4) Institute War Clauses-Cargo;

(5) Institute Strike Clauses-Cargo;

(6) Malicious Damage Clause.

The ICC(A), ICC(B), and ICC(C)) are main coverage, together with the Institute War Clauses-Cargo and Institute Strike Clauses-Cargo, all can be covered independently except the last one — Malicious Damage Clause. Meanwhile, ICC(A) include Malicious Damage Clause, but Malicious Damage Clause should be attached to ICC(B) or ICC(C).

1. ICC(A)

ICC(A) is similar to that of All Risks Insurance under China Marine Cargo Insurance Clauses. The scope of Clause A is comprehensive, so the method of "all risks except exclusions" is adopted, that is to say, except for exclusions, the insurer is responsible for the rest risks. The exclusions include:

(1) General exclusions.

--Loss or damage due to willful misconduct of the insured;

--Ordinary leakage, ordinary losses in weight or volume or ordinary wear and tear;

--Insufficient or unsuitability of packing or preparation of the subject-matter insured;

--Delay;

--Insolvency of the ship owner, the carrier or the charterer;

--Nuclear or atomic weapons.

(2) Exclusions of unseaworthiness and unfitness of the carrying vessel of lighter, including the containers.

If the insured knows beforehand the cargo-carrying ships are unseaworthy, or the cargo-carrying ship transportation vehicle or the container is uncargoworthy, the insurer does not cover the losses or expenses thereby.

(3) Exclusions of War.

The insurer does not cover the losses caused by war, antagonistic activities, capture, or distrait.

(4) Exclusions of Strike.

The insurer does not cover the losses caused by strikes, labor disturbances, civil commotion, or riot.

2. ICC(B)

ICC(B) is similar to WPA Clauses. It lists all risks covered so that the insured may choose the proper insurance cover. The specific coverage includes:

(1) Loss or damage caused by fire, explosion, vessels or craft being stranded, grounded, sunk, capsized, overturning, derailment of land conveyance, collision, contact of vessel craft or conveyance with any external object other than water, discharge of cargo at a port of distress, earthquake, volcanic eruption or lightning.

(2) General average sacrifice, jettison or washing overboard, entry of sea, lake or river water into vessel, craft hold, conveyance, container, lift van or place of storage, total loss of any package lost overboard or dropped whist loading on to, or unloading from, vessel or craft.

ICC(B) is no coverage for theft, shortage and non-delivery.

3. ICC(C)

ICC(C) is similar to FPA Clause. It only covers major casualties. It is not liable for unimportant accidents and natural calamities.

5.4　Insurance Clauses in Sales Contract

1. Insurance Contracts in Sales Contract

The insurance clauses are one of the most important parts of the international sales or purchase contract. They include insurance amount, the risks covered, the insurance premium, the insurance policy and the insurance clauses applied.

In the insurance, the party who insures others against loss or damage and undertakes to make payment in case of loss is called the insurer; the party who is insured against loss and to whom payment covering the loss will be made is the insured; the contract made between the insurer and the insured is the insurance policy; and the sum of money the insured agrees to pay the insurer for an insurance policy is the premium.

Under FOB, CFR, FCA or CPT terms, the insurance clause may simply be stipulated as: "Insurance:To be covered by the buyer". Under CIF or CIP terms, the clause should indicate specific insurance amount, the risks covered, and the insurance clauses adopted. For example, "Insurance is to be covered by the sellers for 110% of the Invoice Value against All Risks and War Risk as per Ocean Marine Cargo Clauses of People's Insurance Company of China dated Jan. 1st, 1981."

2. Insurance Premium

Premium is generally based on the value of goods covered and the statistical probability of loss. Insurance companies take a number of specific factors into consideration when they decide on the rate of insurance premium.

1) Insurance Amount

The insurance amount is the highest amount for which the insurer shall compensate. Usually the buyer requires the seller to apply for insurance from a certain insurance company and for certain coverage. If there is no specific requirement on the insurance coverage, the seller is required to obtain insurance only minimum cover. If the CIF or CIP value cannot be determined, the minimum amount of insurance coverage would be 110% of the amount requested under the L/C for payment, acceptance or negotiation, or 110% of the amount of the invoice, whichever is the greater.

2) Insurance Premium

The insurance premium is calculated upon the insurance amount and the rate.

Insurance amount=CIF (CIP) price × (1 + percentage of addition)

Insurance premium=insurance amount × premium rate

[Case 5-3]

Some 10,000 pieces of cargo exported to the USA by USD10/pc CIF New York are to be covered against All Risks and War Risk and the premium rates are respectively 0.6% and 0.4%.

Question: What's the insurance premium of these cargo?

insurance amount=CIF (CIP) price×(1+percentage of addition)

=10×10,000×(1+10%)

=USD 110,000

insurance premium=insurance amount×premium rate

=110,000× (0.6%+0.4%)

=USD 1,100

---

3. Insurance Documents

An insurance document is the evidence of the insurance contract entered into by the insurer and the applicant or the insurant. It serves as a document defining the obligations of the insurer and the insurant. It is also the document according to which the insurant lodges claim and the insurer settles a claim when the loss or damage which is answerable under the terms of the coverage occurs. Under CIF and CIP contracts, the seller must provide the buyer with insurance documents. And insurance documents are negotiable by endorsement.

According to UCP 600 Section 28 Item "e": "the date of the insurance document must be not later than the date of shipment, unless it appears from the insurance document that the cover is effective from a date not later than the date of shipment."

1) Insurance Policy

Insurance policy is a written document between an insured person and an insurance company specifying the exact losses to be covered and the cost to the insured person. It is the most commonly used document that contains all the details concerning the name, quantity of the cargo, coverage, premium and the insured amount on the face and the detailed contract terms at the back. See Specimen 5-1.

2) Insurance Certificate

It is the simplified form of the insurance policy certifying that insurance has been affected and that a policy has been issued. It does not list all the details at the back but it is of the same legal validity as insurance policy.

PICC 中国人民财产保险股份有限公司

PICC **Property and Casualty Company Limited**

总公司设于北京	一九四九年创立
Head Office: Beijing	**Established in 1949**

货物运输保险单 CARGO TRANSPORTATION INSURANCE POLICY

发票号 （INVOICE NO.） HMHP-2010 270   保单号次

合同号（CONTRACT NO.） MKDOIB-10-043   **POLICY No.** PYCA20104601010050213

信用证号 （L/C NO.） L/C1141750

被保险人

INSURED ① BEIJING ××× IMPORT & EXPORT CO., LTD

中国人民财产保险股份有限公司（以下简称本公司）根据被保险人的要求，以被保险人向本公司缴付约定的保险费，按照本保险单承保险别和背面所载条款与下列特款承保下述货物运输保险，特订立本保险单。

THIS POLICY OF INSURANCE WITNESSES THAT PICC PROPERTY AND CASUALTY COMPANY LIMITED   (HEREINAFTER CALLED "THE COMPANY") AT THE REQUEST OF THE INSURED AND IN CONSIDERATION OF THE AGREED PREMIUM PAID TO THE COMPANY BY THE INSURED ,UNDERTAKES TO INSURE THE UNDER-MENTIONED GOODS IN TRANSPORTATION SUBJECT TO THE CONDITIONS OF THIS POLICY AS PER THE CLAUSES PRINTED OVERLEAF AND OTHER SPECIAL CLAUSES ATTACHED HEREON.

标 记 **MARKS & NOS**	包装及数量 **QUANTITY**	保险货物项目 **DESCRIPTION OF GOODS**	保险金额 **AMOUNT INSURED**
② AS PER INVOICE NO. HMHP-2007 270	③ 1076 CARTONS	④ IRON FLOWER SHELF （TYPE 3）	⑤ USD 20133.00

总保险金额：

TOTAL AMOUNT INSURED: ⑥SAY： U.S. DOLLARS TWENTY THOUSAND ONE HUNDRED AND THIRTY THREE ONLY.

保费：   启运日期：   装载运输工具：

PREMIUM: ⑦ AS ARRANGED   **DATE OF COMMENCEMENT:**   ⑨AS PER B/L   **PER CONVEYANCE:** ⑧WH 0434-748

自   经   至

FROM ⑩ TIANJIN，CHINA   **IVA**   **TO**   PALERMO, ITALY

承保险别：

CONDITIONS: ⑪COVERING INSTITUTE CARGO CLAUSES （B）， INSTITUTE WAR SRCC CLAUSES

所保货物，如发生保险单项下可能引起索赔的损失或损坏，应立即通知本公司下述代理人查勘。如有索赔，应向本公司提交保险单正本（本保险单共有 2 份正本）及有关文件。如一份正本已用于索赔，其余正本自动失效。

IN THE EVENT OF LOSS OR DAMAGE WHICH MAY RESULT IN A CLAIM UNDER THIS POLICY, IMMEDIATE NOTICE MUST BE GIVEN TO THE COMPANY'S AGENT AS MENTIONED HEREUNDER. CLAIMS, IF ANY, ONE OF THE ORIGINAL POLICY WHICH HAS BEEN ISSUED IN TWO ORIGINAL(S) TOGETHER WITH THE RELEVANT DOCUMENTS SHALL BE SURRENDERED TO THE COMPANY. IF ONE OF THE ORIGINAL POLICY HAS BEEN ACCOMPLISHED， THE OTHERS TO BE VOID.

AIG EUROPE, S. A., ITALY BRANCH
VIA DELLA CHIUSA2
20123 ITALY
TEL: 39 02 36901

中国人民财产保险股份有限公司北京市分公司
PICC Property and Casualty Company Limited , Beijing Branch

赔款偿付地点

CLAIM PAYABLE AT/IN ⑫ PALERMO IN USD   (14) *胡华宁* （签字）

出单日期   MANAGER

ISSUING DATE ⑬ AUG .9，2007

地址：中国北京市×××大街 89 号   经办：张克   复核：李利   Settling & Customer Service Centre :

ADD: No.89. ××× Avenue Beijing , China   (理赔/客户服务中心) 86 10 23456789

邮编（**POST CODE**）: 100105

保单顺序号   PICC 0709123

Specimen 5-1

Notes to the Text

I. Vocabulary and phrases.

1. marine cargo insurance   海上货物保险

2. perils of the sea   海上风险

3. extraneous risks   外来风险

4. natural calamities   自然灾害

5. fortuitous accidents   意外事故

6. actual total loss   实际全损

7. constructive total loss   推定全损

8. General Average (GA)   共同海损

9. Particular Average (PA)   单独海损

10. sue and labor expenses   施救费用

11. salvage charges   救助费用

12. China Insurance Clauses (CIC)   中国保险条款

13. Free from Particular Average (FPA)   免单独海损

14. warehousing   储仓

15. a port of distress   避难港

16. "Both to Blame Collision" clause   "船舶互撞责任"条款

17. With Particular Average (WPA)   单独海损

18. All Risks Insurance   一切险

19. general additional coverage   一般外来风险

20. special additional coverage   特殊外来风险

21. theft, pilferage and non-delivery clause   偷窃、提货不着险

22. fresh water and/or rain damage clause   淡水雨淋险

23. shortage clause   短量险

24. intermixture and contamination clause   混杂、沾污险

25. leakage clause   渗漏险

26. clash and breakage clause   碰损、破损险

27. taint of odor clause   串味险

28. sweat and heating clause   受潮受热险

29. hook damage clause   钩损险

30. breakage of packing clause   包装破裂险

31. rust clause   锈损险

32. war risk   战争险

33. strike risk　罢工险

34. on deck risk　舱面险

35. import duty risk clause　进口关税险

36. rejection risk　拒收险

37. alfatoxin risk　黄曲霉素险

38. failure to delivery clause　交货不到险

39. Warehouse to Warehouse Clause (W-W Clause)　仓至仓条款

40. Institute Cargo Clauses (ICC)　协会货物条款

41. malicious damage clause　恶意损害条款

42. exclusions　除外责任

43. major casualties　重大意外事故

44. insurance premium　保险费

45. insurance amount　保险金额

46. insurant　被保险人

47. insurance policy　保险单

48. insurance certificate　保险凭证

II. Sentences and paragraphs.

1. Marine cargo insurance is defined as a contract of insurance whereby the insurance in return for premium collected undertakes to indemnify the insured in a manner and to the extent thereby agreed, against marine losses, that is to say, the losses incidental to marine adventure.

海上货物保险是一种保险合同，作为对所收集的被保险人的保险费的回报合同，它按照双方约定的方式和程度来赔偿被保险人的海上损失。

2. Losses attributable to discharge of the insured goods at a port of distress following a sea peril as well as special charges arising from loading, warehousing and forwarding of the goods at an intermediate port of call or refuge.

船舶发生海难后，被保险货物在避难港卸货造成的损失，以及在中途停靠港或者避难港装卸、仓储、运送货物所发生的特别费用。

3. In the W-W Clause, the insurance company undertakes an insurance liability over the insured cargo from the warehouse or the place of storage of the shipper named in policy until the cargo has arrived at the warehouse or the place of storage of the receiver named in the policy.

仓至仓条款是保险责任起讫的条款，是指自被保险货物运离保险单上载明的托运人的仓库或存放地点时生效，包括正常的运输过程，直至货物到达保险单上载明的收货人的仓库或存放地点为止。

4. If the insured knows beforehand the cargo-carrying ships are unseaworthy, or the cargo-carrying ship transportation vehicle or the container is uncargoworthy, the insurer does not cover the losses or expenses thereby.

如果被保险人事先知道载货船舶不适航或者载货船舶运输工具、集装箱不适航的情况，保险人不承担由此产生的损失或者费用。

5. For example, "Insurance is to be covered by the sellers for 110% of the Invoice Value against All Risks and War Risk as per Ocean Marine Cargo Clauses of People's Insurance Company of China dated Jan. 1st, 1981."

例如："由卖方按发票金额的 110%投保一切险和战争险，按 1981 年 1 月 1 日中国人民保险公司海洋运输货物保险条款负责。"

6. According to UCP 600 Section 28 Item "e": "the date of the insurance document must be not later than the date of shipment, unless it appears from the insurance document that the cover is effective from a date not later than the date of shipment."

根据《UCP 600》第二十八条"e"款规定："保险单据的日期不得迟于装运日期，除非保险单据上表明保险责任不得迟于装运日生效。"

Exercises

I. Match each one on the left with its correct meaning on the right.

1. marine insurance	A. the price paid to the insurer for a policy or damage
2. partial loss	B. failure to delivery risk, war risk, and strike risk
3. insurance premium	C. a voluntary and deliberate loss
4. insurance policy	D. the loss of part of goods
5. special additional risks	E. the insurance contract
6. general average	F. the insurance of ships against specific causes of loss that might be encountered at sea

1. (   )   2. (   )   3. (   ) 4. (   )   5. (   )   6. (   )

II. Decide whether the following statements are True (T) or False (F).

1. WPA provides larger cover than FPA since it includes partial losses and damages resulting from natural calamities.   (   )

2. Three types of risks are covered by marine insurance, namely perils at sea, extraneous risks and force majeure.   (   )

3. All Risks cover literally all risks of physical loss or damage from an external cause, including war, strikes, riots seizure or detention.   (   )

4. Insurance policy is the contract made between the insurer and the insured.   (   )

5. In marine insurance, general average is to be born by the carrier, who may, upon presentation of evidence of the loss, recover the loss from the insurance underwriter.   (   )

6. Under CIF, the buyer should procure insurance for the cargo since the risks transfer from

the seller to the buyer when the cargo passes the ship's rail at the port of shipment. ( )

7. The commencement and termination of three basic CIC insurance coverage use a "warehouse to warehouse" clause. ( )

8. Theft, breakage, leakage, contamination are general extraneous risks. ( )

9. Under constructive total losses, the insured can not ask the insurer to cover the losses. ( )

10. Usually salvage charges can be recovered from the general average. ( )

III. Finish the multiple choice questions.

1. Natural calamities include _____.

    A. tsunami   B. earthquake   C. lightning   D. stranding

2. General extraneous risks include _____.

    A. shortage in weight   B. breakage

    C. war   D. taint of odor

3. An insurance policy is functioned as _____.

    A. evidence of an insurance contract   B. grounds for claims

    C. grounds for indemnity   D. a receipt of premium

4. Which of the following terms can be insured separately? _____.

    A. ICC(A), ICC(B)) and ICC(C)   B. Institute War Clauses-Cargo

    C. Institute Strike Clauses-Cargo   D. Malicious Damage Clause

5. In accordance with ICC conditions, the insurer will not be responsible for the indemnification of _____.

    A. deliberate damage to the subject-matter insured

    B. delay

    C. loss or damage due to willful misconduct of the insured

    D. ordinary losses in weight

微课资源

扫一扫，获取相关微课视频。

5.1.mp4   5.2.mp4

Chapter 6　International Payment

In the sales confirmation signed by the importer and the exporter, the terms of shipment were written as "shipment should be effected in September", soon after the S/C was signed, the importer asked its issuing bank to open the relevant L/C. In the L/C at sight, the time of shipment was also written as "Shipment must be effected on or before September, 2019". The exporter shipped the goods on September 10, and soon got the payment from the issuing bank. On October 10, the importer filed a complaint about late shipment. They insisted that the shipment should not be later than August 31. He said the exporter should pay for compensation for penalty of 0.1% per day for 10 days, which is 1% of the contract value.

Question:

1. Why can the exporter get the payment quickly from the issuing bank?

2. Is the request from the importer reasonable or not? Should the exporter pay for the penalty?

6.1　Payment Options for Domestic Trade

Payment is the central concern for both the buyer and the seller in international transactions. The seller is concerned that he will have certainty of payment after goods have been shipped, and receive that payment in a timely manner. The buyer wants to know that he will receive the goods he has committed to pay for, and further wants to ensure that a secure payment process is neither complicated nor expensive.

This chapter aims to explain the different types of payment methods used in international transactions. It will focus on bills of exchange, documentary collection, and documentary letter credits.

In domestic trade, payment in advance, COD (cash on delivery), open account, collection, are often used. It's easy to understand that for the seller, the risk for open account is the highest among these three, then COD is fair for both the seller and the buyer. Payment in advance is risky for the buyer. Collection is based on the buyer's bank account. If there's enough money in the account, it's safe; if not, it's risky for the seller.

6.2　Payment Instrument

What are the tools of receipt and payment in international trade? As a payment instrument, it should be a financial document with money value, or an evidence of a financial transaction. All payment instruments have two characteristics. One is that they represent a unilateral promise to pay a fixed amount of money to the legitimate holder of the instruments. The other is that they are transferable or negotiable.

1. Bill of Exchange (B/E)

A B/E, sometimes also called a draft or a bill, is a written document which contains an unconditional order whereby the drawer direct the drawee to pay a definite sum of money to the payee or his order.

1) A typical draft bears the following items (Figure 6-1 and Figure 6-2)

The words of "Bill", "Bill of Exchange" or "draft";

The date and place of issuance of draft;

The specific sum which is exactly the same as that indicated on the export invoice;

The tenor, which is the time of the payment, either a sight bill or demand bill;

The name of the drawee;

The name and signature of the drawer;

The name of the payee or the order of the bearer;

The endorsement of the payee when applicable;

The name and signature of the payee.

2) Optional items

The reason of issuing the draft;

The interest clause for time bill;

The total copy of the bill;

The drawee's address etc.

BILL OF EXCHANGE

凭
Drawn Under _____

不可撤销信用证 OUK760981
Irrevocable　L/C　No. _____

日　期 Sept. 12, 2019
Date

支 取
Payable With Interest　　@ _____ % 按　息　付 款

汇
票
号
码
No. 123456

USD 10, 000

September 27, 2019

汇票金额
Exchange for _____

北京
Beijing

见
票
at _____ xxx _____
Being　Unpaid)　Pay　to　the　Order　of

日 后 (本 汇 票 之 副 本 未 付) 付 交
Sight　of　This　FIRST　of　Exchange　(Second　of　Exchange

金额
the sum of US DOLLARS TEN THOUSAND ONLY _____

此致:
付款人
To: _____
Drawee _____

出票人本人或其代表人签章
Drawer's name
Sign/ stamp

Figure 6-1　Bilingual Sight Bill of Exchange Under L/C

ORIGINAL(正本字样)　BILL OF EXCHANGE

No. of the check 汇票号码

DRAWN UNDER　①开证行 _____

L/C NUMBER:　②信用证号 _____

DATED　③开证日期 _____

PAYABLE WITH INTEREST @ _____ % PER ANNUM

NO .④发票号　EXCHANGE FOR　⑤汇票小写金额 ⑥交单地点. 交单日期(汇票出票日期)

⑦票期(即期或远期) OF THIS FIRST OF EXCHANGE　(SECOND OF EXCHANGE BEING UNPAID)

PAY TO THE ORDER OF　⑧ 收款行或其指定人

THE SUM OF　SAY　⑨汇票大写金额　　　　ONLY

TO:　⑩ 付款行 _____

Drawer(beneficiary)出票人本人或其代表人的签章

Figure 6-2　Bilingual Sight Bill of Exchange Under L/C

3) Parties involved

The main parties, illustrated in Figure 6-1 and Figure 6-2, are as follows:

Drawer: the party who issues the draft or bill of exchange.

Drawee: the party who is ordered to pay the funds written on the face of the draft or bill of exchange.

Acceptor: a drawee who agrees to pay the bill when it is due by signing the bill on its face.

Payee: the party who, on the face of the bill, is to receive payment.

Endorser: a payee who has signed (endorsed) and delivered the bill to an endorsee.

Endorsee: a person who receives an endorsed bill from an endorser.

Bearer: a person who has physical possession of a bill that is payable to anyone ("to the bearer") or that has been endorsed without naming an endorsee (endorsed "in blank").

4) Procedure of using a B/E

The acts of a B/E refer to the legal acts carried out to bear obligations to a draft, the main act of which is to issue. Other acts such as presentation, payment, acceptance, endorsement, and dishonor are based on the main act.

Issuance: when a party fills the content of a B/E and signs his name at the right side of the bottom of the paper, this party becomes the drawer if this B/E, normally a B/E or draft, is issued by the exporter in the case of collection and L/C. The party to whom the B/E is addressed to is the drawee, which normally is the importer in the case of collection, and the issuing bank in the case of L/C. The third party is the payee. When the B/E is drawn, it will be sent to the payee. Normally the payee is the exporter's bank in the case of of collection and L/C.

Presentation: the act of taking the bill to the drawee and demanding that he makes the payment or accepts the bill is known as presentation. This results in two different ways: being honored or dishonored.

Payment: under a sight bill, the drawee is required to make the payment when the bill is presented to him. While for a time bill, the drawee is required to accept the bill when the bill is presented to him and make payment at the maturity of the bill.

Acceptance： for a time bill, on the first presentation, the drawee will accept the bill by crossing on the face of the bill and promising to pay on maturity day on the second presentation. The accepted time bill should be returned to the party presenting for acceptance.

Discounting and endorsement: an accepted draft is negotiable in the financial market. In order to receive cash immediately, the holder can sell the draft at a discount rate and transfer the title of the document to the buyer. For the purpose of transfer, the holder needs to sign his name on the back of the draft, and directly to whom he wants to transfer. This is called "endorsement".

Dishonor: dishonor occurs when the drawee refuses to make payment or accept a bill by the payer when it is presented for payment or acceptance. Upon dishonor, the holder of the bill should immediately make the protest or certificate of dishonor, so as to obtain his right of recourse.

5) Classification of a B/E

Banker's draft & commercial draft

According to the drawer and the drawee, a bill can be a banker's draft or a commercial draft.

The former is drawn by a bank on another bank. A banker's draft can be viewed as a bank check which is a secured payment. The latter is drawn by a trader on another trader or a banker.

Documentary Draft & Clean Draft

According to whether or not shipping documents are attached, a bill can be a documentary draft or a clean draft. A documentary draft calls for the attachment of the relevant documents to complete an export transaction. A clean bill is on the other hand without the company of any commercial documents.

Sight Draft & Time Draft/Usance Draft

According to the tenor, bills can be classified into sight draft and time draft (usance draft). Sight draft is payable when presented. On a sight draft, there is the wording as "at sight of this bill of exchange, pay to..." Time draft is payable at a future fixed date. It normally reads as "at 30/60 days' sight of this B/E, pay to..." By signing and writing "accepted" on the draft, the buyer is formally obligated to pay within the stated time.

2. Promissory Note

In the United Nations Convention on International Bills of Exchange and International Promissory Notes, a promissory note is defined as "a written instrument which contains an unconditional promise whereby the maker undertakes to pay a definite sum of money to the payee or to his holder". To put it simple, a promissory note is any written promise to pay. It is a negotiable instrument that is an evidence of debt contracted by a borrower from a creditor, known as a lender of funds. If the instrument does not have all the qualities of a negotiable instrument, it cannot be legally transferred.

There are only two parties concerned in a promissory note, the maker and the payee, which is the most significant difference from the B/E. The maker can be more than one person, who would be either jointly or separately responsible for the payment of the bill.

Promissory notes can be sight promissory notes or time promissory notes. Promissory notes made by the bankers are usually called cashier's check or cashier's order, which are all sight notes and commonly used in international trade. Commercial promissory notes or trader's notes could be accepted as a guarantee for the payment by some sellers in domestic trade.

3. Check

A check is a direction in writing to a bank to pay a stated sum of money on demand to a named party, or to the order of a specified person or a bearer. A check can be seen as a type of B/E drawn on a bank, payable on demand. The drawer of the check must be sure that the sum carried on the check is not more than the amount he has deposited in the bank, otherwise the check will not be honored. If the paying bank marked "certified" with signature on the check, it is a certified check that will not be dishonored.

Apart from the possibility of dishonor, using check in international trade has other disadvantages. A check can be canceled at any time before it is paid. Furthermore, a check has to be sent back through banking channels to the local bank in the importer's country for payment, which is costly and inconvenient for the exporter. As a result, checks are not frequently used in international trade.

6.3   Payment Methods

In international trade, payment methods chiefly conclude remittance, collection and letter of credit. Remittance and collection both depend on commercial credit, namely the promise from the trading partner, and remittance is the simplest one among the methods of payment.

1. Remittance

Remittance refers to the transfer of funds from one party to another among different countries through banks. There are four parties involved in the remittance operation: remitter, remitting bank, paying bank and payee or beneficiary.

1) Workflow of remittance

The major procedure could be illustrated briefly as follows.

First, the importer, as a remitter, comes to the remitting bank to submit a remittance application to effect the payment. Second, the remitting bank upon acceptance, will either issue a remittance instruction by telex or SWIFT to, or draw a demand draft on, one of its overseas branches or correspondent banks in the exporter's country. Third, when receiving the remittance instruction (payment order), the paying bank will credit the exporter's account with relevant amount.

2) Types of remittance

According to the way the remittance instruction delivered from the remitting bank to the paying bank, there are three types of remittance.

Mail Transfer (M/T)

By M/T, the importer will hand over the application of remittance and delivery a sum of certain money to the remitting bank, stating that the remittance should be done by M/T. The remitting bank makes a payment order and sends it to a correspondent bank in the exporter's country by mail, asks the exporter's bank to make the payment to the exporter. M/T is less expensive, but it costs more time. See Figure 6-3.

Telegraphic Transfer (T/T)

By T/T, the importer will hand over the application of remittance and delivery a sum of certain money to the remitting bank, stating that the remittance should be done by T/T. The remitting bank makes a payment order and sends it to a correspondent bank in the exporter's country by telex and SWIFT, asks the exporter's bank to make the payment to the exporter. T/T saves time. See Figure 6-3.

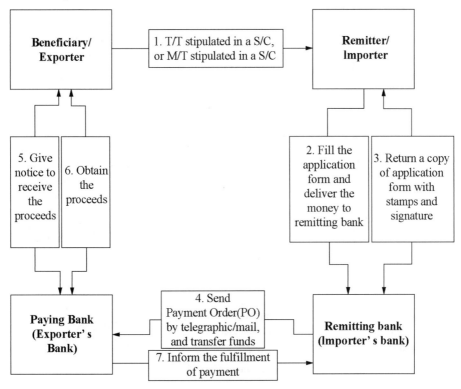

Figure 6-3　Workflow of T/T or M/T

SWIFT is the abbreviation of an Association-Society for Worldwide Inter-bank Financial Telecommunications. It established a shared worldwide data processing and communications link between financial institutions and a common language for international financial transactions. T/T is more expensive but it is much sooner.

Remittance by Banker's Demand Draft (D/D)

By D/D, the buyer will come to the local bank to buy a banker's bill and then deliver it to the seller or beneficiary by mail. When the seller or beneficiary has received it, he will come to the bank designated by the banker's bill of cash. Apart from banker's bill, promissory notes or checks can also be used in this way. See Figure 6-4.

The above types of remittance are applied in payment in advance and open account.

Payment in Advance

Payment in advance is the most secure method for exporters, but the least attractive for importers. Exporters today seldom insist on full advance payment before the shipment, because they may find themselves losing out to competitors who offer more flexible payment methods.

Open Account

This is the least secure method of trading for exporters, but the most attractive to importers. It allows the importer to make payment after he receives the goods without providing any documents evidencing his commitment to payment. Consequently, open account payment should only be considered when an exporter is sufficiently confident that it will be received.

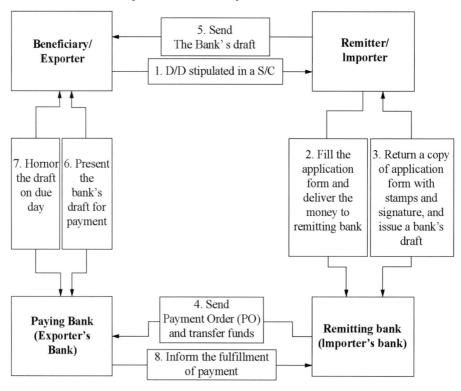

Figure 6-4　Workflow of D/D

It is more sensible to view payment in advance and open account polar opposites. That is why it is more reasonable for traders to consider any alternatives in between the two terms. As a consequence, bills for collection and letters of credit and some other banking products come into play.

2. Collection

By definition, a collection means an arrangement whereby the seller draws a draft on the buyer and authorizes his bank to collect. It is a means of payment ensuring that the goods are handed over to the buyer only when he pays the amount shown on a B/L, or when he accepts the bill and commits to pay by a specified date.

1) The parties involved under collection

In a collection transaction, there are four parties involved, namely, principal, remitting bank, collecting bank, and drawee.

Principal is the one who draws the B/L and authorizes his bank to the effect of the collection. Being the party who is requesting the assistance service from the banks. The seller is called the principal, or sometimes, the remitter, or the drawer.

Remitting bank is the bank authorized by the drawer of the draft to effect collection from the buyer. Usually it is the seller's local bank.

Collecting bank is the bank nominated by the buyer to receive the documents from the **remitting banks** which presents them to the buyer for cash payment or a promise to pay in the future. It is usually the bank in the country of the buyer.

Drawee is usually the buyer of the goods, who is the one owing the indicated amount to the seller. When notified by the collecting bank of the arrival of documents, the drawee has to make immediate cash payment or sign a draft according to the terms of collection order in exchange for the documents from the collecting bank.

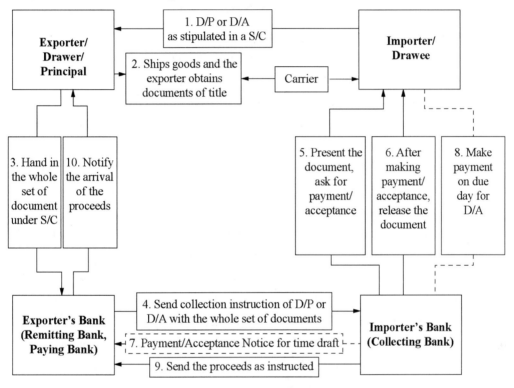

Figure 6-5   Workflow of D/P or D/A

2) Workflow of collection

The exporter and the importer make an agreement in a contract that the payment is effected by collection.

The exporter ships goods and obtains documents of title from the carrier.

The exporter draws a B/E on the importer, and delivers the whole set of documents to his remitting bank, such as documents for goods of title and a collection order containing the exporter's instructions.

The remitting bank forwards B/E with other documents to its correspondent bank—a collecting bank with the collection instruction.

The collecting bank presents draft and documents to the importer upon payments or acceptance from the importer.

The collecting bank remits payments to the remitting bank.

The remitting bank credits payment to the exporter's account.

3) Classification of collection

The difference of draft conducted by the exporter may lead to two primary means of collection: clean collection and documentary collection.

Clean Collection

If the transaction amount is small or if it is impossible to provide commercial documents, the exporter can conduct collection of a draft without the company of commercial documents.

Documentary Collection

Documentary collection is a method of effecting payment for goods whereby the exporter ships goods to the importer, but instructs his bank to collect a certain sum from the importer in exchange for the transfer of title, shipping and other documentation enabling the importer to take possession of the goods. This is much more generally used in international commodity transactions.

There are two main types of documentary collection: documents against payment (D/P), documents against acceptance (D/A).

Documents against Payment (D/P)

Under D/P, the importer can receive the shipping documents after he has duly made the payment of the goods. It can further be of two types: D/P at sight and D/P after sight.

Under D/P at sight, the importer has to effect payment at sight of a demand draft before he obtains the relevant documents. Under D/P after sight, the importer can obtain the document only after he effects payment at the maturity date of a usance draft issued by the exporter. In other words, the importer is not able to obtain the documents only after he accepts the usance draft.

Under D/P after sight, to avoid possible delay and get the goods as soon as possible, the importer can present a trust receipt and borrow the shipping documents from the collecting bank and upon the maturity of the draft, effect the payment of the goods. This is called D/P-T/R. T/R is trust receipt, a written guarantee made by the importer to take the delivery of the goods before the payment. Under D/P-T/R, the exporter must authorize the bank to lend the importer the shipping documents after receiving the latter's T/R and the risks therefore shall be borne by the exporter. See Figure 6-5.

Documents against Acceptance (D/A)

Under D/A, the importer can get the shipping documents from the collecting bank after he has duly accepted the draft, which is only applicable to time draft. This will be greatly convenient for the importer, but means more risks for the exporter, for once he has delivered the shipping documents, he will have lost his title over the goods. See Figure 6-5.

Therefore, to use collection, the exporter needs to have a good understanding of the credit status of the importer. Collection is also a type of payment based on commercial credit.

3. Letter of Credit (L/C)

An L/C is the written promise of a bank on behalf of the buyer to pay a seller the amount specified in the credit provided the seller complies with the terms and conditions set forth in the credit.

An L/C is a method of payment, considered less secure than payment in advance but more secure than documentary collections and open account from the seller's point of view.

From the buyer's point of view, it offers more security than payment in advance but less security than documentary collections or open account terms.

However, it is generally considered that L/Cs offer a good balance of security between the buyer and the seller because both the buyer and seller rely upon the security of banks and the banking system to ensure that payment is received and goods are provided. In an L/C transaction, the goods are consigned to the order of the issuing bank, meaning that the bank will not release control of the goods until the buyer has either paid or undertaken to pay the bank for the documents.

In the event that the buyer is unable to make payment on the purchase, the seller may make a demand for payment on the bank. The bank will examine the beneficiary's demand and if it complies with the terms of the L/C, the bank will honor the demand. Most L/Cs are governed by rules defined by the Uniform Customs and Practice for Documentary Credits 600 (UCP 600).

According to whether the usage of the credit requires the company of documents, L/Cs can be divided into two categories: clean credits and documentary credits. A clean credit does not require the presentation of documents. It is often used as a traveler's check for withdrawing cash abroad, or a bank guarantee for special purpose. In the scope of international trade transaction, the majority of credits are documentary ones to provide the best security for all parties involved.

1) The main items of documentary L/C (See Specimen 6-1)

The parties involved, including the applicant, the issuing bank, the negotiating bank, the paying bank and the like.

Remarks about the L/C: such as the number of the L/C, its type and the issuing date.

The amount of the L/C.

The clauses of the B/E, such as the amount of the bill, the drawer and the drawee, the paying date.

The clauses about the documents, such as the invoice, the B/L, the insurance policy, the packing list, the certificate of origin and inspection certificate. Also, the number of copies of the documents, the description of the goods, specifications, quantity, unit price, total amount, and so on.

Particular clauses, such as the special provisions about the deal in accordance with the particular business or particular situation of the importing country.

LETTER OF CREDIT
-- MESSAGE TEXT --

```
:27: SEQUENCE OF TOTAL
   1/1
:40A: FORM OF DOCUMENTARY CREDIT
   IRREVOCABLE
:20: DOCUMENTARY CREDIT NUMBER
   002/0000026
:31C: DATE OF ISSUE
   180829
:40E: APPLICABLE RULES
   UCP LATEST VERSION
:31D: DATE AND PLACE OF EXPIRY
   20180930  CHINA
:50: APPLICANT
   RIQING EXPORT AND IMPORT COMPANY
   P.O.BOX 1589, NAGOYA, JAPAN
:59: BENEFICIARY
   AIGE IMPORT & EXPORT COMPANY
   ROOM 2501, JIAFA MANSION, BEIJING WEST ROAD, SHANGHAI 200001, P.R.CHINA
:32B: CURRENCY CODE, AMOUNT
   JPY  1200000,
:41D: AVAILABLE WITH BY
   ANY BANK IN CHINA BY SIGHT PAYMENT
:42C: DRAFTS AT
:42A: DRAWEE
   ISSUE BANK
:43P: PARTIAL SHIPMENTS
   ALLOWED
:43T: TRANSSHIPMENT
   ALLOWED
:44E: PORT OF LOADING/AIRPORT OF DEPARTURE
   SHANGHAI,CHINA
:44F: PORT OF DISCHARGE/AIRPORT OF DESTINATION
   NAGOYA,JAPAN
:44C: LATEST DATE OF SHIPMENT
   20180901
:45A: DESCRIPTION OF GOODS AND/OR SERVICES
   01006
   CANNED LITCHIS
   850GX24TINS/CTN
   QUANTITY: 1000CARTONS
   PRICE: JPY1200
   FOB SHANGHAI,CHINA
:46A: DOCUMENTS REQUIRED
   +SIGNED COMMERCIAL INVOICE IN 1 ORAGINAL AND 3 COPIES INDICATING L/C NO. AND CONTRACT NO.SELL001+FULL SET
   OF CLEAN ON BOARD BILLS OF LADING MADE OUT TO ORDER AND BLANK ENDORSED, MARKED "FREIGHT TO COLLECT"
   NOTIFYING THE APPLICANT.
   +PACKING LIST MEMO IN 1 ORAGINAL AND 3 COPIES INDICATING QUANTITY, GROSS AND WEIGHT OF EACH PACKAGE.

   +CERTIFICATE OF QUANTITY/WEIGHT IN 1 ORAGINAL AND 3 COPIES
   +CERTIFICATE OF QUALITY IN 1 ORAGINAL AND 3 COPIES
   +CERTIFICATE OF PHYTOSANITARY IN 1 ORAGINAL AND 3 COPIES
   +HEALTH CERTIFICATE IN 1 ORAGINAL AND 3 COPIES
   +CERTIFICATE OF ORIGIN FORM A IN 1 ORAGINAL AND 3 COPIES
:47A: ADDITIONAL CONDITIONS
   THIRD PARTY AS SHIPPER IS NOT ACCEPTABLE, SHORT FORM/BLANK BACK B/L IS NOT ACCEPTABLE.
   BOTH QUANTITY AND CREDIT AMOUNT 5% MORE OR LESS ARE ALLOWED.
:71B: CHARGES
   ALL BANKING CHARGES OUTSIDE THE OPENING BANK ARE FOR BENEFICIARY'S ACCOUNT.
:48: PERIOD FOR PRESENTATION
   DOCUMENTS MUST BE PRESENTED WITHIN 7 DAYS AFTER DATE OF ISSUANCE OF THE TRANSPORT DOCUMENTS BUT WITHIN
   THE VALIDITY OF THIS CREDIT.
:49: CONFIRMATION INSTRUCTIONS
   WITHOUT
:57D: ADVISE THROUGH BANK
   BANK OF CHINA
   170 PEOPLE AVENUE, SHANGHAI, CHINA
```

Specimen 6-1   Letter of Credit MT 700 Format

Guarantee clauses of the opening bank, which testifies that the opening bank will hold itself responsible for the payment to the beneficiary of the draft.

L/C is of different forms. Most of the issuing banks use their own forms with reference to the standard forms. The legal document concerning the use of L/C is Uniform Customs and Practice for Documentary Credits.

2) The parties to an L/C

Applicant is the party on whose request the credit is issued, and it is the buyer that begins to apply to his bank to open a credit naming the seller as the beneficiary.

Opening Bank or Issuing Bank is the bank issues an L/C at the request of the applicant or on its own behalf. It is usually the bank located in the importer's country.

Advising Bank or Notifying Bank usually is the branch or correspondent bank of the issuing bank in the exporter's country, which verifies the authenticity of the credit and any amendment and advises or transmits them to the beneficiary.

Beneficiary is the party in whose favor a credit is issued and who has the right to demand the proceeds by presenting complying documents.

Paying Bank or Drawee bank is the bank which cashes a check or draft, known as an accepting bank or payer bank too.

Negotiating Bank is the beneficiary's bank which agrees to pay the beneficiary by purchasing a negotiable instrument.

Confirming Bank is the bank that adds its confirmation to a credit upon the issuing bank's authorization or request.

Reimbursing Bank is the bank named in credit from which the claiming banks may request cover after paying or negotiating the documents in compliance with the credit.

Presenting Bank is the bank which receives the package of documents under an L/C and submits it to the paying bank for payment.

Nominated Bank means the bank with which the L/C is available or any bank in the case of a credit available with any bank.

3) Workflow of L/C

After a sales contract has been negotiated and an L/C has been agreed upon as the method of payment, the applicant (importer) will contact a bank to ask for an L/C to be issued, and once the issuing bank has ascertained that the applicant will be able to pay for the goods, it will issue the L/C.

The issuing bank advises the documentary credit to the bank of the exporter, which is called the advising bank or confirming bank.

Once the beneficiary receives the L/C it will check the terms to ensure that it matches with the contract, and will either arrange for shipment of the goods or ask for an amendment to the L/C so that it meets with the terms of the contract.

Once the goods have been shipped, within the validity period of the credit, the beneficiary will present the set of requested documents to its bank, which will perform some document checking to ensure their compliance with the terms of the documentary credit. If they comply with the terms of the L/C the issuing bank is bound to honor the terms of the L/C by paying the beneficiary.

The bank of the exporter is sending the documents to the issuing bank who performs the payment or acceptance after a thorough checking of the documents.

The issuing bank transfers the documents to the importer and proceeds with the debit of its account for the principal amount.

The importer receives the goods, especially thanks to the document of title, the B/L. See Figure 6-6.

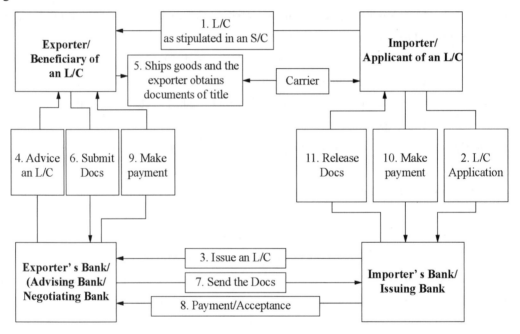

Figure 6-6　Workflow of L/C

4) Types of documentary credit

Revocable Credit: the buyer and the bank that established the L/C are able to amend the L/C or make corrections without informing or getting permissions from the seller. This type of credit is extremely risky for the exporter which explains why it is rarely used.

Irrevocable Credit: any changes (amendment) or cancellation of the L/C (except it is expired) is done by the applicant through the issuing bank. It must be authenticated and approved by the beneficiary. The irrevocable documentary credit cannot be canceled or modified without the express consent from the issuing bank, the confirming bank and the beneficiary.

Confirmed Irrevocable Credit: An L/C is said to be confirmed when a confirming bank adds its confirmation (or guarantee) to honor a complying presentation at the request or authorization of the issuing bank. Under a confirmed irrevocable credit both the issuing bank and the confirming bank undertake to honor a complying presentation, hence providing the beneficiary a double assurance of payment.

Transferable Credit: the exporter has the right to make the credit available to one or more subsequent beneficiaries. Credits are made transferable when the original beneficiary is a middleman and does not supply the merchandise, but procures goods from suppliers and arranges them to be sent to the buyer and does not want the buyer and the supplier to know each other. The middleman is entitled to substitute his own invoice for the supplier's and acquire the difference as profit. According to UCP 600, a transferable credit must clearly state that it is "transferable". Moreover, the credit can only be transferred once. A second beneficiary cannot transfer the credit to a third beneficiary. If the first beneficiary transfers the credit to several parties, all these transferees are considered as second beneficiaries. A bank is not obligated to transfer a credit. A transferable L/C can be transferred to more than one alternate beneficiary as long as it allows partial shipments. The terms and conditions of the original credit must be replicated exactly in the transferred credit. However, to keep the workability of the transferable L/C, some figures can be reduced or curtailed. Non-transferable credit means that the seller cannot assign all or part of the credits to another party. In international commerce, all credits are non-transferable.

Sight Credit and Usance Credit: sight credit is the credit that the bank designated in the L/C immediately pays after inspecting the carriage documents from the seller. The designated bank usually is the advising or confirming bank since it actually resides in the same country as the exporter. Usance credit is the credit that is not paid immediately after presentation, but after an indicated period that is accepted by both the buyer and the seller. Typically, the seller allows the buyer to pay the required money after taking the related goods and selling them.

Back-to-Back Credit: back-to-back credits are used in circumstances very similar to those of the transferable credit where a middle person may be involved in the transaction. A pair of L/Cs in which one is to the benefit of a seller who is not able to provide the corresponding goods for unspecified reasons. In that event, a second credit is opened for another seller to provide the desired goods. Back-to-back credits are issued to facilitate intermediary trade. Intermediate companies such as trading houses are sometimes required to open L/Cs for a supplier and receive export L/Cs from the buyer.

Red Clause Credit: an anticipatory credit is characterized by a special clause, known as "red clause", which is traditionally printed in red ink and authorized the advising bank or the confirming bank to make advances to the beneficiary before his presentation of documents required.

Standby Credit: a standby credit is a clean credit that guarantees the payment for a possible unfulfilled obligation on the part of the applicant. It is especially used as security for open account trading where the exporter requires some kind of "backup" in the event of the importer not paying for the goods. In case of default by the applicant, the beneficiary can demand payment from the guarantor, who is the issuing bank of the standby credit, by presenting a draft, along with a signed statement by the beneficiary about the applicant's failure to pay.

5) Governing rules of L/C

An L/C is governed by a set of rules from the ICC. In this case, the document is called Uniform Customs and Practice, in short UCP 600, which came into effect on 1st, July, 2007.

The fundamental principle of all letters of credit is that L/Cs deal with documents and not with goods, as stated by Article 5 of UCP 600. Accordingly, if the documents tendered by the beneficiary or their agent are in order, then in general the bank is obliged to pay without further qualifications. As a result the buyer bears the risk that a dishonest seller may present documents which comply with the LC and receive payment, only to later discover that documents are fraudulent and the goods are not in accordance with the contract.

With the UCP 600 rules the ICC sought to make the rules more flexible, suggesting that data in a document "need not be identical to, but must not conflict with data in that document, any other stipulated document, or the credit", as a way to account for any minor documentary errors. However in practice many banks still hold to the principle of strict compliance, since it offers concrete guarantees to all parties.

Used by L/C practitioners worldwide, the UCP rules are the most successful private rules for trade ever developed. Bankers, traders, lawyers, transporters, academics and all the like who deal with L/C transactions around the world, will refer to UCP series on a daily basis.

6) Attentions for a documentary credit

The seller is enjoyed with lower risks, high initiative, free transfer and easy finance under a credit. When discussing business terms with the seller, soft clauses should be avoided. At the same time, a safe and convenient way of reimbursement should be confirmed to guarantee a safe collection of payment. Under a credit, the seller needs to present full set of commercial documents and original credit to the nominated bank. If the presentation has discrepancies, it is difficult to handle trade financing.

The bank will also deal with operations such as collection of payment, settlement of payment, credit account according to the state regulations concerning foreign exchange control. If the seller wants to withdraw a credit, he needs to present trust instrument in written form and full set of original credit to the advising bank. If a credit is available by a nominated bank located at the export country, the credit is benefit for the beneficiary instead of the applicant. The seller may choose the best kind of credit, just as the sight payment credit is better than the negotiable credit.

As for the buyer, when issuing a credit, the buyer provides the seller with extra guarantee on payment in cost of more bank charge born by it, so the buyer had better ask the seller for preferential price during the commercial negotiation concerning this point.

4. Letter of Guarantee (L/G)

An L/G is different from an L/C, but to some extent an L/G shares many similarities with a standby letter of credit. An L/G can be used in a wider scope than an L/C, such as trade of commodity, labor and technology, construction project, financing from financial institutions and so on.

There are many differences between an L/G and an L/C. An L/G may allow the importer rather than the exporter as the beneficiary of the instrument. Under an L/C, the exporter can receive the payment as long as the documents they present comply with the terms of credit. In this case the importer may be deceived or defrauded. Under an L/G, when the importer becomes the beneficiary of the L/G, he may have a strong bargaining position and use an L/G to protect his interest.

An L/G can be divided into two types, i.e., credit L/G and payment L/G. L/Gs do not follow any specific format or wording. They tend to be constructed by different cases. But most L/Gs are to follow several essential requirements, such as irrevocable, unconditional, fully transferable, abstract and divisible.

The application of an L/G is subject to the Uniform Rules for Demand Guarantees (ICC Publication No. 758) and the Uniform Rules for Contract Guarantees (ICC Publication No. 325). But some countries, like the USA and Japan, do not allow their banks to get involved in commercial disputes, so the banks of these countries do not issue an L/G, instead they use standby L/C.

5. International Factoring

Apart from using the L/C as an instrument for obtaining loans, exporters can also depend on other approaches for financing. International factoring has developed as a favorable alternative to traditional export finance such as an L/C.

Being able to offer international customers better financing terms so as to maintain and increase sales is now an important part of any international sales package. The obstacles, such as credit risk, economic situation of another country, collecting from foreign accounts and so on, are more often placing the exporters at a competitive disadvantage stand. **Factoring is a complete financial package that combines investigating and assessing the creditworthiness of buyers, giving one hundred percent protection against credit risk, collecting and managing of outstanding receivables and etc.**

There are four parties involved in a transaction: the exporter, the importer, the export factor and the import factor.

Exporter is the client of a factoring transaction, who needs to provide a business license of documents of a similar nature, report of his business operation and financial situation, if required, together with an application form to the local factoring company or bank chosen to initiate the service. Once accepted, the exporter will sign a factoring agreement with the factor to sell all his receivables under agreed terms.

Importer's credibility and performance as well as the scale of business commonly decide how quickly or easily the exporter's application for factoring service.

Export factor could be a local bank or a specialized factoring company in the exporter's country, but must be an FCI member. Following the agreement with the exporter, the factor purchases the exporter's receivables and takes the responsibility for collecting and taking credit risk.

Import factor can be the overseas branch of the exporter factor or a nominated correspondent factor of the export factor, and also should be an FCI member, whose responsibility is to investigate the importer's credit and handle related issues locally.

(1) The procedure of factoring usually includes the following steps.

The exporter and the export factors sign a factoring contract, and to whom assign all agreed receivables. The factors then become responsible for all aspects of the factoring operation.

The export factor chooses an FCI correspondent as an import factor, and reassigns the receivables to him.

The import factor investigates the credit standing of the importer, establishes lines of credit and informs the export factor of the results. This allows the importer to place an order on open account terms without opening L/Cs.

Once the goods have been shipped, the export factor may advance up to 80% to 90% of the invoice value to the exporter.

Once the sale has taken place, the import factor collects the full invoice value at maturity and is responsible for the swift transmission of funds to the export factor who then pays the exporter the outstanding balance.

If 90 days after the due date an approved invoice remains unpaid, the import factor will pay 100% of the invoice value under guarantee.

(2) The advantages of international factoring.

International factoring has many advantages over other methods of international commercial payment. The greatest one is that it allows both exporters and importers to trade on open account terms without risk. International factoring may also bring many other benefits, such as increased sales revenue, risk guarantee, reduced costs, simplified procedures and more profits, etc., to the exporters as well as the importers.

As for exporters, international factoring services can expand sales abroad by offering competitive terms and conditions. They can fully cover credit losses, and offer open account terms by invoicing the importer and granting deferred payments. Moreover, international factoring can have speedy collection and remittance, so as to improve cash flow and enable them to have access to a flexible source of working capital to increase export sales. As for importers, they can expand their purchasing power without using existing lines of credit, and purchase goods without delays which were often encountered when using L/Cs.

Besides the international settlement methods described above, with the development of modern financial services, there are more and better alternatives to the exporters such as packing loan, forfeiting, bill purchase, etc., so that they can improve their operating capital while reducing the settlement risk from the purchasing side. In general, when making export financing decision, the exporter has to take all relevant factors such as risk, cost, availability and credit limit into consideration.

6.4　Payment Clauses in the Contract

Payment can be effected in different ways, therefore, it is imperative to clearly stipulate the specific mode of payment and the detailed requirement. Here are some examples of terms of payment stipulated in the contract.

Examples of Terms of Payment in the Contract are as follows.

(1) The buyer shall pay the total value to the seller in advance by T/T (M/T or D/D) not later than June 30, 2007.

(2) Payment by T/T: payment to be effected by the buyer shall not be later than 30 days after receipt of the documents listed in the contract.

(3) Payment by D/P at sight: upon first presentation the buyer shall pay against documentary draft by the seller at sight. The shipping documents are to be delivered against payment only.

(4) Payment by D/P after sight:The buyer shall duly accept the documentary draft at 60 days sight upon first presentation and make payment on its maturity. The shipping documents are to be delivered against payment only.

(5) Payment by D/A: the buyer shall duly accept the documentary draft drawn by the seller at 90 days sight upon first presentation and make payment on its maturity. The shipping documents are to be delivered against acceptance.

(6) The buyer shall open an irrevocable L/C in favor of the seller before Apr. 15th, 2019. The said L/C shall be available by draft at sight for full invoice value and remain valid for negotiation in China for 15 days after shipment.

(7) 50% by L/C at sight, 50% by D/P at sight.

6.5　Summary Risk Lever of Different Modes of Payment

For exporters, the risk level for different modes of payment is arranged as follows.

100% Payment in advance < L/C< L/G< D/P< COD<international factoring<D/A

The higher the deposit, the more favorable for the exporter because he can use it to buy goods in advance, so for the exporter, he should fully understand the risk for each mode of payment before he signs the contract.

Moreover, exporters should bear in mind that there are always risks that the payment instrument could be dishonored. Receiving a banker's promissory note or a firm's check or an accepted B/L could not ensure the final payment from importers, the possible reasons may be as follows: (1) The check is withdrawn by the drawer, so that the request for payment for goods would be rejected by the paying bank; (2) Even the proceeds has been received by the exporter, the importer could still request his bank to withdraw the payment of the check during a period of time in some countries, so only after the refunding period; (3) Some originals or copies of payment instruments may be forged, the exporter should present them to the bank, and double check to find out the authenticity of them by the banking system.

For importers, they should set high standard of documents and make sure the goods are in exact accordance with the sales confirmation, so that they can reduce the level of risks of loss of both money and goods.

Notes to the Text

I. Vocabulary and phrases.

1. open account　赊销

2. payment in advance　预付款

3. cash on delivery(COD)　货到付款

4. bill of exchange(BE)　汇票，简称 bill 或 draft，常用的国际支付工具之一。在托收和信用证结算中经常会使用到汇票

5. draft　汇票的另外一个英文表达方式

6. promissory note　本票

7. check　支票

8. drawer　出票人，托收和信用证项下的汇票通常是由外销合同的出口商出票

9. drawee　付款人，托收项下的汇票通常是由外销合同的进口商为付款人。信用证项下

的汇票通常由外销合同的信用证开证行为付款人

10. payee 收款人，收款人通常写出口商或出口地银行

11. endorser 背书人，背书是将汇票权利转让给下一手的行为，并且背书人在汇票背面书写记录。第一个背书人是汇票上的收款人 payee

12. endorsee 被背书人，接受背书的人

13. endorsement 背书

14. bearer 在汇票中是指来人。在英国票据法中允许做成以"pay to bearer"这类来人抬头格式，但在日内瓦票据法和我国票据法中不允许

15. presentation 提示，是持票人提示给汇票付款人请求付款的票据行为

16. dishonor 拒付，是付款人拒绝到期付款的行为

17. tenor 期限

18. sight bill (demand draft) 即期汇票

19. time bill (usance draft) 远期汇票

20. maturity 到期

21. acceptance 承兑，是付款人承诺到期付款的行为

22. protest 拒付证明

23. recourse 追索

24. draw by A on B 由 A 开具给 B

25. The United Nations Convention on International Bills of Exchange and International Promissory Notes 《联合国国际汇票和国际本票公约》

26. sight promissory note 即期本票

27. time promissoryrote 远期本票

28. cashier's check (cashier's order) 银行本票

29. commercial promissory note (trader's note) 商业本票

30. on demand 即期

31. certified check 保付支票

32. remittance 汇付

33. collection 托收

34. clean collection 光票托收

35. documentary collection 跟单托收

36. document against payment (D/P) 付款交单

37. document against acceptance (D/A) 承兑交单

38. principal 委托人，在托收方式下是出口商委托出口地银行，故出口商为委托人

39. remitting bank 在汇付方式下是汇出汇款或签发银行汇票的银行(进口地银行)，在托收方式下是帮出口商汇出全套单据的银行(出口地银行)

40. letter of credit 信用证，简称 L/C

41. the beneficiary 受益人，信用证方式下的受益人为出口商

42. issuing bank   开证行

43. issuance   开立

44. advising bank   通知行

45. correspondent bank   代理行

46. confirming bank   保兑行

47. reimbursing bank   偿付行

48. confirm L/C   保兑信用证

49. back to back L/C   背对背信用证

50. documentary L/C   跟单信用证

51. UCP 600   《跟单信用证统一惯例》，国际商会第 600 号出版物，2007 年生效

52. International Commerce Committee(ICC)   国际商会

53. letter of guarantee(L/G)   保函，担保书

54. Uniform Rules for Demand Guarantees (ICC Publication No. 758)   见索即付保函统一规则，国际商会第 758 号出版物，2010 年生效

55. Uniform Rules for Contract Guarantees (ICC Publication No. 325)   合同担保统一规则

56. international factoring   国际保理

57. FCI correspondent bank   国际保理联合会会员银行

II. Sentences and paragraphs.

1. Advising bank or notifying bank usually is the branch or correspondent bank of the issuing bank in the exporter's country, which verifies the authenticity of the credit and any amendment and advises or transmits them to the beneficiary.

通知行通常是开证行在出口商所在地的代理行，便于验证信用证和信用证修改通知书的真实性，并通知、转递给受益人。

2. Once the goods have been shipped, within the validity period of the credit, the beneficiary will present the set of requested documents to its bank, which will perform some document checking to ensure their compliance with the terms of the documentary credit. If they comply with the terms of the L/C，the issuing bank is bound to honor the terms of the L/C by paying the Beneficiary.

当货物出运，受益人应在信用证有效期内提交全套单据给银行，银行需要确保单据与信用证条款一致。如果单据确实与信用证条款一致，开证行必须遵照信用证条款付款给受益人。

3. Factoring is a complete financial package that combines investigating and assessing the creditworthiness of buyers, giving one hundred percent protection against credit risk, collecting and managing of outstanding receivables and etc.

保理业务是一个完整的金融一揽子计划，它结合了买方信用评估、信用风险担保、应收账款管理等财务服务。

Exercises

I. Match each one on the left with its correct meaning on the right.

1. reimburse	A. 议付行
2. beneficiary	B. 可转让信用证
3. issuance	C. 跟单托收
4. comply with something	D. 受益人
5. amendment.	E. 签发
6. irrevocable confirmed letter of credit	F. 修改
7. Uniform Customs and Practice of Documentary Credits	G. 与……相符
8. negotiating bank	H. 偿付
9. transferable credits	I. 跟单信用证统一惯例
10. documentary collection	J. 不可撤销保兑信用证

1. (　　) 2. (　　) 3. (　　) 4. (　　) 5. (　　)

6. (　　) 7. (　　) 8. (　　) 9. (　　) 10. (　　)

II. Finish the multiple choice questions.

1. If there is no specific provision, the draft under an L/C should draw on the _____.

    A. issuing bank   B. paying bank   C. applicant   D. confirming bank

2. _____ is a commercial B/E that requires payment to be made as soon as it is presented to the party obligated to pay.

    A. Time draft   B. Standby L/C   C. Sight draft   D. Clean credit

3. If a bank other than the issuing bank guarantees the payment under an L/C, this L/C is a(an) _____ credit.

    A. revocable   B. revolving   C. confirmed   D. transferable

4. _____ credit is the credit that is not paid immediately after presentation, but after an indicated period that is accepted by both the buyer and the seller.

    A. Time   B. Usance   C. Clean   D. Red clause

5. The B/E used in D/A must be a _____.

    A. sight bill   B. clean bill   C. bank bill   D. usance bill

6. If an L/C is "irrevocable", this means that _____.

    A. an importer may cancel a bank's authority to make payment

    B. an importer may not change his method of payment at any time

    C. an importer may change credit terms by giving notice

D. an exporter will grant only the most favorable terms of credit

7. When an L/C is confirmed, all of the risks of the issuing bank are then born by _____.

    A. the issuing bank free of charge   B. the importer free of charge

    C. the confirming bank for fee   D. the exporter for a fee

8. If the seller finds any discrepancies in the L/C, whom does he write to ask for an amendment? _____.

    A. The issuing bank   B. The advising bank

    C. The buyer   D. The negotiating bank

9. The irrevocable L/C can _____.

    A. neither be amended nor canceled without agreement of all parties

    B. be amended or canceled at any moment without prior notice to the beneficiary

    C. be amended or canceled if the buyer notifies the seller

    D. only be amended but not be canceled

10. An American company has ordered a parcel of garments from Tianjin Garments Imp. & Exp. Corporation. Payment will be made by a sight L/C. When will the American company pay for the garments? _____.

    A. When the goods have been loaded onto the vessel at the port of shipment

    B. When the bank has the shipping documents covering the shipment

    C. When the buyer receives the shipment of garments

    D. When the goods have arrived at the port of destination

11. The description of merchandise on the L/C must be identical to that on the _____.

    A. insurance policy   B. sales contract

    C. invoice   D. certificate of origin

12. In international trading transactions under L/Cs delivery of the goods is usually effected by _____.

    A. the seller handing over the documents representing the goods

    B. the seller loading the goods onto the ship

    C. the buyer taking delivery of the goods at the port of destination

    D. the buyer receiving the B/L through the bank

III. Answer the following questions according to the information you have got.

1. What are the paying instruments mostly used today?

2. What is the B/E?

3. What is promissory note?

4. What are main modes of payment in trade?

5. What are the differences among T/T, M/T and D/D?

6. What are the differences between D/P and D/A?

7. What is the L/C?

8. What is the most frequently used L/C?

9. What is the major difference between L/C and collection?

10. What are the advantages of international factoring?

 微课资源

扫一扫，获取相关微课视频。

6.1.mp4

6.2.mp4

Chapter 7 Inspection and Going Through Customs

Leading in

Dalian Xinhua Wireless Power Plant is a private enterprise. The plant ordered a batch of cold rolled stainless steel strips from Japan and entrusted Dalian Dacheng Trading Company to import. Dacheng Trading Company entrusted the customs declaration affairs to Sanchuan Customs Broker, which will handle the import declaration procedures with Dalian Customs on May 25, 2018. Specific documents include B/L, commercial invoice and packing list.

Question: How Li Li, as a customs declarant of Sanchuan Customs Broker, to complete the customs declaration business?

7.1　Commodity Inspection

1. Definition of Commodity Inspection

Commodity inspection, refers to the inspection and accreditation conducted by the authoritative specialized import and export commodities inspection agency in accordance with the provisions of laws, regulation or contracts during the process of international sales of goods.

Such inspection activities may involve the quality, quantity, weight, packaging, health and safety, as well as issuing of the inspection certificates.

Commodity inspection is one of key steps during the sales of goods in international trade.

Commodity inspection is an additional term that is used between buyers and sellers. The scope of commodity inspection depends on the buyers. Some buyers hire the inspection agencies only for pre-shipment inspections, such as visual quality, quantity, packing, marking and loading inspections and some others request for higher level inspections and ask inspection agencies to stay in the vendors' factories and inspect commodities during manufacturing processes.

Normal inspection is done based on an agreed inspection and test plan (TP).

An inspection may be performed at the destination port. For arrived goods inspection may include close inspection and functional testing, or may only consist of counting the units received and performing a surface inspection of shipping containers to assess whether any damage may have occurred in transit.

2. Main Scope of Commodity Inspection

1) Quality Inspection

Product quality inspection employs a variety of testing methods, including chemical testing, instrument analysis, and physical testing to inspect the quality, size and grade of commodities so as to determine whether they meet the standards the buyer and the seller have agreed.

2) Quantity and Weight Inspection

The quantity and weight of goods are measured by agreed measurement units and methods specified in the contract to determine whether they meet the requirements of the contract.

3) Package Inspection

Package inspection refers to the one in which the inside and outside packages and marks are inspected by commodity inspection agencies according to trade contracts, standards or other relevant provisions.

4) Damaged Goods Surveying

Damaged goods surveying is to survey the imported damaged goods to understand the cause of damage and its impacts on the value and fixed-damaging level and to issue a certificate as a basis.

5) Sanitary Inspection

For the claim to the relevant health inspection of goods is to do import and export inspection for food, fruits and other products to determine whether they meet the sanitary conditions of the human consumption.

6) Safety Inspection

Safety inspection of goods is carried out over the inspection of safety aspects of the import and export of goods in accordance with national regulations and foreign trade contracts, standards and legal requirements.

3. Common Inspection Agencies

The first category is to be the official inspection agencies. These official inspection agencies generally focus on certain commodities such as food and medicines. Food and Drug Administration (FDA) is the most common one in practice.

The second category is the private or non-governmental organizations (NGOs). Most of the commodity inspections are undertaken by NGOs, and these private inspection agencies have the legal status of a notary public.

In common practice, the most famous of these institutions are:

SGS (Societe Generale de Surveillance);

OMIC (Overseas Merchandise Inspection Co., Ltd);

UL (Underwriters Laboratories);

Lloyd's Surveyor:

BV (Bureau Veritas) and so on.

The third category is some enterprises or factories which have their own testing rooms, laboratories and so on.

4. Inspection Certificate

It is a collective name for various import and export commodity inspection certificates, appraisal certificates and other certificates.

It is a valid document with legal basis for parties involved in international trade to fulfill contractual obligations, handle disputes for claims, arbitration, and litigation. The necessary proof of tariff and preferential tariff reduction and exemption.

1) Certificate of Quality

Certificate of quality is an effective document for payment settlement and imports of goods. Release permit issued by the commodity inspection authorities or, clearance seal has the same effects as a commodity inspection certificate; a notice issued by the inspection authorities also have the same nature as an inspection certificate.

2) Weight or Quantity Certificate

Weight or quantity certificate is a valid document for goods delivery, payment settlement, issuing B/L, which is also a certificate for calculation of foreign taxation, freight and handling charges.

3) Veterinary Inspection Certificate

Veterinary inspection certificate is a certificate certifying that the exported animal products or food have passed the quarantine inspection. It is suitable for export commodities such as frozen meat, frozen poultry, canned poultry, frozen rabbits, hides, wool, velvet, bristles, casings, etc. It is an important document for external delivery, bank settlement and importation of importing countries.

4) Sanitary Certificate

Sanitary certificate is a document for animal products to prove that it is edible after quarantine. This kind of certificate is applied to those goods like sausages, canned poultry, frozen fish, shrimps and eggs. This kind of certificates are valid identifications for goods delivery, customs clearance and bank's settlement.

5) Disinfection Certificate

Disinfection certificate is a certificate that proves that the exported animal products have been disinfected to ensure safety and hygiene. It is suitable for commodities such as bristles, horsetails, leather sheets, goat hair, feathers, human hair, etc. It is a valid certificate for external delivery, bank settlement and foreign customs clearance.

6) Fumigation Certificate

Fumigation certificate is to show the goods have been experienced fumigation, such as the grain, oil seeds, pulses, hides and other commodities, as well as the wooden packages and the filling materials of plant.

7) Inspection Certificate on Damaged Cargo

Inspection certificate on damaged cargo is the certificate of damaged cargo. This kind of certificate applies to circumstances like imported goods' incompleteness, shortage stain and damages. It is an effective certificate to be used by the consignee to claim the shipper, the carrier, the insurer or other relevant responsible parties.

8) Certificate of Origin

It is the certificate of export goods imported through customs clearance of the importing country and enjoying preferential treatment of tariff reduction and exemption and proof of the origin of the goods.

5. Export Inspection

Compulsory commodity inspections performed by government agencies of exporting countries in accordance with law are to ensure that export commodities can comply with government regulations.

Its purpose is to improve the quality of commodities, establish credibility in the international market, promote foreign trade, and protect the interests of domestic and foreign consumers.

All export commodities listed in the "List of Entry and Exit Commodities for Inspection and Quarantine by Entry-Exit Inspection and Quarantine Institutions" and other export commodities required by the laws and regulations to be inspected, or commodities stipulated in the contract that must be inspected and issued by the customs are completed after preparation after that. It should apply to the inspection agency for inspection within the specified location and time limit.

1) The scope of inspections

The scope of implementing statutory inspections includes:

① Export commodities included in the "Catalogue of Entry and Exit Commodities for Inspection and Quarantine by Entry-Exit Inspection and Quarantine Organizations" ("Catalogue Table");

② Hygienic inspection of exported food;

③ Quarantine of trade exported animal and plant products;

④ Performance inspection and use appraisal of export dangerous goods and product packaging containers in the "Catalogue Table";

⑤ Cargo inspection of shipping vehicles such as cabins and containers for export of perishable and spoiled foods and frozen products;

⑥ Export commodities that are subject to inspection by the inspection and quarantine agency as required by relevant international trade treaties and L/Cs;

⑦ Export commodities subject to customs inspection as required by other laws and administrative regulations.

2) Inspection period

Outgoing goods to be inspected should be submitted for inspection seven days before customs declaration or shipment at the latest.

For individual goods with a long inspection and quarantine period, corresponding inspection time shall be reserved. Export commodities issued with inspection certificates or release slips after passing the customs inspection shall generally be shipped for export within two months from the date of issuance of the certificate, and fresh and exported commodities shall be shipped for export within two weeks.

Those who exceed the above-mentioned time limit shall report to the customs for re-inspection and return all the original inspection certificates and release notes issued.

3) Export inspection procedures

The inspection procedures of China's export commodities mainly include three links: application for inspection, inspection, and visa and release.

Application for inspection

① For the products subject to export inspection, the inspector should fill in "Application for Certificate of Export Inspection" in detail before export. Each application for inspection and quarantine of outbound goods is limited to one contract and one L/C. For the same contract and the same L/C, but with different mark numbers, the corresponding application form should be filled in separately.

② In addition to the application form, relevant documents and materials should also be submitted at the same time, such as foreign trade contracts and contract annexes signed by the two parties, L/C, commercial invoices, packing list and factory inspection orders, performance inspection of export goods transportation packaging documents, apply for inspection to the inspection agency where the commodity is stored, and pay inspection fees.

Inspection

The inspection agency shall accept the inspection of the batch of commodities after reviewing that the above documents meet the requirements.

① Sampling.

After the inspection agency accepts the inspection, it dispatches personnel to the cargo storage site for on-site inspection and identification in time. The on-site inspection generally adopts the sampling method commonly used in international trade (except for individual special commodities). When sampling, a certain number of representative products shall be drawn from different parts of the goods according to different cargo forms, and a certain ratio samples (specimens) of the whole batch of goods are for inspection according to the prescribed method. The inspector should provide information on the location of the inventory and cooperate with the inspector to do sampling work.

② Inspection.

The inspection agency should first carefully study the declared inspection items, determine the inspection content, carefully review the provisions on quality, specifications, and packaging in the contract (L/C), clarify the basis of inspection, and determine the inspection standards and methods; then use a variety of technical means from sensory to chemical analysis and instrumental analysis to inspect export commodities. The forms of inspection include commodity inspection, self-inspection, joint inspection, on-site inspection and origin inspection.

Visa and release

Customs will issue corresponding inspection and quarantine certificates to the products that have passed the inspection, and the exporting enterprise will then declare the export within the prescribed validity period.

6. Import Inspection

According to China's current "Implementation Regulations of the People's Republic of China on the Import and Export Commodity Inspection Law" and other relevant regulations, import commodities included in the statutory inspection scope must be subject to mandatory inspection by the General Administration of Quality Supervision, Inspection and Quarantine according to the regulations.

The goods that need to be inspected must pass the inspection and obtain a certificate before they can handle customs clearance and delivery.

For imported commodities that are not subject to statutory inspection, the inspection agency may conduct sample inspection and implement supervision and management.

Import inspection procedures are as follows.

Application for inspection—sampling—inspection

1) Application for inspection

① For the commodities subject to import inspection, the importer shall complete the application for inspection and quarantine of the imported goods, prepare relevant import documents, and apply for inspection to the inspection agency located at the port of entry.

② Pay the inspection fee.

2) Sampling

① Sampling according to national standards and regulations.

② Before the inspection is passed, the goods may not be moved without permission.

3) Inspection

① If the consignee of imported commodities other than the imported commodities that must be inspected by the customs finds that the quality of the imported commodities is unqualified or damaged and needs to be issued by the customs for compensation, it shall apply to the customs for inspection and certification.

② For important imported commodities and large-scale complete sets of equipment, the consignee should carry out pre-inspection, supervision or supervision before shipment in the exporting country according to the foreign trade contract, and the customs can send inspectors to participate as needed.

7.2   Going Through Customs

1. Definition of Customs Declaration

Broadly speaking, customs declaration refers to the whole process that the person in charge of inbound and outbound transportation vehicles, the consignor and the consignee of inbound and outbound goods, the owner of inbound and outbound articles, or their agents to go through customs formalities for entry and exit of transportation vehicles, goods, and articles with the customs.

Among them, the person in charge of the inbound and outbound transportation means, the consignor and the consignee of the import and export goods, the owner of the inbound and outbound articles, or their agents are the bearers of the customs declaration and the main body of the declaration, that is, the customs declaration person, also known as the customs declaration unit.

The customs brokers include both legal persons and other organizations, such as import and export enterprises and customs declaration enterprises, as well as natural persons, such as the owners of goods.

The objects of customs declaration are inbound and outbound transportation vehicles, goods and articles.

The content of customs declaration is to handle the entry and exit formalities of transportation vehicles, goods and articles and relevant customs formalities.

2. Scope of Customs Declaration

All inbound and outbound transportation vehicles, goods, and articles need to go through customs declaration procedures.

1) Inbound and outbound transportation vehicles

Refer to all kinds of domestic and overseas ships, vehicles, aircraft and pack animals used to carry people, goods and articles in and out of the country and operate internationally.

2) Inbound and outbound goods

Mainly include general imported goods, bonded goods, temporary (quasi) import and export goods, specific tax-exempt goods, transit, transshipment and transit goods and other inbound and outbound goods. In addition, some special goods, such as water, electricity, etc. transported in and out of the country through cables and pipes, and intangible goods, such as software attached to the goods carrier, are also objects of customs declaration.

3) Entry and exit items

Refer to luggage, postal items and other items entering and leaving the country. Items that enter and leave the country by way of entry and exit personnel to carry consignment are luggage items; items that enter and leave the country by post are postal items; and other items mainly include privileged and official supplies or self-use items of foreign institutions or personnel and international express delivery part of the express shipment, etc.

3. Customs Declaration for Export Goods

1) Customs declaration for import and export goods

The last step before the goods are shipped is to handle customs clearance (Export Customs Clearance) with the customs.

When the goods or means of transport enter and leave the country, the consignor or their agents must send the goods to the container yard, container terminal or terminal warehouse designated by the customs, request the declaration to the customs of the entry and exit port, and submit the required documents for inspection, accept the inspection of the goods and transportation means by customs personnel, and pay customs duties and other taxes levied by the customs according to law, and then the customs can release the goods and transportation means.

After the release, the exporter may handle the export shipment of goods.

2) Preparation before export declaration

Exporters must be prepared before customs declaration. Preparations include:

(1) To complete export goods;

(2) To acquire customs clearance qualifications, or commissioned customs declaration if needed;

(3) To prepare customs documents: including basic documents, special documents, and preparatory documents.

① Basic documents refer to commercial and freight documents directly related to export goods, mainly including commercial invoices, packing list, loading cargo vouchers (or waybills, parcels), tax exemption certificate issued by customs for export goods;

② Special documents refer to the documents that are regulated by relevant laws and regulations of the country, mainly including quota license management documents and other types of special management documents;

③ Preparatory documents refer to documents for inspection or collection when the customs deem necessary, including trade contracts, certificates of origin of the goods, certificate of the industrial and commercial license of the entrusting unit, account information of the entrusting unit and other relevant documents.

(4) Fill in the export goods declaration form and other customs declaration documents.

Pre-entry of customs declaration refers to the customs that implements the "customs declaration of import (export) goods" in the implementation of the customs automation system, and the customs declaration unit or the customs person will enter the data and content declared on the customs declaration into the electronic computer, and transfer the data and content to the customs declaration automation system.

The above work is completed, you can go through customs declaration formalities for entry and exit transportation vehicles and goods.

3) Export customs clearance procedures

Customs clearance procedures for exporters can be divided into four steps:

(1) declaration;

(2) inspection of goods;

(3) payment of taxes and fees;

(4) and release of shipments.

From the standpoint of customs, they can be divided into four steps as:

(1) receipt;

(2) inspection of goods;

(3) valuation;

(4) and release.

For the four steps, please refer to Figure 7-1.

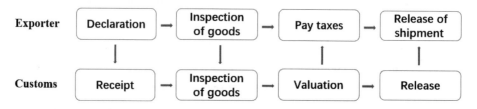

Figure 7-1   Export customs clearance procedures

① Declaration.

Persons in charge of inbound and outbound transportation vehicles, consignors of export goods and articles, or their agents, when exporting goods pass through customs-controlled ports, in the form of written or electronic data interchange (EDI) within the time limit set by the customs, report to the customs about the export of goods, accompanied by relevant freight and commercial documents, apply for customs review and release, and take legal responsibility for the authenticity and accuracy of the reported content.

When the exported goods leave the country, the consignor should declare to the customs 24 hours before loading. Specifically, after the export goods are shipped to warehouses and venues such as docks, stations, airports, and post offices, they must be declared to the customs 24 hours before the customs limitation.

The contents of the declaration include the business unit of export goods, the receiving and delivery unit, the declaration unit, the mode of transportation, the mode of trade, the country of trade and the actual status of the goods (mainly including the name, specifications, models, quantity, weight, price, etc.)

② Inspection of goods.

After accepting the declaration of the customs declaration unit, the customs determine whether the nature, origin, status, quantity and value of the inbound and outbound goods, transportation means and articles are on the declaration, the content that has been filled in is consistent with the administrative law enforcement behavior of the inspection of the goods.

The inspection of the goods can prevent subcharging, illegal entry and exit, smuggling, violation of regulations, and evasion of tariffs, ensure that tariffs are levied according to rates, and maintain the normal development of international trade.

Exports of goods, except those that have been exempted from inspection by the General Administration of Customs for special reasons, should be inspected by the Customs. The inspection of exports should be carried out at the time and place specified by the Customs, generally at shore terminals, stations, airports, post offices or other customs supervision places in the customs supervision zone.

Export of bulk goods, dangerous goods, fresh and live goods can be inspected on the job site upon application. Under special circumstances, upon application and approval by the Customs, it may also send personnel to the factory, warehouse or construction site outside the specified place to inspect the goods at the prescribed time and collect the fees according to the regulations.

③ Pay taxes.

Export tariffs are levied by the customs on exported goods in accordance with relevant national policies and regulations. The main purpose is to control the blind export of some commodities. Except for a few commodities, most exports are exempt from customs duties.

China's tariffs are ad valorem, which is based on the FOB price of the exported goods as the duty-paid price, and the taxable amount as a percentage of the goods-paid value as the tax rate.

④ Release shipment.

Release means the customs accepting the declaration of export goods. After reviewing the customs declaration documents, inspecting the goods, and collecting taxes and fees according to law, the customs site supervision decision is made on the export goods.

For general export goods, after the consignor or its agent truthfully declares to the customs, and fully pays the taxes and relevant fees, the customs signs the "customs clearance" on the export freight document or special release strip "Chapter", the shipper of the exported goods will leave the country by shipment.

After the customs release, the exporter can handle the shipment of the goods.

4. Customs Declaration for Imported Goods

When goods or vehicles enter or leave the country, their consignors or their agents must deliver the goods to the container yard, container depot or terminal warehouse designated by the customs as required, request declaration to the customs at the port of entry and exit, submit the required documents for inspection, accept the inspection of the goods and means of transportation reported by customs personnel, and pay customs duties and other taxes levied by the customs in accordance with the law. After the release of means of transportation and the goods, the importer may handle matters such as picking up the goods.

Customs clearance procedures for imported goods, as far as importers are concerned, they can generally be divided into four steps: declaration of entry; delivery of goods; payment of taxes; and vouchers.

From the standpoint of customs, it can be divided into four steps: acceptance of declaration; inspection of goods; taxation; *customs clearance and release.

Please refer to the Figure 7-2.

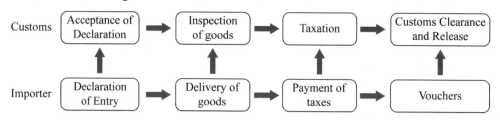

Figure 7-2　Import customs clearance procedures

1) Declaration of entry

After the imported goods arrive at the port, the import enterprise or its agent can declare and release to the customs in accordance with the provisions of the national customs decree.

(1) Declaration time limit.

"Customs Law of the People's Republic of China" stipulates that the customs declaration time limit for imported goods is 14 days from the date of declaration of entry of the transportation means. If the declaration is overdue, the customs will charge a certain percentage of stagnation according to the CIF or CIP price of the imported goods reimbursement; if it has not been declared for more than three months, the customs can sell it. After deducting transportation, loading, unloading, storage and other expenses and taxes, if there is a surplus, it will be returned to the applicant within one year after the goods are sold. For the consignee, if there is no application for overdue, it will be turned over to the treasury.

(2) Fill in the declaration form.

When import companies or their agents handle import declarations within the statutory period, they need to truthfully fill out the "Imported Goods Declaration Form".

(3) Submit inspection documents.

The relevant documents declared refer to the documents that correspond to the goods being declared and support the declaration form.

In addition to customs declarations, customs declaration documents can be divided into three categories: basic documents, special documents, and preparatory documents.

① Basic documents mainly include import commercial documents (such as invoices, packing list, bills of lading, etc.) resulting from import transactions such as goods transactions, packaging, transportation, settlement, and insurance.

② Special documents are the documents that the state stipulates to implement special control. They mainly include import goods licenses and other special management certificates.

③ Preparatory documents are the documents that the customs needs to check or collect when they need to go through the formalities of importing goods. Preparatory documents mainly include contract, certificate of origin, etc.

2) Inspection review

(1) Review of customs declaration.

The review of customs declaration documents is the core link of import declaration. In actual business, the customs first conduct a preliminary review of the customs declaration documents, and then conduct a comprehensive and detailed review in terms of form and content.

(2) Inspection of imported goods.

Except for the imported goods exempted from inspection approved by the Customs, they must be inspected by the Customs at the time and place specified by the Customs. After the Customs Confirms the inspection, the on-site customs officer shall print the inspection notice. During customs inspection, the consignee or his agent of imported goods must be present and cooperate with the Customs in inspection as required. After the inspection, the accompanying personnel shall sign and confirm on the inspection record sheet.

3) Pay taxes

China implements a two-column system of general and preferential tariffs. The tariff classification commodity catalogue adopts the internationally implemented commodity

classification catalogue, and the internationally applicable principle of origin is adopted in principle in the application of the tariff regulations.

4) Release

After the preliminary review of the documents and inspection of the goods, if no abnormalities are found, the customs will send a special person to carry out a comprehensive compound review of all documents and inspection of the imported goods to confirm if the customs declaration procedures are complete, the documents are complete, the goods are legal, and the tax has been paid according to the regulations, the freight documents will be signed and released, or the customs will issue the B/L to release them to show that the customs agrees to enter the goods.

However, the customs still have to carry out follow-up supervision on the goods imported with specific tax reduction and exemption treatment after it is released. After the customs release, the importer can pick up the goods.

Notes to the Text

I. Vocabulary and phrases.

1. inspection   检验

2. quality inspection   质量检验

3. quantity and weight inspection   数量与重量检验

4. package inspection   包装检验

5. damaged goods surveying   货损调查

6. sanitary inspection   卫生检验

7. safety inspection   安全检验

8. SGS (Societe Generale de Surveillance)   (瑞士)通用公证行

9. OMIC (Overseas Merchandise Inspection Co., Ltd)   (日)海外货物检查株式会社

10. UL (Underwriters Laboratories)   (美国)保险商实验室

11. Llody's Surveyor Bureau Veritas   (英国)劳氏公证行

12. Veterinary Inspection Certificate   兽医检验证书

13. Disinfection Certificate   消毒证书

14. Fumigation Certificate   熏蒸证书

15. luggage   行李

16. procedures   程序

17. release   放行

18. vouchers   凭证

19. preferential tariffs   优惠关税

II. Sentences and paragraphs.

1. Veterinary inspection certificate is a certificate certifying that the exported animal products or food have passed the quarantine inspection. It is suitable for export commodities such as frozen meat, frozen poultry, canned poultry, frozen rabbits, hides, wool, velvet, bristles, casings, etc. It is an important document for external delivery, bank settlement and importation of importing countries.

兽医检验证书是证明出口动物产品或食品经过检疫合格的证件。适用于冻畜肉、冻禽、禽畜罐头、冻兔、皮张、毛类、绒类、猪鬃、肠衣等出口商品，是对外交货、银行结汇和进口国通关输入的重要凭证。

2. Disinfection certificate is a certificate that proves that the exported animal products have been disinfected to ensure safety and hygiene. It is suitable for commodities such as bristles, horsetails, leather sheets, goat hair, feathers, human hair, etc. It is a valid certificate for external delivery, bank settlement and foreign customs clearance.

消毒检验证书是证明出口动物产品经过消毒处理、保证安全卫生的证件。适用于猪鬃、马尾、皮张、山羊毛、羽毛、人发等商品，是对外交货、银行结汇和国外通关验放的有效凭证。

3. The inspection agency should first carefully study the declared inspection items, determine the inspection content, carefully review the provisions on quality, specifications, and packaging in the contract (L/C), clarify the basis of inspection, and determine the inspection standards and methods; then use a variety of technical means from sensory to chemical analysis and instrumental analysis to inspect export commodities. The forms of inspection include commodity inspection, self-inspection, joint inspection, on-site inspection and origin inspection.

检验机构首先应当认真研究申报的检验项目，确定检验内容，仔细审核合同(信用证)中关于品质、规格、包装的规定，弄清检验的依据，确定检验标准、方法；然后使用从感官到化学分析、仪器分析等各种技术手段，对出口商品进行检验。检验的形式有商检自验、共同检验、驻厂检验和产地检验。

4. China implements a two-column system of general and preferential tariffs. The tariff classification commodity catalogue adopts the internationally implemented commodity classification catalogue, and the internationally applicable principle of origin is adopted in principle in the application of the tariff regulations.

我国实行普通与优惠两栏的复式税则制。税则商品分类目录采用国际实行的商品分类目录，在税则适用的原则上采用国际通行的原产地原则。

Exercises

I. Finish the multiple choice questions.

1. The main scope of commodity inspection include _____.

　A. equality inspection　　　　　B. quantity and weight inspection

　C. package inspection　　　　　D. safety inspection

2. The most famous of these institutions are _____.

　A. SGS　　　　B. OMIC　　　　C. UL　　　　D. Loyd's Surveyor

3. The inspection procedures of China's export commodities mainly include three links

_____.

　A. application for inspection　　　B. inspection

　C. visa　　　　　　　　　　　D. release

4. The forms of inspection include _____.

　A. commodity inspection self-inspection

　B. joint inspection

　C. on-site inspection

　D. origin inspection

5. Customs clearance procedures for exporters can be divided into _____.

　A. declaration　　　　　　　B. inspection of goods

　C. payment of taxes and fees　　　D. release of shipments

II. Decide whether the following statements are True (T) or False (F).

1. The competent department of China's entry-exit inspection and quarantine is the customs. 　　　　　　　　　　　　　　　　　　　　　　(　)

2. The scope of commodity inspection depends on the buyers. Some buyers hire the inspection agencies only for pre-shipment inspections, and ask inspection agencies to stay in the vendors' factories and inspect commodities during manufacturing processes. 　(　)

3. The quantity and weight of goods are included in the scope of commodity inspection.

　　　　　　　　　　　　　　　　　　　　　　　　　　　　(　)

4. SGS (Societe Generale de Surveillance) is a Swedish official inspection agency. 　(　)

5. Outgoing goods to be inspected should be submitted for inspection 14 days before customs declaration or shipment at the latest. 　　　　　　　　　　　　(　)

6. For imported commodities that are not subject to statutory inspection, the inspection agency can not conduct sample inspection and implement supervision and management. 　(　)

7. All inbound and outbound goods and articles need to go through customs declaration

procedures, but transportation vehicles are not needed. ( )

8. Special documents for customs declaration mainly includes quota license management documents and other types of special management documents. ( )

9. China's tariffs are based on the CIF price of the exported goods as the duty-paid price, and the taxable amount as a percentage of the goods-paid value as the tax rate. ( )

10. "Customs Law of the People's Republic of China" stipulates that the customs declaration time limit for imported goods is 7 days from the date of declaration of entry of the transportation means. ( )

III. Answer the following questions according to the information you have got.

1. What's the main scope of commodity inspection?

2. Please list common inspection certificates and indicates their uses.

3. What's the purpose of compulsory export commodity inspections performed by government agencies?

4. What's the scope of customs declaration?

5. What preparation must be made before export declaration?

6. What are the customs clearance procedures for imported goods from the standpoint of both the importer and the customs?

 微课资源

扫一扫，获取相关微课视频。

7.1.mp4

7.2.mp4

Chapter 8   Disputes, Claims and Arbitration

Leading in

A foreign trade company in Country A imported 20,000 metric tons of ordinary bean cakes from Company B overseas and delivery was arranged in August. However, in April, production areas for bean cakes were hit by flood, thus the bean cakes acquisition plan failed. Company B requested to exempt it from the delivery responsibility based on the principles of force majeure.

Question: Is it a valid request? Why?

8.1   Disputes

In international trade, disputes arise from time to time for various reasons. For instance, a buyer may breach a contract by refusing to accept goods with improper reasons or failing to pay for the goods when payment is due; a seller may violate a contract by failing to make an agreed delivery or delivering goods that do not conform to the contract. **Breach of contract means the refusal or failure by one party of a contract to fulfill an obligation imposed on him under that contract. In international trade practice, the main reasons for disputes can be concluded into three categories: breach of contract by the seller, breach of contract by the buyer and breach of contract by both the seller and the buyer.**

Breach of Contract by the Seller

A seller may be considered to have breached a contract if he fails to

- make delivery of the goods or deliver them within the shipment time stipulated in the contract;
- deliver the goods that are in conformity with the contract or the L/C in respect of quality,

specifications, quantity and packing, etc.;

- present the complete and adequate shipping documents or present them within the stipulated time period.

Breach of Contract by the Buyer

Considering the different obligations undertaken by a buyer, the buyer may breach a contract if he fails to

- open the relevant L/C or open it within the stipulated period under an L/C payment;
- accept the goods without sufficient reasons under an L/C payment;
- dispatch the vessel or notify the seller with sufficient information about the vessel song according to the stipulations in the contract under FOB terms.

Breach of Contract by Both Parties

Misunderstanding or miscomprehension of a contract with vague expressions can lead to trade disputes.

As the sales contract has a legal binding force upon both contracting parties, any party who has violated the contract shall be legally held responsible for the breach, and the injured party is entitled to remedies according to the stipulations of the contract or relevant laws.

8.2   Claims

When disputes arise, the injured party usually will lodge a claim against the party concerned for compensation. **Thus, claim can be defined as a demand made by one party upon another for a certain amount of payment on account of a loss sustained through its negligence. There are generally three types of claim related to international trade practice: claim regarding selling and buying, claim regarding transportation and claim concerning insurance. In this section, only the first type of claim will be covered as this is the only type of claim that is made between the two parties of the sales contract.**

In import and export trade, claims regarding quality and quantity or weight are common, even though proper inspection of the goods has been conducted by designated surveyors or public inspection bureaus. The goods may have been damaged or lost during transit. In case the goods delivered are inconsistent with the contract stipulations, the buyer should make a claim against the seller within the time limit of re-inspection under the support of an inspection certificate or survey report.

As is well known, disputes are very common in international trade and are detrimental to the business relationship between the buyer and the seller. To avoid or to properly handle future disputes, it is necessary to include a claim clause in a contract. Normally, there are two ways to stipulate claim clause in the contract: discrepancy and claim clause and penalty clause.

1) Discrepancy and Claim Clause

In most trade contracts, it is only the discrepancy and claim clause that is stipulated. The clause in this respect normally stipulates the relevant evidences or proofs to be presented and the relevant authoritative body for issuing the certificate. The evidences or proofs provided should be complete and clear, and the authority should be competent in issuing the relevant certificates. Otherwise, claims can be refused by the other party.

Besides the evidence to be presented, this clause shall also include a period within which a claim is lodged. Technically, the period for claim refers to the effective period in which the claimant can make a claim against a party for breach. Claims made after the agreed period can be refused by the party in breach. Generally speaking, a period that is too long may put the seller under a heavy responsibility and a period that is too short may make it impossible for the buyer to file a claim. Therefore, the period for a claim should be made as specific as possible in the clause. See an example in Example 8-1.

> **[Example 8-1] An Example of Discrepancy and Claim Clause in a Sales Contract**
>
> Any claim by the buyer regarding the goods shipped shall be filed within 30 days after arrival of the goods at the port of destination specified in the relative B/L and supported by a survey report issued by a surveyor approved by the seller. Claims in respect of matter within responsibility of the insurance company, shipping company/other transportation organization will not be considered or entertained by the seller.

If a claim is justified, prompt and well-supported, it can be settled in the following ways: making a refund, compensating for direct losses or expenses, selling the goods at lower prices or replacing the defective goods with good ones. As the discrepancy and claim clause is closely related to the inspection clause, they are combined as the inspection and claim clause in some contracts.

2) Penalty Clause

For transactions where goods in substantial quantity or large pieces of mechanical equipment are concerned, a penalty clause is expected to be stipulated in the contract together with a Discrepancy and claim clause in case one party fails to implement the contract such as non-delivery, delayed delivery, delayed opening of L/C, etc., the injured party can get compensation to a certain degree. Under this clause, the party who has failed to carry out the contract must pay the other party a fine, a certain percentage of total contract value. The provisions for the amount and the penalty ceiling should also be included in the clause. See an example in Example 8-2.

[Example 8-2] An Example of Penalty Clause

Should the buyers for their own sake fail to open the L/C within the time stipulated in the contract, the buyers shall pay a penalty to the sellers. The penalty shall be charged at the rate of 0.5% of the amount of the L/C for every ten days of delay in opening the L/C. However, the total penalty shall not exceed 5% of the total value of the credit which the buyers should have opened. Any fractional days less than ten days shall be deemed to be ten days for the calculation of penalty. The penalty shall be the sole compensation for the damage caused by such delay.

8.3   Arbitration

If one party is found to have breached the contract, the other party of the contract who suffers loss or damage therefore will lodge a claim against the former for refund or compensation. However, in most cases. the claim is not able to be settled smoothly as expected due to various reasons. Then what are the usual ways to settle disputes in international trade?

1. Methods of Dispute Settlement

In international trade practice, when disputes arise between exporters and importers, they can be settled through negotiation, mediation, arbitration or litigation.

Friendly negotiation is the best method of all and beneficial to both parties because the parties concerned are most familiar with the problem and dealing with it personally can avoid damage to their friendship.

If the parties involved are not able to reach any agreement between themselves, they can then seek the help of a third party for mediation. This third party can be any impartial party or international chamber of commerce or a government trade authority. As these experts are skilled and experienced mediators, having a competent third party to speak as an intermediary is often more effective than speaking for oneself. A large portion of the disputes in international trade practice is settled this way because it helps maintain friendly business relations between exporters and importers. However, mediation only facilitates negotiation, no award or opinion on the merits of the disputes is given.

If the disputes cannot be settled through amicable negotiation or mediation, arbitration is the next best alternative. What arbitration differs from mediation is that the third party to whom the dispute is submitted decides the outcome. Arbitration clause is often stipulated in advance in a sales contract. However, if no such clause is included in advance, parties concerned can choose to have their dispute arbitrated after it has arisen.

In case the three alternatives are not workable for the settlement, the parties involved can resort to the last one — litigation. However, litigation is usually costly and time-consuming and what's more, detrimental to the relationship between the parties concerned. Therefore, it is not suggested to use if other ways to settle the disputes are workable.

2. Arbitration Procedure

Internationally, the main arbitration body is the International Court of Arbitration. In China, the main arbitration body is China International Economic and Trade Arbitration Commission (CIETAC). Pursuant to the current arbitration rules of CIETAC which took effect on January 1st, 2015. The general arbitration procedures are: applying for arbitration, forming arbitration tribunal, hearing of an arbitration case, issuing an award, setting aside an award and enforcing an award.

1) Applying for an arbitration

When applying for an arbitration, the claimant must submit to the Secretariat of the Arbitration Commission an arbitration agreement, an application for arbitration in writing, and the facts and evidence on which his claim is based. At the same time, he shall also pay an arbitration fee in advance to the Arbitration Commission.

The application for an arbitration shall include such information as the name and address of the claimant and those of the claimee, the arbitration agreement relied upon by the claimant, the facts of the case and the main points of dispute, and the claimant's claim and the facts and evidence on which his claim is based.

2) Forming arbitration tribunal

After receiving the notice of arbitration, an arbitration tribunal should be formed. There are normally two types of arbitration tribunal: sole-arbitrator tribunal with one arbitrator and collegiate tribunal with three arbitrators. An arbitrator (or arbiter) is the impartial third party chosen by a higher or neutral body, or by the two parties in dispute to deal with a claim.

In the case of sole-arbitrator tribunal, both parties concerned may jointly appoint or authorize the chairman of the arbitration body to appoint a sole arbitrator to hear the arbitration case alone.

A collegiate tribunal, on the other hand, normally consists of three arbitrators. The claimant and the claimee each should appoint an arbitrator from among the panel of arbitrators. The third arbitrator however shall be jointly appointed by both parties or appointed by the chairman of the arbitration body. The arbitration tribunal formed by the three arbitrators shall jointly hear the arbitration case. Most cases to which the normal procedure applies shall be examined and heard by a collegiate tribunal with three arbitrators unless otherwise agreed by the parties.

3) Hearing an arbitration case

After an arbitration tribunal is formed, it is time to arrange the hearing of an arbitration case. However, if an oral hearing is needed, before hearing, the arbitration tribunal shall fix the date of the oral hearing after consultation with the Secretariat of the Arbitration Commission, and then communicate to the parties 30 days (for foreign economic cases and maritime cases) or 15 days (for domestic economic cases) before the date of the hearing so that the parties concerned may have sufficient time to make necessary arrangements.

However, at the request of the parties or with their consent, oral hearings may be omitted if the arbitration tribunal also deems that oral hearings are unnecessary. In this case, the arbitration tribunal may examine the case and make an award on the basis of documents only.

4) Issuing an award

As conclusion of the hearing, an award will be issued. An arbitration award (or arbitral award) is a determination on the merits by an arbitration tribunal in an arbitration, and is analogous to a judgment in a court of law. For international arbitration cases, the time limit of the issuing of such an award is within 9 months from the date on which the arbitration tribunal is formed. In case of oral hearing, the arbitration tribunal shall make an award within 30 days from the date of the oral hearing. The date on which the arbitral award is made is the date on which the arbitral award is final and the award comes into effect. The arbitration award is final and binding upon both parties. Neither party may bring a suit before a law court or make a request to any other organization to revise the arbitral award.

5) Setting aside an award

Although the arbitration award is final and binding upon both parties, if one party deems that there are matters not in conformity with the statutory procedure in the award, after receipt of the arbitral award, he can apply for setting aside the arbitral award. For example, the parties have neither included an arbitration clause in their contract nor subsequently concluded a written arbitration agreement or the formation of an arbitrator or arbitration tribunal is not in conformity with arbitration rules.

6) Enforcing an award

If no award is set aside, the parties must execute the arbitral award within the time limit specified. In case one party fails to execute the arbitral award, the other party may apply to the competent court for enforcement. If the residence or the properties of the losing party is located within the territory of China, the other party may apply to the Intermediate People's Court for enforcement of the award; if the residence of the losing party or the properties of the losing party is located outside China, the other party may apply to the competent court in that country for enforcement. Whenever one party applies for enforcement to the competent court, he shall submit a written application for enforcement together with the arbitration agreement and the original copy of arbitral award.

3. Arbitration Costs

Arbitration cost consists of two parts: arbitration fee and actual cost. As mentioned above the arbitration fee shall be paid in advance by the claimant when applying for arbitration.

The actual costs include the costs of making investigations and collecting evidence, costs of engaging experts to make appraisals, etc. The arbitration tribunal shall decide in the arbitral award which party shall bear the actual fees and expenses, and how much each party should bear. For example, the arbitration tribunal has the power to decide that the losing party shall pay the winning party a proportion of the expenses reasonably incurred by the winning party in dealing with the case as compensation. The amount of such compensation shall not in any case exceed 10% of the total amount awarded to the winning party.

4. Arbitration Clause in the Sales Contract

An arbitration clause or agreement expresses the willingness of the parties to submit the disputes for arbitration. Different from other clauses in the sales contract, an arbitration clause shall be regarded as existing independently and separately from the other clauses of the contract. Similarly, an arbitration agreement attached to a contract shall be treated as a part of the contract, but existing independently and separately from the other parts of the contract.

An eligible, effective, complete and accurate arbitration agreement or arbitration clause should have the following elements: place of arbitration, arbitration body, applicable arbitration rules, arbitration award, etc. See an example in Example 8-3.

[Example 8-3] Example II of Arbitration Clause

"Any disputes arising from or in connection with this contract, shall be settled amicably through negotiation. In case no settlement can be reached through negotiation, the case shall then be submitted to the China International Economic and Trade Arbitration Commission of the China Council for the Promotion of International Trade, Beijing for arbitration which shall be conducted in accordance with the Commission's Arbitration Rules in effect at the time of applying for arbitration. The arbitral ward is final and binding upon both parties."

8.4　Force Majeure

The term "Force Majeure", also known as "Greater Force", refers to change occurrence, unavoidable risks which prevent the parties from fulfilling their duties and obligations under the project agreements.

1. Features of a force majeure event

(1) It happens after the contract is signed;

(2) It is not resulted from the negligence or malfeasance of the parties involved;

(3) Neither the buyer nor the seller can control the situation.

2. Consequences of force majeure

1) Termination of contract

In case of natural disasters or other events that have made it impossible to fulfill the contract, the contract can be terminated.

2) Postponement of contract

In case of events (such as transportation stoppage caused by an earthquake) that will only delay the fulfillment of a contract, the contract can be postponed but not terminated since it is still possible for the seller to carry out his contract obligations.

3. Types of force majeure events

Force majeure events generally can be divided into two basic types: natural events and political events.

1) Natural events

These may include tsunamis, hurricanes, floods, plague, earthquakes, etc. These are events which are not within the control of the host government. The parties shall look at the availability and cost of insurance, the likelihood of the occurrence of such events and any mitigation measures which can be carried out.

2) Political and special events

These may include terrorism, riots or civil disturbances, wars, strikes, change of law or regulation, nuclear or chemical contamination, failure of public infrastructure, etc.

These risks are generally considered to be beyond the control of the parties involved.

4. Force majeure clause

A force majeure clause is a contractual provision that specifies what happens under the contract in case a "force majeure" event occurs. See Example 8-4 and Example 8-5.

[Example 8-4] Example I of Arbitration Clause

All claims and disputes arising under or relating to this Agreement are to be settled by binding arbitration in the state in which parties agree to arbitrate or another location mutually agreeable to the parties. The arbitration shall be conducted on a confidential basis pursuant to the Commercial Arbitration Rules of the American Arbitration Association. Any decision or award as a result of any such arbitration proceeding shall be in writing and shall provide an explanation for all conclusions of the law and fact and shall include the assessment of costs, expenses and reasonable attorneys' fees. Any such arbitration shall be conducted by an arbitrator experienced in industry or legal experience required for arbitrator and shall include a written record of the arbitration hearing. The parties reserve the right to object to any individual who shall be employed by or affiliated with a competing organization or entity. An award of arbitration may be confirmed in a court of competent jurisdiction.

[Example 8-5]　An Example of Force Majeure Clause

Neither party shall lose any rights hereunder or be liable to the other party for loss or damage on account of failure of performance by the defaulting party if the failure is occasioned by government action, war, terrorism, fire, explosion, flood, strike, lockout, embargo, act of god, or any other cause beyond the control and without the fault or negligence of the defaulting party, provided that the party claiming force majeure has exerted all reasonable efforts to avoid or remedy such force majeure; provided, however, that in no event shall a party be required to settle any labor dispute or disturbance. Such excuse shall continue as long as the condition preventing the performance continues. Upon cessation of such condition, the affected party shall promptly resume performance hereunder. Each party agrees to give the other party prompt written notice of the occurrence of any such condition, the nature thereof, and the extent to which the affected party will be unable to perform its obligations hereunder. Each party further agrees to use all reasonable efforts to correct the condition as quickly as possible and to give the other party prompt written notice when it is again fully able to perform its obligations.

Notes to the Text

I. Vocabulary and phrases.

1. dispute　争议

2. breach of contract　违约

3. claim　索赔

4. discrepancy and claim clause　异议和索赔条款

5. penalty clause　罚金条款

6. negotiation　协商

7. mediation　调解

8. litigation　诉讼

9. arbitration　仲裁

10. arbitration agreement　仲裁协议

11. apply for arbitration　提出仲裁申请

12. form arbitration tribunal　组织仲裁庭

13. hearing an arbitration case　审理仲裁案件

14. issue an award　做出裁决

15. enforce an award　执行裁决

16. set aside an award　撤销裁决

17. arbitrator　仲裁人

18. claimant　申诉人

19. claimee　被申诉人

20. CIETAC　中国国际经济贸易仲裁委员会

II. Sentences and paragraphs.

1. Breach of contract means the refusal or failure by one party to a contract to fulfill an obligation imposed on him under that contract. In international practice, the main reasons for disputes can be concluded into three categories: breach of contract by the seller, breach of contract by the buyer and breach of contract by both the seller and the buyer.

违约是指合同一方拒绝或不履行合同规定的义务。在国际惯例中，争议的主要原因可归结为三类：卖方违约、买方违约和买卖双方违约。

2. Thus, claim can be defined as a demand made by one party upon another for a certain amount of payment on account of a loss sustained through its negligence. There are generally three types of claim related to international trade practice：Claim regarding selling and buying, claim regarding transportation and claim concerning insurance. In this section, only the first type of claim will be covered as this is the only type of claim that is made between the two parties of the sales contract.

因此，索赔可以定义为一方因疏忽造成的损失而向另一方要求支付一定数额的款项。与国际贸易惯例有关的三种索赔有买卖索赔、运输索赔和保险索赔。在本节中，仅涵盖第一种索赔，因为这是唯一的销售合同双方之间的索赔类型。

3. In most trade contracts, it is only the discrepancy and claim clause that is stipulated. The clause in this respect normally stipulates the relevant evidences or proofs to be presented and the relevant authoritative body for issuing the certificate.

在大多数贸易合同中，只规定了不符点和索赔条款。这方面的条款通常规定了应提交的相关证据或证明以及签发证书的相关权威机构。

4. Internationally, the main arbitration body is the International Court of Arbitration. In China, the main arbitration body is China International Economic and Trade Arbitration Commission (CIETAC). Pursuant to the current arbitration rules of CIETAC which took effect on January 1st, 2015. The general arbitration procedures are: applying for arbitration, forming arbitration tribunal, hearing of an arbitration case, issuing an award, setting aside an award and enforcing an award.

在国际上，主要的仲裁机构是国际仲裁院。在中国，主要的仲裁机构是中国国际经济贸易仲裁委员会(CIETAC)。根据 2015 年 1 月 1 日起生效的 CIETAC 现行仲裁规则，一般仲裁程序为：申请仲裁、成立仲裁庭、审理仲裁案件、做出裁决、撤销裁决和执行裁决。

Exercises

I. Finish the multiple choice questions.

1. The disagreement resulted from one party of a transaction totally or partially unable to

perform the obligation and liability stipulated in the contract is _____.

    A. claim   B. dispute

    C. breach of contract   D. settlement of disputes

2. Which of the following may possibly result in disputes between sellers and buyers ? _____.

    A. Breakage of the package   B. Rising of price

    C. Fluctuation of exchange rate   D. Quota

3. Which of the following is a clause in a contract and meanwhile a law itself ? _____.

    A. Arbitration clause   B. Claim clause

    C. Dispute clause   D. Force majeure clause

4. The main arbitration body in China is _____.

    A. MOFTEC   B. CCPIT   C. CIETAC   D. ICC

5. According to usual practice, the penalty of a contract shall not exceed _____ total value of the goods.

    A. 3%   B. 4%   C. 5%   D. 5.5%

6. After a dispute, in case that the parties concerned are unable to reach an agreement, they can ask a third party to help settle the dispute. But the result has no binding effect on either party. This action is called _____.

    A. negotiation   B. mediation   C. arbitration   D. litigation

7. Before going for arbitration, both parties involved in a dispute need to make an arbitration agreement in written form, in which they agree to refer the subject in dispute to a third party. This indicates the _____ nature of arbitration.

    A. flexible   B. simplified   C. compulsory   D. voluntary

8. The award of arbitration is final and binding on both parties. This shows the _____ nature of arbitration.

    A. flexible   B. swift   C. enforceable   D. voluntary

9. In international trade, the most preferred method of setting disputes is _____.

    A. negotiation   B. litigation   C. lawsuit   D. arbitration

10. Force Majeure Clause is a clause that mainly _____.

    A. protects the right of the seller

    B. protects the right of the buyer

    C. enables the seller to avoid his contractual obligations

    D. enables the buyer to avoid his contractual obligations

II. Decide whether the following statements are True (T) or False (F).

1. Reasons resulting in disputes in international trade can be classified into three categories: breach of contract by the seller, breach of contract by the buyer and breach of contract by both the seller and the buyer.   ( )

2. One of the ways to stipulate period for claim is "Claim should be filed within 90 days after shipment".   ( )

3. The best way to stipulate force majeure events in the Force Majeure Clause of a contract is to stipulate them in a synthesized way. (　　)

4. The arbitration award is final and binding on both parties, therefore should be enforced without any doubt. (　　)

5. There are two main types of arbitration body: governmental body and non-governmental body. (　　)

6. Inspection on import and export commodities in China falls into two categories: statutory inspection and non-statutory inspection. (　　)

7. If a claim is well-supported, the claimant shall pay a fine, a certain percentage of total contract value. (　　)

8. The main ways to settle disputes in international trade are negotiation, mediation, arbitration and litigation. (　　)

9. When a force majeure event takes place, the party concerned has no choice but to terminate the contract. (　　)

10. The arbitration tribunal has the power to decide that the losing party shall pay the winning party the arbitration fee incurred in dealing with the case. (　　)

III. Answer the following questions according to the information you have got.

1. What are the reasons that cause disputes in international trade?

2. What are the ways to stipulate a claim clause?

3. What are the differences between arbitration and litigation?

4. What is the content of an arbitration clause?

5. What are the procedures of arbitration?

 微课资源

扫一扫，获取相关微课视频。

8.1.mp4

8.2.mp4

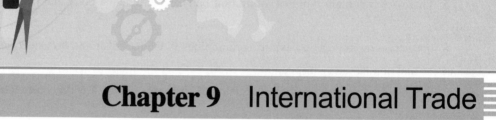

Chapter 9　International Trade Procedures and Documentation

Leading in

Our company exported a batch of motors by irrevocable L/C at sight, and the contract stipulated that the time of shipment was August, 2003. After signing the contract, we shipped and exported the goods in time according to the requirements of the L/C opened promptly by the other party. However, when making documents, the documentary staff made the commodity name on the commercial invoice into "MACHINERY AND MILL WORKS, MOTORS" according to the L/C, while the marine B/L only filled in the general designation of the commodity: "MOTORS."

Question: Can the paying bank refuse to make the payment based on this discrepancy? Why?

9.1　Procedures of an Export Transaction

The purpose of export trade is to transfer domestic goods to foreign buyers. From the perspective of trade operation, the seller must have the goods available for sale, find the intention to purchase goods from foreign customers, and carry out trade negotiations and reach agreements which both parties are willing to. After the agreement, the seller must supply goods in accordance with the agreement and receive the funds safely.

1. Preparation for exporting

When companies or traders determine to promote their products abroad for the first time, they will find themselves facing many problems which do not exist in domestic market. Besides the additional transportation, customs entry, etc., they are not familiar with the overseas market, local preference and business customs of the local merchants. In order to operate successfully abroad, traders must prepare for their market entry. Besides plans for export such as commodity production (acquisition), formalities for export, etc., other essential factory in the preparation are the conduct of research to build a knowledge base of specific country issues, specific market opportunities or concerns and a plan for marketing and promotion.

2. Business Negotiation

After the establishment of business relationship between the foreign trade enterprise and the selected foreign customers, the foreign trade enterprise may negotiate with the other party on the specific content of the export transaction. Trade negotiation can be carried out either in the form of exchange of letters or data messages (including telegram, telex, fax, EDI and e-mail) or by telephone or face-to-face. Business negotiation generally contains the inquiry, offer, counter-offer, acceptance and other sectors. Unless otherwise agreed, contracts for the international sale of goods shall enter into force once the offer is accepted. However, in the actual business, in order to clarify responsibility to fulfill, both parties usually need to sign a written contract, such as the export sales contract or sales confirmation.

3. Implementation of Contract (under CIF term; payment by L/C)

Under CIF contract with terms of payment by L/C, the implementation of export contract usually goes through the steps of reminding of L/C, examination and modification of L/C, goods preparation, inspection application, chartering and booking shipping space, insurance, shipment, customs formalities, documents preparation for bank negotiation and settlements of disputes, etc.

1) Reminding on issuing of L/C

It is the usual practice that the L/C is to be opened and reach the seller a couple of days ahead of shipment so as to give the seller enough time to make preparation for shipment, such as making the goods ready and booking shipping space. For prompt shipment, it is advisable that the L/C should be issued on time.

Reminding on Opening of L/C from the Exporter to the Importer

In order to make shipment promptly, please open your L/C according to the Sales Confirmation... No. TOY20150405: The buyer shall open an irrevocable L/C in favor of the seller before Apr. 15th, 2015 and reach the seller 45 days ahead of time of shipment. The said L/C shall be available by draft at sight for full invoice value and remain valid for negotiation in China for 15 days after shipment.

2) Examination and amendments of L/C

Upon receipt of an L/C, the seller must examine it very carefully to make sure that all terms and conditions are stipulated in accordance with the contract. If any discrepancies exist, the seller should contact the buyer immediately for necessary amendments so as to guarantee the smooth execution of the contract.

> **A Reminder in a Notification of Documentary Credit by Bank of China**
>
> If you find any terms and conditions in the L/C which you are unable to comply with and/or any error(s), it is suggested that you contact the applicant directly for necessary amendment(s) of as to avoid any difficulties which may arise when documents are presented.

3) Preparation of goods

After the contract is concluded, it is the main task for the exporter to prepare the goods for shipment and check them against the terms stipulated in the contract. The quality, specification, quantity, marking and the packing should be in line with the contract or the L/C. The date for goods preparation should agree with the shipping schedule.

4) Inspection application

If required by the stipulations of the states or the contract, the exporter should obtain a certificate of inspection from the institutions concerned where the goods are inspected. Usually, the commodity will be released only after the issuance of the inspection certificate by the inspection authority.

5) Chartering and booking shipping space

After receiving the relevant L/C, the exporter should contact the shipping agent or the shipping company for chartering and booking space. Chartering is required for goods of large quantity which needs full shipload; and for goods in small quantity, space booking would be enough.

6) Insurance

International trade may be subject to many risks. For example, ships may sink or cargoes may be damaged or lost in transit, exchange rates may alter, buyers default or government may suddenly announce an embargo, etc. It is customary to insure goods against the perils of the journey. The coverage will vary according to the types of goods and other circumstances. If the consignment is covered by cargo insurance, the party who is insured will be reimbursed for the losses.

7) Customs formalities

Before the goods are loaded, certain procedures in customs formalities have to be completed. As required, completed declaration forms giving particulars of the goods exported together with the sales contract, invoice, packing list or weight memo, inspection certificate and other relevant documents, have to be lodged with the customs. The goods will be on board on time of shipment after the release by the customs.

8) Documents preparation for bank negotiation

The relevant shipping documents required by the L/C will be submitted to the negotiating bank for negotiation after shipment is made. Shipping documents usually include commercial invoice, packing list, B/L, insurance policy, certificate of origin, certificate of inspection, etc. Documents should be correct, complete, concise and clean. Only after the documents are checked to be fully in conformity with the L/C, can the issuing bank reimburse the payment. Payment shall be dishonored by the opening bank for any discrepancies in the documents.

4. Business Aftermath

1) Settlement of disputes

Sometimes complaints or claims inevitably arise in spite of the careful performance of a contract by the exporter and the importer. They are likely to be caused by various reasons such as more or less quantity delivered, wrong goods delivered, poor packing, inferior quality, discrepancy between the samples and the goods which actually arrived, delay in shipment, payment not made, etc. In accordance with specific conditions, complaints and claims may be made to the exporter or the importer, the insurance company of the shipping company. Once disputes arise, it is advised that arbitration is better than litigation, and conciliation is better than arbitration. Details of this part are given in Chapter 8 *Disputes*, *Claims and Arbitration* of this book.

2) Export verification and tax rebate

As long as the export enterprises receive money smoothly after they complete the delivery of goods in accordance with the terms and conditions of the sales confirmation and/or the L/C, they should go to the foreign exchange management department (i.e. State Administration of Foreign Exchange) and tax department (i.e. State Administration of Taxation) timely for export verification and tax rebate.

9.2   Procedures of an Import Transaction

The business procedure of the import trade is also divided into four stages: preparation before the transaction, transaction negotiation and contract conclusion, contract fulfillment and business timely aftermath. The specific contents of them are almost the same as the export trade, such as market research, customers identification, business relations establishment, trade negotiations, signing contracts, etc. However, due to different statuses, some contents are different. The basic business procedure of import trade is shown in Figure 9-1.

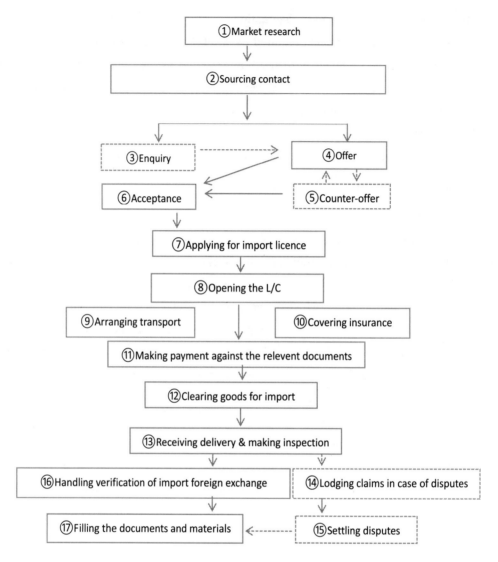

Figure 9-1   Flow chart of import procedures
(On the FOB basis, payment of L/C)

General import procedures in trade term FOB with payment method of L/C are as follows.

① Market research;

② Sourcing contract with potential partners;

③ Enquiry;

④ Offer;

⑤ Counter-offer;

⑥ Acceptance and establishment of a contract;

⑦ Applying for import license;

⑧ The buyer opens the L/C;

⑨ The buyer books a ship and notifies shipping information to seller;

⑩ The buyer arranges cargo marine insurance;

⑪ The buyer pays for complying documents;

⑫ The buyer makes customs clearance;

⑬ The buyer receives goods and makes inspection;

⑭ Lodging claims in case of disputes;

⑮ Settling disputes;

⑯ handling verification of import foreign exchange receipt;

⑰ Filling the documents and materials.

9.3　International Trade Documentation

Documentation is an invisible part of international trade. It refers to the preparation and examination of documents involved in a transaction. The major purpose of documentation is to provide a specific and complete description of the goods so that they can be correctly processed for customs clearance, transport, insurance, payment, etc. For most transactions in international trade today, without documentation there will be no possibility of transactions. Considering its importance, this chapter is solely devoted to the introduction to the basic requirements and information sources of export documentation and the explanation of major documents used in export trade.

1. Significance of Export Documentation

The importance of documentation, in a sense, can be amplified by saying that the exchange of documents takes priority over the exchange of goods in some international transactions. This is well illustrated in those contracts signed under the trade terms such as FOB/FCA, CFR/CPT and CIF/CIP, where the delivery of goods from the seller to the buyer is symbolized by the handover of title documents, rather than the actual delivery of goods. As these types of transactions take a large portion of the total volume of trade, the importance of documentation hence can not be underestimated.

Without proper documents, a seller would be unable to send the goods abroad and collect payment, neither could the buyer claim the goods at the destination. A smooth transaction heavily relies on the correct preparation and presentation of relevant documents at different stages. It is crucial for both the seller and the buyer to acquire sufficient documentation skills to be qualified practitioners. In the meantime, compared with importers, exporters are more susceptible to the impact of documentation. It is an essential condition for exportation in the first place. In order to get through the mandatory supervision and control of the customs, presentation of required documents is the prerequisite. Lack of necessary documents or presentation of wrongly made documents is among the most common reasons for delayed release of cargos from the customs. This also applies to importers when they are handling the import customs formalities. In addition, documents serve as the proof of fulfillment of contract for the seller. Most of the obligations listed on the sales contract could be reflected on the availability of certain documents or the certain content of a document. A B/L, for example, indicates the details of sellers' performance of transportation. Sometimes the buyer requires some documents to ensure that the goods delivered are what he expects. A certificate of quality may be required to guarantee the quality of the product. As a result, by evidence of documents, exporters prove that they have delivered the right goods at the right time to the right place in the right manner. Furthermore, in most cases exporters have to use documents in their collection of payment. Most of the popular payment terms ask for documents of the company, especially the title document such as B/Ls. Unable to provide the required documents, the exporter will have trouble in settling payment for his goods delivered.

2. Basic Requirements for Export Documentation

In view of the importance of documentation, it is essential for trade practitioners to learn about the basic requirements for them. So far, there has been no well-established standard for documentation in international trade. In addition, documentary requirements may differ from transaction to transaction and from country to country, largely. The differences mainly lie in areas such as the types needed, the forms, contents and languages used, etc. Whatever differences there might be, generally speaking, documentation for every transaction should meet the following basic requirements: correctness, completeness, conciseness, cleanness and promptness.

Documents are correct and accurate if the content (including the exact words used) conforms to that in the L/C and the format of the documents is in line with the requirement. Aside from these, correctness is met when the right types of documents are prepared and the right number of the originals and duplicates are presented.

Documents are considered complete when all necessary documents (including the types and number of originals and duplicates) are prepared and presented in a complete set.

To be concise, the seller shall make sure that all documents should avoid redundant, unnecessary or ambiguous words or expressions. Meanwhile, to be clean, documents should bear no marks of correction on the face.

When the above "Cs" are all met, the seller should then prepare the documents in time and present them within the time period for presentation stipulated in the L/C. This lives up to the requirement of promptness.

In brief, exporters should attach great importance to documentation and make sure all documents meet the above requirements in order to ensure the smoothness and success of every single transaction. To achieve this, the seller has to check very carefully so that all documents for a transaction should not only be in strict compliance with the stipulations in the relevant contract and L/C but also be in consistency with each other.

3. Export Documents

The successful completion of a single transaction may involve many documents. They may include government granted documents such as export license and quota, commercial documents such as commercial invoice and packing list, transportation documents such as B/L and shipping advice, insurance documents such as insurance policy or insurance certificate and financial documents such as B/E. Some documents are used for very specific reason and then only required at a certain stage, others such as commercial invoice and packing list are of more general use, appearing at most of the stages throughout the performance of a transaction. To fully illustrate the sophistication of export documentation, the next part will develop an extensive discussion about the various kinds of documents, following the fulfillment of a CIF contract which requires payment by L/C. The reason to choose such a contract is two folded. On the one hand, transactions of this type are very common in practice; on the other hand, such contract requires the use of documents of the greatest number and variety when comparing with others. It can provide a full picture of the documentation practice with considerable satisfaction.

1) Documents required before or at contract negotiation

Before the negotiation of a contract, a seller is expected to apply for an export license or at least make sure that he is able to obtain it if the commodity he is to sell falls under the export control. During the negotiation of the terms and conditions of a contract, sometimes offers are made on a proforma invoice, which in this case should only be seen as a form of quotation. After acceptance is made at the end of the negotiation, the seller and the buyer will draft a sales contract including all the necessary information for a transaction.

- export license

An export license is the first document a seller has to prepare when he intends to export commodities that are under export control of his country. Export licenses are issued by the government or its authorized institutions and required at the time of export customs clearance. The goods under export control normally include the main raw materials, machinery or equipment in short supply, military or other goods relating to national security, and works of art and antiques which are of national, cultural or historical importance. In some cases the licensing system is used to implement government policy such as economic sanctions against certain countries.

- proforma invoice

A proforma invoice is issued by the seller as a response to an inquiry from the potential buyer. It is a document similar to a commercial invoice and it contains the same information as those in the commercial invoice. It is a statement of sales, issued before a transaction has been concluded rather than a record of sales already effected.

A proforma invoice is needed in the following circumstances. If an irrevocable L/C is required by the exporter, the importer will use a proforma invoice to substantiate the need for an L/C to his bank. Sometimes it is needed by the importer to apply for the import license and foreign exchange. A proforma invoice, in some other circumstances, may be required by an importer to help him apply for the relevant L/C. Therefore, a proforma invoice has no legal status and serves only as a means to facilitate an importer's accomplishment of the above-mentioned tasks.

2) Documents involved in goods preparation

After a seller has got the goods prepared and packed, he will then issue a commercial invoice and a packing list. Both documents are very important and required in all main stages of an export procedure.

- commercial invoice (Specimen 9-1)

A commercial invoice is an exporting firm's invoice, made out to his foreign importer, describing key transaction details particularly the total value. It is one of the most important documents used in international trade. It is used as the foundation for keeping accounts and making declarations to the customs. It is often one of the documents required for payment settlement. A commercial invoice serves as a record of the essential details of a transaction.

Commercial invoices are usually required by all relevant parties involved in a transaction such as buyers, the paying bank, sellers and their bank, customs authorities in the exporting and importing countries, carriers and their agents at the port of shipment and discharge. For instance, the buyer needs the commercial invoice to check whether the goods delivered to him conform to the terms and conditions stipulated in the contract. The bank needs the commercial invoice together with other documents such as the B/L and the insurance certificate to effect payment. The customs needs the commercial invoice to calculate duties.

In the case of a transaction on L/C payment, it should be noted that according to UCP 600, a commercial invoice must be issued by the beneficiary to the applicant stated in the L/C.

- packing list (Specimen 9-2)

A packing list is a document made out by the seller stating the detailed content of each individual shipment. It is a supplementary document to the commercial invoice used to make up the deficiency of an invoice by giving all the necessary particulars of the goods. A packing list is one of the documents required for mandatory inspection, export and import customs formalities and negotiation of payment. It is also used to facilitate the general checking of goods before shipment by the seller. The buyer also needs the packing list to check the goods on their arrival at the destination. In addition, packing lists can facilitate insurance claims and claims settlements in case of loss or damage.

3) Documents concerning mandatory inspection

If the goods need to go through mandatory inspection required by the stipulations of the government or the contract, the seller has to apply for it by filling out an inspection application form also known as proposal form. After inspection, if the goods are up to the required standard, the seller will receive the relevant inspection certificate from the inspection body.

- export commodity inspection application (Specimen 9-3)

Export commodity inspection application is one of the essential domestic documents for the export of many commodities in China. The State Administration for Commodity Inspection, in the light of the needs in the development of foreign trade, makes, adjusts and publishes "A List of Import and Export Commodities Subject to Inspection by the Commodity Inspection Authorities". The export of commodities on this list is not allowed until they have been inspected. Therefore, if the goods of the seller are on this list, he is required to fill out an application form to apply for inspection upon submission, he will also be asked to present other documents such as the sales contract, the L/C, the commercial invoice, and the packing list. In some cases, only the inspection report supplied by the manufacturer is required.

- certificate of inspection

An inspection certificate is a document indicating the results of the inspection of the goods in terms of quality, quantity or any other element that has been specified. An inspection certificate may be issued by a government institution, surveyors of chamber of commerce or an independent service company. Inspection certificates are required when the goods are cleared for export and import and when the seller negotiates payment at the bank. Its primary function is to ensure that the goods in question are meeting the relevant requirements stipulated by certain authorities.

The types of inspection certificates used in international trade vary greatly. They include certificates to cover such issues as quality, weight, quantity, veterinary standards, health, disinfection, fumigation and phytosanitary. Common types of inspection certificates include Inspection Certificate of Quality, Inspection Certificate of Weight, Inspection Certificate of Quantity, Inspection Certificate of Health, and Veterinary, Inspection Certificate of Quarantine and so on. The employment of certificates differs greatly among categories of products.

4) Documents involved in transportation

For booking shipping space or chartering vessel, the seller is required to fill out a booking note. In return, the seller will receive a shipping order from the carrier or the agent.

- booking note

A booking note is a form which is to be filled out by the exporter providing the carrier or the shipping agent all the necessary particulars about the shipment when an exporter intends to book shipping space on a liner or charter a ship for the carriage of export goods. When shipping space is booked or a ship is chartered, the carrier or the agent will inform the exporter of the particulars by means of a shipping order.

- shipping order

A shipping order is a notice to the shipper (exporter) from the carrier or the agent, indicating that goods have been received for loading. Thus a shipping order contains detailed information concerning the sailing, goods, place of loading, etc. When the carriers or the agents are in receipt of the goods, they will mark and sign the shipping order properly so that the goods can be ready for export clearance. After the customs clearance, the Customs will stencil on the face of the shipping order evidencing that goods are cleared for export. This shipping order will be presented to the carrier at the time of loading. Without a shipping order, goods are not allowed to be loaded on board.

5) Documents needed for export customs clearance

The export goods can not be loaded for shipment until they are cleared for export. To clear goods for export, exporters should declare the export goods to the Customs by filling in the relevant customs forms such as the Customs Declaration for Export Commodity (used in China). After customs clearance, the Customs or the authorized institution will either stencil on the face of the shipping order or issue a customs clearance for export commodity to the seller, evidencing that goods are cleared for export.

customs declaration for export commodity (Specimen 9-4).

To clear the export commodity for export customs, the seller should fill out a customs declaration, which will be submitted to the Customs or relative authorized institutions. In addition, some supporting documents may need to be submitted as well as a commercial invoice, a packing list, an export license (if required), a copy of the sales contract and an inspection certificate (in case of mandatory inspection) and a shipping order.

6) Documents received after shipment

After they are cleared for export and the customs clearance is obtained, the goods can be arranged to be loaded on the vessel. For his goods to be loaded, a seller shall produce the shipping order and/or the customs clearance to the carrier. To ensure sufficient notice about the shipment, a shipping advice which is issued by the carrier or the shipping agent at the time of loading shall be forwarded to the importer by the seller without delay. Upon completion of the shipment, the exporter will get a B/L issued by the carrier.

- mate's receipt

A mate's receipt is a document issued and signed by the mate of the shipping vessel indicating that the goods have been received by the vessel for loading or that the goods have been loaded on board the vessel. The seller can exchange the mate's receipt for the on-board B/L at a later time.

- shipping advice/shipping notice

A shipping advice, also known as a shipping notice, is a notice of the shipment details which is issued by the carrier when goods are loaded on board the vessel. A shipping advice is to be forwarded by the seller (shipper) to the buyer (consignee). The purpose of the shipping advice is to notify the buyer that goods are loaded and that he can proceed to prepare for making payment and for receiving the goods at the destination. If the contract is concluded under FOB, FCA, CFR or CPT, the seller also has to pass the shipping advice to the buyer without delay so as to facilitate the buyer to arrange insurance.

- B/L (Specimen 9-5)

A B/L is a document which is issued by an ocean carrier to a shipper with whom the carrier has entered into a contract for the carriage of goods. It evidences the receipt of goods by the carrier and serves as a contract of carriage between the shipper and the carries at the same time. Most importantly, a B/L is a property document representing title to the goods, thereupon the most needed document for the settlement of payment.

7) insurance documents

Under a CIF contract, it is the exporter's obligation to cover insurance for the export goods. Insurance is normally obtained after the completion of the loading at the port of shipment. To take out insurance, an insurance application form, also known as the proposal form has to be filled out and submitted to an insurance company for the purchase of cargo insurance. When the application is accepted, an insurance policy or certificate will be issued by the insurer.

- insurance application form

An insurance application form, also known as insurance proposal form, is to be filled out by the insured, providing all information about the parties concerned and the shipment involved. The specific information may cover the name of the insured party, the description of the cargoes insured, the voyage insured, the insurance amount, the insurance coverage, etc. Documents needed for submission are the commercial invoice, the packing list, the port of shipment and destination, etc. After all necessary formalities concerning insurance is completed, insurance documents such as insurance policy are to be issued by the insurance company or the agent.

- insurance policy (Specimen 9-6)

An insurance policy is the contract made between the insurer and the insured, which is issued by the insurer and confirmed by the insured. In an international trade transaction, an insurance policy or certificate forms part of the chief documents for transactions on a CIF or CIP basis. In addition, in case of loss or damage the insurance policy or certificate is the essential basis for insurance claim and claim settlement.

8) Documents for bank negotiation

The last and most important thing a seller has to do is to collect and check all documents specified in the L/C and present them within period required to the negotiating bank for payment settlement. While doing so, he should also fill out a B/E (a draft). The documents needed for submission generally include the commercial invoice, the packing list, the B/L, the insurance policy, etc. Apart from these documents, there are also other types of documents required by the buyer and submitted to the bank for negotiation. Among them, the certificate of origin, consular invoice and customs invoice are worth mentioning.

● B/E or draft

A B/E or draft is an unconditional order in writing signed by one party (drawer) requesting a second party (drawee/payer) to make payment in lawful money immediately or at a determined future time to a third party (payee).

Usually, a draft is drawn and presented by the seller to the buyer or their banks as the payment instrument. Strictly speaking, a draft drawn under L/C is a payment instrument rather than a kind of documents, though in practice it is accepted as one of the documents required for payment.

It should be noted that a draft drawn under L/C is usually required to indicate the relevant L/C in the drawn clause and the B/E amount should in no case exceed the L/C amount.

● certificate of origin (Specimen 9-7)

A certificate of origin is a document certifying the origin of the goods or the place/country of manufacturing. It should state the nature, quantity, value, and the place of manufacture. In many countries the certificate of origin is usually prepared by the exporter, signed in the presence of a notary public institution and certified by a non-governmental commercial organization acceptable to the destination country. In China the certificate of origin is generally issued by two governmental authorities: one is Entry-Exit Inspection and Quarantine of the People's Republic of China (CIQ), and the other is China Council for the Promotion of International Trade (CCPIT).

There are normally two types of certificates of origin: one is the Certificate of Origin; the other is the generalized system of preferences certificate of origin (GSP Certificate of Origin) (Specimen 9-8). The GSP Certificate of Origin is a special type of certificate of origin available from Entry-Exit Inspection and Quarantine of the PRC and used to obtain the preferential customs duty treatment imposed by some developed countries on import commodities from some developing countries. The main purpose of the certificate of origin is to prove the origin of the goods based on which the import customs can set import duties and implement the applicable import controls such as sanctions, quotas, anti-dumping duties or favorable treatments.

9) Other documents

- consular invoice

A consular invoice is a form, usually only obtainable from the importing country's consulate in the exporting country, on which the seller or its agent must enter a detailed description of the goods being shipped. Such a form is required by certain countries in order to compile statistics, control imports, collect import duties and check the origin of goods and the credit of the exporter. A consular invoice shall carry such information as the name of the goods, the number of the items, their weight, the value and origin of the goods and a declaration that the information given is correct. Most of the consular invoices are in the language of the country to which the goods are shipped so it is usually considered as the most difficult document of all and must be filled in with special care.

- customs invoice

A customs invoice is one of the documents made out on a special form prescribed by the customs authorities of the importing country. Generally, the invoice may include information required by the import customs that is not stated on an ordinary commercial invoice. This invoice is usually required by some importing countries such as the USA, Canada, New Zealand, Australia and some African countries and used to clear customs, to verify the country of origin for import duty and tax purposes, to compare export prices and domestic prices and to fix anti-dumping duties.

4. Clause Concerning Documents in the Sales Contract

In trade practice, stipulations concerning documents may not necessarily appear in every contract. In some cases, documents required are stipulated in the contract. They may constitute part or whole of the contents under the column "Remarks" or they may be mentioned in the attachment to a contract. And it is not uncommon, however, that there are no such stipulations in the contract at all. In that case, the agreement concerning documents remains an oral one between the buyer and the seller and is binding upon the parties concerned. Still, it is advisable that the relevant stipulations should be laid down in the contract in terms of the types, issuing authorities, number of originals or copies, etc.

While it may not appear in a sales contract, the stipulation "Documents Required" is always an necessary part of a documentary L/C. Under an L/C transaction, sellers are paid against documents presented; buyers pay and receive goods against documents released; and the banks deal in the documents instead of the goods. Documents play such an essential role in L/C transaction that documents to be presented (or to be required) should be clearly stipulated in the relevant L/C.

Notes to the Text

I. Vocabulary and phrases.

1. export procedure   出口流程

2. business negotiation   商业谈判

3. letters of credit   信用证

4. sales contract   买卖合同

5. financial documents   金融单据

6. export formalities   出口手续

7. export license   出口许可证

8. commercial invoice   商业发票

9. proforma invoice   形式发票

10. packing list   装箱单

11. inspection certificate   检验证明

12. shipping order   装货单

13. export customs clearance   出口报关

14. mate's receipt   大副收据

15. shipping advice/shipping note   装船通知

16. bill of lading   海运提单

17. booking note   订舱单，托运单

18. insurance policy   保险单

19. bill of exchange (a draft)   汇票

20. certificates of origin   原产地证明

21. consular invoices   领事发票

22. customs invoices   海关发票

II. Sentences and paragraphs.

1. The purpose of export trade is to transfer domestic goods to foreign buyers. From the perspective of trade operation, the seller must have the goods available for sale, to find the intention to purchase goods from foreign customers, and carry out trade negotiations and reach agreements which both parties are willing to. After the agreement, the seller must supply goods in accordance with the agreement and receive the funds safely.

出口贸易的目的是将国内货物转让给外国买主。从贸易经营的角度来看，卖方必须有

可供销售的货物，从国外客户中找到有意向购买货物的买主，并进行贸易谈判，根据双方意愿达成相应协议。协议签订后，卖方必须按协议规定提供货物，并安全收到货款。

2. A commercial invoice is an exporting firm's invoice, made out to his foreign importer, describing key transaction details particularly the total value. It is one of the most important documents used in international trade. It is used as the foundation for keeping accounts and making declarations to the customs. It is often one of the documents required for payment settlement. A commercial invoice serves as a record of the essential details of a transaction.

商业发票是出口企业开给国外进口商的发票，它显示了一些关键的交易细节，特别是总价值。商业发票是国际贸易中最重要的单据之一；是记账和向海关申报的基础单据；通常还是支付结算所需要的单据之一，负责记录交易基本细节。

3. A B/L is a document which is issued by an ocean carrier to a shipper with whom the carrier has entered into a contract for the carriage of goods. It evidences the receipt of goods by the carrier and serves as a contract of carriage between the shipper and the carries at the same time. Most importantly, a B/L is a property document representing title to the goods, thereupon the most needed document for the settlement of payment.

提单是由海上承运人签发给与承运人订立货物运输合同的托运人的单证。提单作为承运人收到货物的凭证，同时作为托运人和承运人之间的运输合同。最重要的是，提单是代表货物所有权的物权凭证，因此是结算货款的必备文件。

4. An insurance policy is the contract made between the insurer and the insured, which is issued by the insurer and confirmed by the insured. In an international trade transaction, an insurance policy or certificate forms part of the chief documents for transactions on a CIF or CIP basis. In addition, in case of loss or damage the insurance policy or certificate is the essential basis for insurance claim and claim settlement.

保险单是保险人与被保险人之间签订的合同，由保险人签发并经被保险人确认。在国际贸易中，保险单或保险凭证构成 CIF 或 CIP 条件下交易的主要单据的一部分。此外，在发生损失或损害时，保险单或保险凭证是保险索赔和理赔的必要依据。

Exercises

I. Finish the multiple choice questions.

1. Under a _____ contract with payment by L/C, the exporter has to go through the comparatively more complicated procedure of documentation.

    A. EXW   B. FOB/FCA

    C. CFR/CPT   D. CIF/CIP

2. If a transaction is concluded on _____ term, the exporter is obliged to obtain an insurance policy or certificate.

    A. EXW   B. FOB/FCA

    C. CFR/CPT   D. CIF/CIP

3. For all export transactions, documents required need to be prepared largely on the basis of the _____.

    A. sales contract   B. letter of credit

    C. commercial invoice   D. packing list

4. A(An) _____ is the first document a seller has to prepare when he intends to export commodities that are under export control of his country.

    A. commercial invoice   B. export license manufacturing

    C. proforma invoice   D. customs invoice

5. A (An) _____ is a document certifying the origin of goods or the place/country of manufacturing.

    A. commercial invoice   B. inspection certificate

    C. packing list   D. certificate of origin

6. To clear the commodity for export customs, the seller should fill out a (an) _____ as an application which will be submitted to the customs or relevant authorized institutions.

    A. commercial invoice   B. export license

    C. customs declaration   D. customs invoice

7. _____ is a document made out by the seller as a supplementary document to the commercial invoice to make up the deficiency of an invoice by giving all the necessary particulars of the goods.

    A. Consular invoice   B. Proforma invoice

    C. Customs invoice   D. Packing list

8. A _____ is dispatched by the carrier or the agent to inform the exporter of the particulars of shipment arrangement after shipping space is booked.

    A. booking note   B. bill of lading

    C. shipping advice   D. shipping order

9. A(An) _____ is a document indicating the results of the inspection of the goods in terms of the quality, quantity or any other element that has been specified.

    A. inspection certificate   B inspection application

    C. certificate of origin   D. inspection certificate of quality

10. In international trade practice, stipulations concerning documents are an indispensable part of _____.

    A. the sales contract

B. the documentary L/C

C. either the sales contract or the documentary L/C

D. both the sales contract and the documentary L/C

II. Decide whether the following statements are true (T) or false (F).

1. Insurance policy is one of the basic documents required by buyers for all transactions on FOB, CFR and CIF basis. (   )

2. Export documents should be made out based on the information either in the sales contract or in the L/C. (   )

3. The commercial invoice serves as a record of the essential details of a transaction. (   )

4. Export of commodities is possible only after the commodities have been inspected. (   )

5. Commodities are not allowed to be loaded on the ocean vessel until they have been cleared for customs. (   )

6. A booking note is a form which is to be filled out by the carrier providing all the necessary particulars about the shipment to facilitate booking shipping space or chartering. (   )

7. The amount on a B/E (draft) must be exactly the same as the amount shown in the relevant commercial invoice. (   )

8. If there is a discrepancy between the amount on a draft and that in the L/C, this draft is not acceptable to the issuing bank. (   )

9. According to Article 18 of UCP 600, a commercial invoice must be issued by the beneficiary named in the L/C. (   )

10. A certificate of origin can be used to certify the time when the export commodities are produced. (   )

III. Answer the following questions according to the information you have got.

1. How many steps are involved in export trade process?

2. What are the differences between the import trade and the export trade in view of their procedures?

3. What is the importance of export documentation?

4. What are the information sources for export documentation?

5. What documents is the exporter normally asked to submit when he charters or books shipping space?

6. What are the main documents required for the negotiation of payment?

7. What should the sellers do to ensure that the documents required can be presented correctly, completely and promptly?

COMMERCIAL INVOICE

TO:

INV No.: _____
DATE: _____
S/C No.: _____
L/C No.: _____

FROM_____VIA_____TO_____BY_____

MARKS & NUMBERS	DESCRIPTION OF GOODS	QUANTITY	UNIT PRICE	AMOUNT

TOTAL VALUE (IN WORDS)	

_____
(SIGNATURE)

Specimen 9-1

PACKING LIST

TO:

INVOICE No.:

INVOICE DATE:

S/C No.:

B/L No.:

SHIPMETN FROM: _____ TO: _____

L/C No.: _____ DATE OF SHIPMENT: _____

MARKS & NUMBERS	DESCRIPTION OF GOODS	QAUANTITY	G.W.	N.W.	MEAS.
	TOTAL				

TOTAL PACKAGE IN WORDS:

(SIGNATURE)

Specimen 9-2

中华人民共和国出入境检验检疫
出境货物报检单

报检单位(加盖公章):   *编号

报检单位登记号: 联系人: 电话: 报检日期: 年 月 日

发货人	(中文)	
	(外文)	
收货人	(中文)	
	(外文)	

货物名称(中/外文)	H.S.编码	产地	数/重量	货物总值	包装种类及数量

运输工具名称号码		贸易方式		货物存放地点	
合同号		信用证号		用途	
发货日期		输往国家(地区)		许可证/审批号	
启运地		到达口岸		生产单位注册号	
集装箱规格、数量及号码					

合同、信用证订立的检验检疫条款或特殊要求	标 记 及 号 码	随附单据(画"✓"或补填)
		□合同 □包装性能结果单 □信用证 □许可/审批文件 □发票 □ □换证凭单 □ □装箱单 □ □厂检单

需要证单名称(画"✓"或补填)		*检验检疫费	
□品质证书 __正__副	□植物检疫证书 __正__副	总金额 (人民币元)	
□重量证书 __正__副	□熏蒸/消毒证书 __正__副		
□数量证书 __正__副	□出境货物换证凭单 __正__副		
□兽医卫生证书 __正__副	□	计费人	
□健康证书 __正__副	□		
□卫生证书 __正__副	□	收费人	
□动物卫生证书 __正__副	□		

报检人郑重声明:	领 取 证 单	
1. 本人被授权报检。	日期	
2. 上列填写内容正确属实,货物无伪造或冒用他人的厂名、标志、认证标志,并承担货物质量责任。 签名:_____	签名	

注:有"*"号栏由出入境检验检疫机关填写   ◆国家出入境检验检疫局制

[1-2 (2000.1.1)]

Specimen 9-3

中华人民共和国海关出口货物报关单

预录入编号：   海关编号：

收发货人		出口口岸		出口日期	申报日期
生产销售单位		运输方式	运输工具名称		提运单号
申报单位		监管方式		征免性质	备案号
贸易国(地区)	运抵国(地区)		指运港		境内货源地
许可证号	成交方式	运费		保费	杂费
合同协议号	件数	包装种类		毛重(千克)	净重(千克)
集装箱号	随附单据				生产厂家
标记唛码及备注					

项号	商品编号	商品名称、规格型号	数量及单位	最终目的国(地区)	单价	总价	币制	征免

特殊关系确认：   价格影响确认：   支持特许权使用费确认：

录入员	录入单位	兹声明对以上内容承担如实申报、依法纳税之法律责任	海关批注及签章
报关人员		申报单位(签章)	

Specimen 9-4

Shipper	B/L No.
Consignee	**中 国 对 外 贸 易 运 输 总 公 司** China National Foreign Trade Transportation Corporation **CARRIER** 联 运 提 单 **COMBINED TRANSPORT** **BILL OF LADING**
Notify address	

Pre-carriaged by	Place of receipt	RECEIVED the foods in apparent good order and condition as specified below unless otherwise stated herein. The Carrier, in accordance with the provisions contained in this document,
Ocean vessel	Port of loading	1) undertakes to perform or to procure the performance of the entire transport form the place at which the goods are taken in charge to the place designated for delivery in this document, and 2) assumes liability as prescribed
Port of discharge	Place of delivery	in this document for such transport. One of the bills of Lading must be surrendered duty endorsed in exchange for the goods or delivery order.

Marks and Nos.	Number and kind of packages	Description of goods	Gross weight(kg.) Measurement(m^3)

Total number of packages(in words):

ABOVE PARTICULARS FURNISHED BY SHIPPER

Freight and charges	Freight prepaid at	Number of original B/L	IN WITNESS whereof the number of original bills of lading stated above have been signed, one of which being accomplished, the other(s) to be void.
Place and date of issue			Signed for or on behalf of the Carrier **OCEAN SHIPPING AGENCY CO.** AS AGENT FOR THE CARRIER NAMED ABOVE

Specimen 9-5

	中国人民保险公司 The People's Insurance Company of China
PICC	
	总公司设于北京　　　　　一九四九年创立 Head Office Beijing　　　　Established in 1949

货物运输保险单
CARGO TRANSPORTATION INSURANCE POLICY

发票号 (INVOICE NO.)		保单号次 POLICY NO.	
合同号 (CONTRACT NO.)			
信用证号(L/C NO.)			
被保险人： INSURED:			

中国人民保险公司(以下简称本公司)根据被保险人的要求，由被保险人向本公司缴付约定的保险费，按照本保险单承保保险别和背面所载条款与下列特款承保下述货物运输保险，特立本保险单。

THIS POLICY OF INSURANCE WITNESSES THAT THE PEOPLE'S INSURANCE COMPANY OF CHINA (HEREINAFTER CALLED "THE COMPANY") AT THE REQUEST OF THE INSURED AND IN CONSIDERATION OF THE AGREED PREMIUM PAID TO THE COMPANY BY THE INSURED, UNDERTAKES TO INSURE THE UNDERMENTIONED GOODS IN TRANSPORTATION SUBJECT TO THE CONDITIONS OF THIS OF THIS POLICY AS PER THE CLAUSES PRINTED OVERLEAF AND OTHER SPECIAL CLAUSES ATTACHED HEREON.

标　记 MARKS & NOS	包装及数量 QUANTITY	保险货物项目 DESCRIPTION OF GOODS	保险金额 AMOUNT INSURED

总保险金额 TOTAL AMOUNT INSURED:			
保费： PERMIUM:	AS ARRANGED	启运日期 DATE OF COMMENCEMENT:	装载运输工具： PER CONVEYANCE:

Specimen 9-6

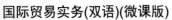

自 FROM:		经 VIA		至 TO	

承保险别：

CONDITIONS:

　　所保货物，如发生保险单项下可能引起索赔的损失或损坏，应立即通知本公司下述代理人查勘。如有索赔，应向本公司提交保单正本(本保险单共有　份正本)及有关文件。如一份正本已用于索赔，其余正本自动失效。

IN THE EVENT OF LOSS OR DAMAGE WITCH MAY RESULT IN A CLAIM UNDER THIS POLICY, IMMEDIATE NOTICE MUST BE GIVEN TO THE

COMPANY'S AGENT AS MENTIONED HEREUNDER. CLAIMS, IF ANY, ONE OF THE ORIGINAL POLICY WHICH HAS BEEN ISSUED IN　ORIGINAL(S)

ORIGINALCS TOGETHER WITH THE RELEVANT DOCUMENTS SHALL BE SURRENDERED TO THE COMPANY. IF ONE OF THE ORIGINAL POLICY HAS BEEN ACCOMPLISHED. THE OTHERS TO BE VOID.

中国人民保险公司

The People's Insurance Company of China

赔款偿付地点 CLAIM PAYABLE AT			
出单日期 ISSUING DATE			

Authorized Signature

Specimen 9-6(continued)

1. Exporter (full name and address)	Certificate No.
2. Consignee (full name, address, country)	**CERTIFICATE OF ORIGIN** **OF** **THE PEOPLE'S REPUBLIC OF CHINA**
3. Means of transport and route	5. For certifying authority use only
4. Country/Region of destination	

6.Marks and number of packages	7. Description of goods; number and kinds of packages	8. H.S. code	9. Quantity or weight	10. Number and date of invoice

11. **Declaration by the exporter**	12. **Certification**
The undersigned hereby declares that the above details and statements are true and correct; that all the goods were produced in China and that they comply with the Rules of Origin of the People's Republic of China	It is hereby certified that the declaration by the exporter is true and correct.
-- Place and date, signature and stamp of authorized authority	-- Place and date, signature and stamp of certifying authority

Specimen 9-7

1. Goods consigned from (Exporter's business name, address, country)	Reference No.
	GENERALIZED SYSTEM OF PREFERENCES CERTIFICATE OF ORIGIN (COMBINED DECLARATION AND CERTIFICATE)
2. Goods consigned to (Consignee's name, address, country)	FORM A ISSUED IN THE PEOPLE'S REPUBLIC OF CHINA (country)
3. Means of transport and route (as far as known)	SEE NOTES OVERLEAF
	4. For official use

5.Item number	6.Marks and numbers of packages	7.Number and kinds of packages; Description of goods	8. Origin criterion (see notes overleaf)	9. Gross weight or other quantity	10. Number and date of invoice

11.Certification	12.Declaration by the exporter
It is hereby certified, on the basis of control carried out, that the declaration by the exporter is correct	The undersigned hereby declares that the above details and statements are correct; that all the goods were produced in
	CHINA
	(country) and that they comply with the origin requirements specified for those goods in the generalized system of preference for goods exported to
-----------------------------	-----------------------------
Place and date, signature and stamp of certifying authority	(importing country)

	Place and date, signature of authorized signatory

Specimen 9-8

微课资源

扫一扫，获取相关微课视频。

9.1.mp4

9.2.mp4

参 考 文 献

[1] 帅建林. 国际贸易实务(英文版)[M]. 4 版. 北京：对外经济贸易大学出版社，2020.

[2] 杨智华. 进出口贸易实务(英文版)[M]. 北京：清华大学出版社，2020.

[3] 易露霞，陈新华，尤彧聪. 国际贸易实务双语教程[M]. 5 版. 北京：清华大学出版社，2020.

[4] 黎孝先，石玉川，王健. 国际贸易实务[M]. 7 版. 北京：对外经济贸易大学出版社，2020.

[5] 周瑞琪，王小鸥，徐月芳. 国际贸易实务(英文版)[M]. 4 版. 北京：对外经济贸易大学出版社，2019.

[6] 张素芳. 国际贸易理论与实务(英文版)[M]. 4 版. 北京：对外经济贸易大学出版社，2018.

[7] 谢桂梅. 国际贸易实务(英文版)[M]. 2 版. 北京：清华大学出版社，2015.

[8] 国际商会. International Chamber of Commerce. https://iccwbo.org.

[9] 徐进亮，张啸晨. 国际贸易实务(双语版)[M]. 北京：对外经济贸易大学出版社，2019.

[10] 孙智慧. 国际贸易实务(双语)[M]. 北京：对外经济贸易大学出版社，2018.

[11] 易露霞，方玲玲，尤彧聪. 国际贸易实务案例教程(双语)[M]. 2 版. 北京：清华大学出版社，2016.

[12] 傅龙海，丛晓明. 国际贸易实务双语教程[M]. 3 版. 北京：对外经济贸易大学出版社，2018.